HISTORY OF TECHNOLOGY

History of Technology

Volume 31, 2012

Edited by
Ian Inkster

B L O O M S B U R Y
LONDON · NEW DELHI · NEW YORK · SYDNEY

Bloomsbury Academic

An imprint of Bloomsbury Publishing Plc

50 Bedford Square	175 Fifth Avenue
London	New York
WC1B 3DP	NY 10010
UK	USA

www.bloomsbury.com

First published 2012

British Library Cataloguing-in-Publication Data
A catalogue record for this book is available from the British Library.

ISBN: HB: 978-1-4411-5279-4

Typeset by Newgen Imaging Systems Pvt Ltd Chennai, India
Printed and bound in Great Britain

Contents

The Contributors

Karel Davids
Professor of Economic and Social History
Afdeling Geschiedenis VU University
Amsterdam
1081 HV The Netherlands
Email: c.a.davids@vu.nl

Anna Guagnini
Dipartimento di Filosofia
Università di Bologna
Via Zamboni 3840126 Bologna
Italy
Email: anna.guagnini@unibo.it

Ian Inkster
Research Professor of International History
Nottingham Trent University
Nottingham UK NG11 8NS and
Professor of Global History
Department of International Affairs
Wenzao Ursuline College of Languages
Kaohsiung 80793 Taiwan
Email: *ian.inkster@ntu.ac.uk*

Pamela O. Long
Independent Historian
3100 Connecticut Ave. NWApt. 137
Washington, DC 20008
Email: pamlong@pamelaolong.com
Website: *www.pamelaolong.com*

Manuel Márquez
L. L. & M. M. Consultores S. C.
Managing Partner
Email: manuel_marquez@ll-mm.com

David Pretel
Economic History Society Research Fellow and Trinity Hall Research Associate.
University of Cambridge
Email: *dp393@cam.ac.uk*

Lissa Roberts
Professor of Long Term Development of Science and Technology
Department of Science, Technology and Policy Studies
University of Twente
POB 2177500 AE Enschede, The Netherlands
Email: l.l.roberts@utwente.nl

Patricio Sáiz
Professor of Economic History.
Universidad Autónoma de Madrid
Facultad de CC. EE. y EE.
Campus Cantoblanco,
28049 – Madrid
Email: patricio.saiz@uam.es

Dr. Simona Valeriani
Research Officer, URKEW Project
London School of Economics
Houghton Street, Room V203WC2A
2AE, London, UK

Introduction: 'Useful Knowledge' Reconsidered

KAREL DAVIDS

Afdeling Geschiedenis VU University, Amsterdam

The following four essays in this volume of *History of Technology* deal in various ways with the theme of 'useful knowledge' in the pre-industrial period. 'Useful knowledge', or 'useful and reliable knowledge', has in the past decade become a term of choice in historical debates on the relation between economic growth and technological change. Although the origin of the term reaches back to at least the seventeenth century, its modern currency owes much to its appearance in the classic book by Simon Kuznets on economic growth published in 1965.[1] Following from Kuznets, Joel Mokyr, Larry Epstein, Ian Inkster and other scholars have employed 'useful knowledge' as a fruitful concept in economic history, the history of technology and the history of science. One of the main reasons why the notion has quickly caught on is probably precisely its potential bridging function between various historical disciplines. 'Useful knowledge' is a flexible, inclusive term and appears to be less burdened by associations with hierarchies of knowledge than concepts such as 'science' or 'technology'.

For Joel Mokyr, the notion of 'useful knowledge' and its subdivision in 'prop-ositional' and 'prescriptive' knowledge formed the main building blocks in a sweeping argument about the dynamics of technological change before and after the Industrial Revolution.[2] Larry Epstein discussed 'useful' or 'experien-tial' knowledge as part of an overarching argument about the institutional con-text of innovation in pre-industrial Europe. He saw craft guilds as the principal institutions that created a favourable environment for gradual technical change through the formation of human capital via apprenticeship systems and the circulation of knowledge via migration of trained craftsmen, especially jour-neymen.[3] Ian Inkster stressed the 'historical exceptionality' of early modern Europe by its 'potential' for future economic growth as a result of the spread of 'social and spatial locations and applications' of 'useful and reliable knowl-edge'. Within Europe, eighteenth-century Britain was a special case due to its 'unusual amount of institutional innovation across a range of socio-cultural sites and activities' which fostered the growth of this sort of knowledge close to 'places of production and industrial innovation'.[4]

In 2007, *History of Science* devoted a special issue to Mokyr's *The Gifts of Athena*, in which the concept of 'useful knowledge' figured prominently.[5] The present volume of *History of Technology* takes up the theme of 'useful knowledge', but from a different angle than the issue of *History of Science*. The intention of the following articles is not primarily to examine the connections between 'useful knowledge' and the Industrial Revolution or the rise of the knowledge economy (although these kinds of issues come up for discussion, too, as we will see shortly) but rather to take a closer look at the notion of 'useful knowledge' itself. They contextualize, elaborate and re-evaluate the concept itself. What does 'useful knowledge' mean? How can this concept aid our understanding of the development of knowledge and skills?

In the opening article of this section Pamela O. Long discusses the ambience in which knowledge and expertise was exchanged in the late medieval and early modern period. She suggests that the notion of 'trading zone' can be helpful in understanding how the transition from scholastic methods of knowledge production to empirically based inquiries about the natural world could occur. 'Trading zones' can be defined as 'arenas in which the learned taught the skilled and the skilled taught the learned', via face-to-face communication, writing books, creating things or in other ways. Long argues that the number and range of such sites of exchange of knowledge, values and skills in fifteenth- and sixteenth-century Europe greatly increased. Arsenals, mines, ore-processing sites and capital cities, she demonstrates in her essay, were particularly important cases in point.

Simona Valeriani looks at the media by which different categories of knowledge got connected. She argues that the emergence of a new culture for the investigation of nature in early modern Europe was a result of a combination of categories of knowing that had been separate in the Middle Ages, such as 'theory/praxis, intellectuals/artisans/speculative knowledge/skill'. An important role in the coming together of these different categories was played by what she calls 'in-between objects' such as maps, instruments or three-dimensional models. Models are a location where 'minds' meets 'hand' and where knowledge is exchanged between actors from different backgrounds and different 'epistemic traditions'. The mediating function of models between categories of knowledge is particularly evident at an early date in architecture, which Valeriani illustrates with a case study on the use of models by Christopher Wren.

Lissa Roberts concentrates on the aspect of circulation. She examines how exactly '(useful and reliable) knowledge' circulated in the early modern period and where and in what ways 'that which circulated' was learned and appropriated. Circulation of knowledge could only take place by some form of physical embodiment (in humans, books, machines, instruments, etc.) and the very fact of embodiment implied that the knowledge which was embodied could be formed or transformed. Embodiment thus was not a neutral phenomenon. What circulated, Roberts insists, was not ready-made, stable knowledge but 'multi-valent', 'dynamic' knowledge or knowing that was being shaped in the process of circulation itself. Moreover, learning or appropriating knowledge should not be viewed as an act of cognition by individual, closed minds but as an ongoing process in which a variety of actors, human and non-human, were involved and which could assume both tacit and articulate forms. This process of knowledge-formation occurred in a complex interplay with economic interests and power relations.

In the last essay of this thematic issue Karel Davids sets out to historicize the notion 'useful knowledge' itself by raising the question who defined 'useful knowledge' in early modern times, how and on the basis of what criteria they did it and which variations in definition occurred and why. Davids argues that 'utility' of knowledge has for a long time carried a variety of meanings but that the range of meanings was progressively narrowed in the late seventeenth and eighteenth century. The emergence of 'useful' knowledge in the sense employed by present-day historians is in his view thus also a story of loss. A whole set of meanings has been discarded or forgotten. Variations in the definition of 'usefulness' can according to Davids be explained by the rise and fall of different groups of 'gatekeepers' of knowledge, which were underpinned by changes in social, political or institutional power.

These different perspectives on the concept of 'useful knowledge' may also have implications for debates on the very issues for which the notion proved to be so fruitful to begin with, such as the sources of economic growth, the origins of the Industrial Revolution or the emergence of new ways to investigate nature. They generate all sorts of fresh questions, which may be the starting point for new directions of research. For example: under what circumstances could 'trading zones' of knowledge expand or contract? Under what conditions did the *concept* of 'useful knowledge' interact with technology in *practice*? To what extent were particular notions of 'usefulness' instrumental in stimulating, hampering or redirecting technological change or economic growth? How did the formation of 'useful knowledge' interact with political power? How did global travelling affect the development of 'useful knowledge'? Under what circumstances could 'in-between objects' actually bring together different categories of knowledge and create a favourable environment for new ways to study nature?

Such questions may be helpful in investigating even bigger issues as well. In November 1834, British and American missionaries and merchants in Canton founded the Society for the Diffusion of Useful Knowledge in China. 'In our days', the founders stated, 'many nations have begun the race for improvement; and are now moving onward in swift career, their course being constantly made more luminous by the light of science, and more rapid by the force of truth. This has resulted from the *diffusion of useful knowledge* among them'. The aim of the new society was to help the Chinese to join 'the other nations in the march of intellect'and rouse 'their sleeping energies to inquiries after knowledge'.[6] Studying questions such as those mentioned above may help us to understand why Westerners in the early nineteenth century took it for granted they were achieving ever faster 'improvement' thanks to something called 'useful knowledge' and why they thought China could benefit from the pursuit of this sort of knowledge as well. But these questions should not only be addressed for Europe or for the United States, they should be approached from the Asian side, too. To what extent, for example, were particular notions of 'usefulness' instrumental in stimulating, hampering or redirecting technological change or economic growth in China or other regions in Asia? How did the formation of 'useful knowledge' in those parts of the world interact with political power? And under what circumstances could 'in-between objects' bring together different categories of knowledge in Asia? Answers to those questions are equally urgent as in the case of Europe or the United States. In this way, the study of 'useful knowledge' doubtless makes a significant contribution to the ongoing debate about the origins of the Great Divergence.

Notes

1. Simon Kuznets, *Economic Growth and Structure* (New York, 1965), 85–7.

2. Joel Mokyr, *The Gifts of Athena. Historical Origins of the Knowledge Economy* (Princeton, 2002).

3. Stephan R. Epstein, 'Journeymen Mobility and the Circulation of Technical Knowledge, XVI–XVIIth Centuries', in, *Les chemins de la nouveauté. Innover, inventer au regard de l'histoire*, eds Liliane Hilaire-Pérez and Anne-Françoise Garçon (Paris, 2003), 411–30, idem, 'Property Rights to Technical Knowledge in Premodern Europe, 1300–1800', *American Economic Review*, 2004, 94: 382–7, idem, 'Labour Mobility, Journeymen Organisations and Markets in Skilled Labour Markets in Europe, 14th–18th Centuries', in *Le technicien dans la cité en Europe Occidentale, 1250–1650*, eds Mathieu Arnoux and Pierre Monnet (Rome, 2004), 251–69, Stephan R. Epstein and Maarten Prak, 'Introduction: Guilds, Innovation, and the European Economy, 1400–1800', in, *Guilds, Innovation, and the European Economy, 1400–1800*, eds idem (Cambridge, 2008), 1–24.

4. Ian Inkster, 'Potentially Global: "Useful and Reliable Knowledge" and Material Progress in Europe, 1474–1914', *The International History Review*, 2006, 28: 237–86, esp. 283–5.

5. 'Reflections on Joel Mokyr's The Gifts of Athena', special issue *History of Science*, 2007, 25: part 2, number 148.

6. Michael C. Lazich, 'Placing China in its "Proper Rank among the Nations": The Society for the Diffusion of Useful Knowledge in China and the First Systematic Account of the United States in China', *Journal of World History*, 2011, 22: 527–51, esp. 536.

Trading Zones: Arenas of Exchange during the Late-Medieval/Early Modern Transition to the New Empirical Sciences

PAMELA O. LONG*

Independent Historian

The focus of this paper is the transition from the text- and commentary-based methods of knowledge production in the late medieval universities to the 'new sciences' that developed from the mid-sixteenth through the seventeenth centuries. The paper takes up in a new way, the Zilsel thesis of artisanal influence on the 'scientific revolution'.[1] It suggests that an important aspect of the transition from scholastic to empirically based investigations of the natural world was the growing importance of 'trading zones' in which skilled individuals, who had acquired their skill in apprenticeship relationships, either informal or formal, increasingly engaged in substantive communication with more 'learned' individuals educated in universities, and with elite individuals.

At the outset it is important to recall the complexity of a transition that spanned several centuries, involved numerous disciplines, occupations and activities, both traditional and innovative, and encompassed fundamental social and economic as well as intellectual changes. No single explanation suffices. Further, current scholarship rejects a starkly contrasting picture of medieval versus early modern attitudes towards investigating the natural world. Empirical traditions developed in antiquity. They continued through the medieval centuries, especially within certain Arabic traditions, within specific disciplines such as optics, and, as William Newman especially has shown, within the practices of alchemy.[2] Moreover, as has long been recognized, Aristotelianism and the scholastic practices of the universities enjoyed influence through the seventeenth century, were capable of considerable change and innovation and related in complex ways with more empirical approaches – sometimes in conflict, at other times in harmony or creative dialogue.[3]

Other issues concern the relationships of specific investigative endeavours, such as astronomy or natural history, to the values and attitudes of the broader culture. In general, I suggest that empirical values – the belief in the efficacy of individual experience and experiment, observation, measurement, the use of instruments and precision – became, by the late sixteenth century, values that prevailed in the broader society. Thus, they became more readily available for use by particular individuals and groups for the investigation of the natural world.

The cultural and intellectual movement of humanism was particularly relevant to this development. With its emphasis on rhetoric, history, moral philosophy and Ciceronian Latin, humanism initially developed in the fourteenth century outside of the universities but by the late fifteenth century exerted significant influence within them. The humanist interest in particular actions, in practice, in history, in how to live a good life and in Greek and Roman antiquity,[4] including ancient objects like coins, statues and ancient ruins,[5] encouraged the investigation of particular objects and specific phenomena. Humanist study of certain texts – for example the *De architectura* of Vitruvius[6] – led to friendships and joint investigative ventures between university-trained men and workshop-trained artisans. Together men of diverse backgrounds physically examined and measured ancient ruins with Vitruvius's often obscure text in hand. Examples of friendships and substantive communication between artisan-trained men and university-trained men abound – Alberti and Brunelleschi, Antonio Averlino, called Filarete, and Filelfo, Raffael and Marco Fabio Calvo, Titian and Pietro Aretino, Palladio and Daniele Barbaro, to mention a few of the best-known examples.[7]

Such friendships were one result of changes in the visual arts in the fifteenth century, including the discovery of artist's perspective and the investigation and adoption of classical forms.[8] The increasing cultural importance of vision and the renaissance of the visual arts brought with it the rising status of practitioners associated with its various arts and an expansion of writings on the visual arts and other topics having to do with fabrication and practice, including engineering and machines.[9] (Such – for the modern world – diverse practices were in this period not strictly separated from each other; artisans trained as painters often became proficient in engineering and architecture as well.) The lure of the machine becomes ever more evident as manuscript and then printed books come to be filled with discussions of and illustrations of machines and mechanical devises from gears to springs to mills, to carriage mechanisms, to guns. The spectacular 'theatres of machines' that appeared in the last quarter of the sixteenth century, often in large folio editions, are the end products of a long tradition.[10] At the same time the mathematical arts were transformed and came to be applied in a thoroughgoing way to mechanical and engineering problems.[11]

The emerging importance of trading zones, then, is just one aspect of a complex, long-term cultural development (the broad outlines of which I have suggested above) and are familiar to historians and historians of science. Yet the proliferation of 'trading zones' between the learned and the skilled has not received sufficient attention as an aspect of this cultural development through two centuries between 1400 and 1600. Turning to this phenomenon, it needs to be emphasized that the categories themselves began to erode. Some learned men acquired skill. Some of the skilled worked to learn Latin and acquired some of the basics of humanist learning.

TRADING ZONES

The metaphor of the trading zone refers to arenas – symbolic or actual places – where people from different backgrounds who might hold quite different views and assumptions communicate in substantive ways. Peter Galison, deriving the idea from anthropological studies, developed the concept for the history of science and applied it to studies of twentieth-century particle physics to explain how subspecialist groups of physicists who took very different approaches to their subject could communicate with each other and with engineers about how to develop particle detectors and radar; and how experimenters, instrument makers and theorists could communicate without changing their diverse theoretical orientations or practices, while maintaining different ideas about what they were doing and what their results meant.[12]

'Trading zones' as I use the phrase here with reference to fifteenth- and sixteenth-century Europe differs from Galison's meaning in that he deals with highly developed professional groups working within ever-more-specialized subdisciplines. In contrast, the earlier period that is my focus precedes the development of professionalization especially in areas such as architecture and engineering. There was a kind of fluidity and openness to discussion concerning issues of design and construction and problems in engineering in which a variety of people from diverse backgrounds offered opinions, suggested alternatives, conversed with one another, and produced relevant writings and drawings. What passed for 'expertise' could vary from one situation to another and was far more diverse and fluid than has been the case since the full development of professionalism (and its requisite educational and licensing requirements) in modern times.[13]

To demarcate 'trading zones' more precisely, they must be distinguished from patron/client relationships. In the latter, certainly there is communication or exchange between two individuals, one with greater power and resources than the other. The patron gives money, employment, or some other benefit, while the client provides a service, or some kind of compensatory gift such as the dedication of a treatise.[14] Yet unlike in a trading zone, this type of communication does not involve the reciprocal exchange of substantive knowledge or expertise. Likewise, a trading zone is not identical to a gift exchange. In such exchanges, the donor bestows a gift accompanied by the expectation (as Marcel Mauss explicated) of something in return.[15] Such gift items could involve a great variety of objects including books and natural history specimens. But, in a trading zone, what is traded is substantive knowledge or expertise.

Early modern trading zones consisted of arenas in which the learned taught the skilled, and the skilled taught the learned, and in which the knowledge involved in each arena was valued by both kinds of 'traders'. (However, this statement must be qualified because increasingly the boundaries between the two became less clear as the two types of individuals acquired each other's skills and practices.) This exchange often involved direct one-to-one oral communication, but it could also involve indirect forms of exchange such as writing a book, which is later read, or the discussing, editing, translating and commentating of the kind that occurred in the Vitruvian tradition. What was required was that learned individuals valued practical and technical knowledge, not only for what it could achieve in the material world (such as palaces or fine jewelry) but also as a form of knowledge. Similarly, artisan/practitioners valued knowledge of classical texts, archaeology and other kinds of knowledge traditionally belonging to learned humanists who knew Latin and had received a university education.

I suggest that the number and range of trading zones between the learned and the skilled increased dramatically in fifteenth- and especially sixteenth-century Europe. Within such trading zones, the people 'trading' tended to become more like one another and to lose the distinguishing characteristics deriving from their particular backgrounds. Many activities and particular places became trading zones during these two centuries. They include princely courts; print shops that saw extensive collaboration among authors, printers, designers, engravers, woodcutters, copy editors, patrons and proofreaders; instrument makers' shops; and coffee shops.[16] In these 'trading zones', both practitioners and learned humanists moved closer together in terms of their empirical values, their knowledge base and their habitual practices having to do with reading and writing, and with designing and fabricating or constructing physical things. Trading zones became middle grounds where learned and skilled individuals interacted and exchanged substantive knowledge as they often also engaged in constructive and productive activities, created innovative technologies and wrote tracts, pamphlets and books on the topic at hand. In this essay I focus on three kinds of locales that became trading zones – first, arsenals, then mines and metal-processing sites throughout Europe, and finally, the city. Concerning the third zone, I focus on one example – Rome in the late sixteenth century and more specifically hydraulic engineering efforts in Rome directed at flood control.

ARSENALS: SITES OF INNOVATION AND EXCHANGE

Arsenals proliferated throughout Europe in the fifteenth century and expanded in the sixteenth. They became sites for carrying out multiple tasks and for experimentation involving the manufacture of both guns and gunpowder. Men at arsenals tested ballistics, trained gunners, and designed and supervised the construction of fortifications. Some arsenals, including the famed Venetian arsenal, functioned in addition as dockyards in which ships were designed, constructed and outfitted. The varied activities at arsenals were complemented by a great expansion of writings on artillery and ballistics, fortification and shipbuilding and other maritime activities.[17]

Testing, precision measurement and experimentation became necessary aspects of the wide-ranging development of artillery. A late fourteenth-century record exists that shows that the city of Nuremberg had test-fired guns for both the quality of the metal and accuracy before delivering them to the duke of Bavaria. Such testing became standard procedure in arsenals throughout the empire from the fifteenth century through the seventeenth. Empirical practices of gun founding entailed a performance evaluation that involved precision measurement with regard to aim as well as a consideration of metallurgical materials and work methods.[18]

The active experimentation that characterized the development of artillery was evident in many parts of Europe. In the gun foundries of Flanders and Brabant, for example, a series of experiments and inventions brought about the improvement of gun carriages. Gun founders developed a variety of devices that stabilized the gun on the carriage, aided in handling the perennial problem of recoil and facilitated accurate aiming and firing. Ongoing experimentation also involved the production of gunpowder. By the mid-fifteenth century, the process of corning had been invented. Corned or granulated gunpowder replaced powdered gunpowder, thereby reducing the risk of accidental firing. Another innovation from the mid-fifteenth century created longer cannon, which improved the trajectory of the shot. As the use of artillery expanded, so also did the construction of arsenals. Along with these developments, numerous writings on artillery and gunpowder appeared.[19]

One of the most important arsenals of Europe was created by the Emperor Maximilian I (1459–1519) in Innsbruck in the Tyrol. Mines in nearby Schwaz supplied copper to the gun foundries and silver to pay for them. Large foundries in Innsbruck manufactured guns. Other shops forged, rolled and beat armour, and fabricated pikes and swords for the infantry. Specialists in workshops in the nearby town of Absam manufactured cannonballs. The great development of the Innsbruck arsenal was in large part the work of the master founder Gregor Löffler (ca. 1490–1564), the first master gunner to become an arms manufacturer. Löffler transformed his foundry in Innsbruck from an artisanal craft workshop to a large industrial plant, a change that met the needs of increasing demand from the mid-sixteenth century.[20]

The Innsbruck arsenal actively experimented and pursued innovations and improvements in the development of artillery, which included ongoing efforts to standardize the calibre of guns. The arsenal also designed wheeled carriages for guns. Similar developments occurred in the growing number of arsenals in other parts of Europe. The problem of multiple calibres, which led to inefficiency and slowness of fire in battle, was addressed in many arsenals, for example in England by Henry VIII (1491–1547) and in France. The French also worked successfully to achieve greater gun mobility and, like the arsenal at Innsbruck, developed a system in which different types of guns retained the same length barrel. Spanish arsenals paid particular attention to light field artillery and small arms. The Spaniards also developed their own unique gun barrels that were widest in the center and double tapered towards the breach and towards the muzzle.[21]

Georg Hartmann (1489–1564), a mathematician and instrument maker, had studied theology and mathematics at the University of Cologne. After a sojourn in Italy, he moved to Nuremberg in south Germany and set up an instrument shop where he made globes, astrolabes, sundials and quadrants. In

1540 he invented a calibre scale, a metal rule that showed the internal diameter of a cannon and the corresponding weights of stone, iron and lead shot. This instrument made it unnecessary to weigh the shot before loading guns, thus simplifying its use in battle. In England, in the same decade, the gun founder Ralph Hogge of Buxted (fl. 1540s) succeeded in casting guns in iron. During the sixteenth century, the kings of Spain were offered and reviewed numerous military inventions – from rapid-firing artillery to transportable bridges, to a portable mill for grinding grain in a fortress under siege. Models, demonstrations and tests of new devices were commonplace. The crown often referred proposals to the Council of War, which included military experts, for further consideration. Monopolies were granted for devices deemed workable and useful, the most important being an improved match for arquebuses (an early muzzle-loaded firearm), and a new technique of careening, that is, the cleaning and repairing of ship bottoms.[22]

Spanish ship construction in the late sixteenth and seventeenth centuries centered on two basic types of ship. The galley, an oared ship also powered by sails, had a shallow draft and was suitable for use in the Mediterranean. The centre for galley construction, especially during the rule of Philip II (1527–98), was the arsenal of Barcelona. Philip II began the reform of Spanish naval power, and by 1574 had built a fleet of 150 galleys. However, as Spain turned towards the Atlantic, the high-velocity tidal currents, gales and huge waves made the galley unsuitable. A second type of ship, the galleon, came into use. It was a large three-masted sailing ship suitable for Atlantic seafaring. Invented either by the Venetians around 1520 or developed from the Portuguese caravel (its precise origins are unclear), it was adopted by Spain. Spain's north coast became a center for building galleons. Ongoing discussion, debate and experiment focused on the best way to build a galleon for stability, manoeuvrability and ability to carry sufficient cargo and guns.[23]

In England the ordnance office created during the reign of Henry VIII was located in the Tower of London. Officers of the ordnance included individuals responsible for technical matters. The surveyor was a mathematical practitioner skilled in measurement and surveying, who tested the quality and quantity of armaments and other goods when received. He also supervised the proof master's testing of goods and ammunition, and he surveyed the land and building work in the construction of forts. The office also employed engineers who designed and built forts, fire masters (in charge of gunpowder and explosives), master gunners and ordinary gunners. All needed some degree of mathematical training. Some carried out skilled mathematical practices in the ordnance office as they also disseminated their knowledge by writing books on mathematical and mechanical topics. For example, in the early seventeenth century, the surveyor of the ordnance, Jonas More (1617–79), pursued wide-ranging interests in practical mathematics and wrote books on mathematics and fortification.[24]

The Venetian arsenal, key to the defence of the Venetian state and to Venetian cultural pride, was famous throughout Europe. By the sixteenth century it had become a vast, multifaceted enterprise. Occupying about 20 hectares of land, the arsenal was surrounded by more than four kilometres of walls and moats. It employed hundreds of artisans called *arsenalotti*, skilled workers who received the only guaranteed wage in Venice. The arsenal was organized to include three largely separate spheres of production. The largest section was devoted to building, repairing and outfitting ships. Another department manufactured ropes and cables, and a third was charged with the manufacture of arms and gunpowder.[25]

From the early fifteenth century, shipbuilders in the Venetian arsenal experimented with a variety of ship designs, often in rivalry with one another. Notable is a dynasty of Greek masters starting with Teodoro Baxon or Bassanus (d. ca. 1407), who brought techniques to the arsenal from the island of Rhodes. Baxon created a number of new designs, including a light galley that he made wider and heavier than the traditional vessel without sacrificing speed. The Venetian Senate, which governed Venice and controlled the arsenal, encouraged Baxon as well as native Venetian shipbuilders to produce innovative designs that were seaworthy. After Baxon's death the Venetian Senate attempted to lure his nephew Nicolò Palopano from the island of Rhodes, and finally succeeded in 1424. Palopano and Bernardo di Bernardo, the foreman of the ship carpenters of the arsenal, began a long rivalry encouraged by the Venetian Senate. It continued until Palopano's death in 1437.[26]

It was within the ambience of the Venetian arsenal during the time of Palopano that the earliest extant treatise on shipbuilding was composed. Its author was Michael of Rhodes (d. 1445), a mariner who created and illustrated his book for the most part in the 1430s. Although he did not work directly for the arsenal, Michael wrote his book in its shadow and was probably assisted, at least with information, by someone inside. Presumably from the island of Rhodes, Michael hired on to a Venetian galley in 1401 in the low position of oarsman, when he was about 16 years old. Thereafter, he worked his way up into various officer positions in over 40 voyages, which he carefully recorded in the autobiographical service record that he wrote into his book. He gave his position on board, as well as the names of the captain and noble patrons of most of the ships on which he served.[27] His book contains an abacus or mathematical treatise of more than 200 pages, revealing that he was a good mathematician[28]; a portolan (navigational directions),[29] a section on the zodiac with charming illustrations of the zodiacal signs[30]; and much calendrical material concerning such matters as the date of Easter and the dates of the full moon.[31] He created his own unique coat-of-arms (arrogating to himself a privilege allowed only to nobles) with a mouse eating a cat perched on top, two turnips on the side and an M blazed in the middle.[32] The shipbuilding section, which treats the construction of three types of galley and two diverse round ships, contains numerous drawings with measurements, such as those related to the construction of the hull.[33]

Michael probably wrote his book as a way to impress the Venetian nobles who hired officers for their ships for each yearly voyage. Although he was a practitioner – a navigator and mariner – and although his book concerned the practices with which he was involved, Michael's book is not a practical manual; rather it served different cultural uses within wider social spheres within the culture of Venice and the Venetian maritime enterprise. It is a book by a practitioner that, as Piero Falchetta in particular has shown, is a step on the way to luxury navigational books destined for the library shelves of elite merchants and oligarchs. Indeed, Michael's book is evidence of a trading zone. It shows his learning of mathematics, astrology, calendrical matters and shipbuilding and that this knowledge went beyond the strictly practical aspects of his occupation as a mariner. It seems to have been written with the nonpractitioner in mind – elite Venetians who themselves would have been impressed and interested in the practical and technical aspects of shipbuilding and navigation.[34]

Michael in general was an autodidact whose great skill in mathematics suggests that at some point he may have found instruction from one of the many abacus masters who worked in Venice and elsewhere. Probably a native Greek speaker, he wrote (or sometimes copied from other texts) in Venetian. As he worked his way up from the very low position of oarsman, he clearly laboured to acquire graphic skill and become knowledgeable in diverse areas. He eventually attained, for some voyages, the highest officer position possible for non-noble mariners; officers in this position and for some of his other positions were permitted to eat at the captain's table. Whether he actually instructed the young Venetian nobles and other travellers in mathematics, as David McGee has speculated, is unknown.[35]

An intriguing coincidence puts Michael of Rhodes in the same convoy as Nicholas of Cusa, perhaps the greatest philosopher of the fifteenth century. Both men were in the same convoy of four ships sent to fetch the Byzantine emperor John VIII Palaiologos and his party of 700 traveling from Constantinople to Venice in 1437. The purpose of the trip was to bring the emperor to the Council of Ferrara-Florence, which many hoped would unite the Catholic and eastern Orthodox churches.[36] Whether the two men were on the same ship and, if so, whether they conversed is unknown. Nevertheless, Cusanus later wrote a treatise, *Idiota: De sapientia, de mente, de staticis experimentis* in which he advocated the knowledge of the 'unlearned' (the *Idiota*, that is, one without knowledge of Latin) and promoted the value of practical mathematics. The first two of the four books take the form of a dialogue between an unlearned man (the *idiota*) and an orator. The *idiota* shows the way to wisdom by rejecting the learning of the orator based on the authority of books. He suggests instead, that wisdom can be found in the streets and marketplaces where ordinary weighing and measuring occur.[37] An intriguing, but undocumented possibility is that the *idiota* in the dialogue could have been modelled on Michael of Rhodes.

Although Michael was an excellent mathematician, he was not a shipbuilder and would not have been able to build a ship. He undoubtedly obtained drawings and other information concerning ship construction from someone, probably one of the Rhodians, working in the arsenal. After the death of the Rhodian master shipbuilder Palopano in 1437, shipbuilders in the Venetian arsenal through the fifteenth and sixteenth centuries continued to produce innovations with, as we have seen, the active involvement of the Venetian Senate. Within this atmosphere of self-conscious rivalry and experimentation, shipwrights created new versions of great merchant galleys, an armed sailing ship called the *barza* (a round ship designed for fighting pirates in the Mediterranean) and light galleys. New ideas often required the presentation of models and arguments in favour of the efficacy of the design over the objections of detractors. This long tradition of naval construction and experimentation at the arsenal provided the ideal setting for Vettor Fausto (after 1480–ca. 1546). Fausto was a humanist who won the position of public lecturer of Greek eloquence in Venice and then embarked on a project to design and then improve on the quinquereme, an oared ship with five rows of oars that had been used by the Greeks in antiquity. Fausto had studied both literature and mathematics and had produced a text and translation of the pseudo-Aristotelian *Mechanics*. The Venetian Senate reviewed his model, and after much debate, provided him with the materials, space and personnel at the arsenal to build it. Launched in 1529 to great public fanfare, Fausto's quinquereme was taken to be a victory in the revival of Greek science.[38]

Fausto eventually was given a permanent position in the arsenal, and he continued to produce innovations as he directed the construction of ships. He is a figure for whom it would not be possible to separate his learning and his technical skill – he seems to have fully possessed both. His influence was still in evidence at the end of the sixteenth century. In 1593, one of his pupils, the shipwright Giovanni di Zaneto, applied some of the principles of the quinquereme to the design of the *galeazza*, a great galley adapted specifically for war. Zaneto's goal was to make this ship as mobile as light galleys. Among the individuals consulted in this matter was the local professor of mathematics, Galileo Galilei (1564–1642). Galileo concerned himself with other military matters as well, such as his invention of a military compass, about which he also wrote a small book. Jürgen Renn and Matteo Valleriani have argued that early in his career Galileo was closely connected to the arsenal and that the development of his thought was strongly influenced by the practical problems, especially concerning the strength of materials that he confronted there.[39]

Although the book of Michael of Rhodes remained in manuscript form until the twenty-first century, Venice in the sixteenth century functioned as one of the great printing centres of Europe and produced large numbers of practical and technical books, many on topics relevant to the arsenal. They included books on artillery, fortification and other aspects of the military arts, such as the posthumously published *Pirotechnia* by the metallurgist Vannoccio Biringuccio (1480–ca. 1537), who headed the armoury at Rome in his last years. The *Pirotechnia* contained the first detailed description of the casting of bronze cannon and also described boring methods and explained how to produce standard calibres.[40] Niccolò Tartaglia (1500–57), a mathematics teacher from Brescia who worked in Venice, produced two works on mechanics and mathematics that investigated problems of ballistics: *Nova scientia* (1537) and *Quesiti et inventioni diverse* (1546). Tartaglia uses the dialogue form in his tracts. He depicts himself and others such as gunners discussing a variety of questions with noble princes and dukes. The conversations between gunners and nobles concern topics such as the mathematical trajectories of cannon balls, the best angle for aiming the cannon barrel and other issues of ballistics. Tartaglia worked on both theoretical and practical mathematical problems. He devised a gunner's quadrant that could help determine the correct position and angle for the efficacious firing of cannon. He also made diagrams of ballistics and analyzed ways of aiming accurately. He produced a table of calibres that mentions 24 kinds of guns.[41]

MINES AND ORE-PROCESSING SITES

Mining in late medieval Europe was closely associated with arsenals because guns, large and small, were made of metal – either iron or bronze. Eventually cannonballs were made of iron rather than stone. By the mid-fifteenth century the expanded manufacture of gunpowder artillery and the proliferation of princely and noble mints for the production of specie led to a scarcity of metals. Scarcity provided princely and wealthy investors with motivation to take on the cost and technical problems associated with digging deeper mines, and as a result, mining changed radically in the mid-fifteenth century. Medieval mining had usually constituted a local, often family based, small-scale enterprise, sometimes carried out seasonally as a supplement to agriculture, and it was limited to shallow mines. The new capitalist mining enterprises, in contrast, constituted large-scale operations that employed many workers for wages. These operations profited in part by digging deeper mines and solving the technical problems of ventilation, water removal and ore removal that accompanied greater depth. To support such endeavours, princes and wealthy entrepreneurs invested money, buying shares in mine operations. For about a hundred years, between 1450 and 1550, they were richly rewarded by a central European mine boom with greatly increased production of silver, copper, iron, tin and lead.[42]

To solve the problem of removing water and extracting ore from deep mines, miners employed large pumps and other machinery, often powered by waterwheels. Types of water-removing machinery illustrated in Georg Agricola's famous *De re metallica* (1556) include piston pumps made from hollowed-out tree trunks, endless bucket chains and reversible hydraulic wheels. The most productive mines were in central Europe, in the Erzgebirge, at Schwaz in the Tyrol and in Hungary. These locations were the sites of large-scale operations such as excavation and processing of silver-bearing copper. Several thousand workers, women as well as men, might work at a single mine; some worked underground; some carried materials; some prepared charcoal; and some were involved in, separating, smelting and refining ores.[43]

The largest ore-processing operations involved the production of silver and copper after the discovery of new methods for processing silver-bearing copper ores. *Saigerhütten*, as they were called in central Germany, were constructed in Saxony, the Tyrol and elsewhere. These large plants included many hearths, furnaces, bellows, hammers, stamping machinery (most driven by waterwheels), crucibles and many kinds of tools. Other metal-producing regions included Sweden and Alsace for silver production and Italy for alum, discovered in Civita Vecchia around 1462 and essential in the textile industry for fixing dyes. Iron production expanded rapidly in many areas of Europe in the sixteenth century. Iron processing was transformed by the development of the blast furnace, invented through a process of modifying the traditional bloomery furnace. The bloomery furnace produced a spongy iron called a bloom that was further worked by hammering at a forge. The blast furnace achieved higher heats by means of larger bellows, higher chimneys, and other modifications. Instead of the bloom, it produced molten iron that poured into forms known as pigs. Blast furnaces required greater capital investment and had to be operated continuously for effective production. By the mid-sixteenth century, cast-iron production included products such as cannonballs, pots and pans and guns. Liège, France, became a site for a large-scale coal-mining operation. Tin was produced in large quantities in the English counties of Cornwall and Devon.[44]

Technical innovation and mechanization were hallmarks of early modern mining and ore processing. Mines were dug deeper; galleries and shafts were improved; winches and hoists were installed for ore removal; waterpower was increasingly employed to power pumps and other water-removal equipment, with the more efficient overshot wheel gradually replacing the undershot. Blast furnaces were improved and increasingly used in iron production. Experiments in making alloys and compound metals were ongoing and often entailed the modification of existing techniques. In one innovation, lead was used to make tinplate. Bismuth, discovered in the thirteenth century, was developed commercially for the first time in the sixteenth when it was added to lead and tin to make metal type. Printers' type was later fabricated from harder alloys of lead and antimony, which were also cheaper.[45]

Perhaps the most important innovation came out of a series of experiments that resulted in a technique of processing argentiferous copper ores by alloying copper and lead to produce silver. The three-stage process entailed the addition of lead. First the ore was melted at high temperatures, creating an alloy of lead and argentiferous copper. As the ore cooled, the different temperatures at which copper and lead melt allowed separate crystallizations of copper and silver-bearing lead. This product was then heated in a roasting oven, wherein the lead ore gave off copper crystals. The copper was refined in a drying oven, and the silver was separated from the lead in cupellation ovens. The elements of this complex system developed from alchemical traditions and from the expanding cumulative knowledge acquired from minting coins. It is first documented in Nuremberg in the mid-fifteenth century. It is an invention at the heart of the central European mine boom, producing much higher yields of silver and thereby increasing the profitability of silver and copper mining. It could not be adopted straightforwardly to particular mining operations but often had to be modified to take into account the specific qualities of various local ores. Such modifications required ongoing experimentation. There is evidence that princes were directly involved in initiating experiments by goldsmiths, metallurgists and others to adapt the process to local conditions in planning mines and ore-processing operations.[46]

Mines constituted important early modern sites for technical experimentation and innovation. Their cultural significance increased with the proliferation of pamphlets and books on mining and metallurgy, especially important from the early sixteenth century. Mine overseers, assayers and other practitioners, learned humanists, and occasionally nobles, wrote books ranging from small pamphlets to detailed and lavishly illustrated treatises on mining, ore processing, assaying, mine organization and mine law. Of the printed books, an early Italian treatise that became well-known in German territories was Biringuccio's *Pirotechnia*, mentioned above. Far more extensive than previous writings, the *Pirotechnia* treated ores and ore processing, assaying, gold and silver refining, alloys, the art of casting, methods of melting metals, small casting, procedures of working with fires, gunpowder and fireworks. Biringuccio's extensive textual descriptions of many of these processes were illustrated by woodcuts.[47]

Biringuccio was a practitioner and overseer, but other authors of books on mining and metallurgy were university-trained humanists. Calbus of Freiberg (d. 1523) wrote a small dialogue about mining and ores (*Bergbüchlein*). The well-known humanist and physician Georg Agricola (1494–1555) wrote a dialogue titled *Bermanus* (1530), in which three interlocutors, two physicians and a mine overseer (Bermanus), discuss regional ores and those mentioned in ancient texts, as they wander in the Erzegebirge. Agricola portrays Bermanus as combining direct observation and experience with knowledge of ancient texts. Agricola's famous treatise on mining and metallurgy, *De re metallica*, was published posthumously in 1556. The humanist Latin treatise contained a defence of mining modelled after the ancient author Columella's defence of agriculture. It also contained rich detail concerning various mine and metallurgical operations and spectacular illustrations of the machines, furnaces and various processes involved in mining and ore processing. Lazarus Ercker (ca. 1530–94), an assayer and overseer, wrote a number of books on assaying and ore processing, the last of which was an expansive treatise with illustrations in which the author emphasizes the importance of his own practical experience. Most sixteenth-century mining and metallurgical treatises were printed, but some, such as the *Schwazer Bergbuch*, were written expressly as manuscript books. The copies of the *Schwazer Bergbuch* are adorned with beautifully hand-painted miniature illustrations of various mine operations. It was written by Ludwig Lässl (d. 1561), an official in the mine court of Schwaz in the Tyrol.[48]

Books on mining, ore processing and metallurgy were written mostly for princes and for a far-flung group of investors in mining, most of whom did not possess mining skills or specialized expertise. The books set out many technical processes in written form, rationalizing the disciplines of mining and metallurgy, using and in part creating precise technical vocabulary. Many of the treatises contained illustrations that provided vivid visual detail of machines and operations. The books often described with great clarity technical operations and equipment. Illustrations were often essential for making complex machinery comprehensible, but they also made the mechanical arts of mining and metallurgy dramatically appealing to the unskilled.

THE CITY – ROME IN THE LATE SIXTEENTH CENTURY

A very different kind of location that became a trading zone was the city. Cities were expanding in the late sixteenth century, becoming sites of building construction, hydraulic engineering projects and other projects of urbanization, such as the construction and paving of streets.[49] Here I discuss Rome in the late sixteenth century. As a capital city headed by the pope, Rome cannot be called typical, although it did share some characteristics with other expanding cities of the same period.

Rome in this period became a particularly important centre of communication between the skilled and the learned. The urban space was in the process of being transformed by intense activity involving building construction and urban projects – the construction and renovation of churches and palaces; the repair and reconstruction of two great aqueducts, the Acqua Vergine and the newly named Acqua Felice; the creation of new fountains made possible by the greatly augmented water supply; the widening and paving of streets; the redesign of squares; the transport of obelisks from their ancient sites to new locations; and numerous projects aimed at preventing the periodic disastrous flooding of the Tiber River. The goal of such activities was the renewal and transformation of the city.[50]

Especially after the reform of the Catholic Church undertaken after the conclusion of the Council of Trent in the early 1560s, the popes renewed their efforts to create a splendid city consonant with its role as the capital of the Christian world. The intense activity of construction and engineering, combined with the complex patronage situation characteristic of Rome, not only transformed the urban landscape but also brought about the production of numerous writings and images, including cartographical images, related to the practical and engineering concerns of the city. In many urban projects learned individuals interacted with engineers and artisans in significant ways.[51] This extensive interchange between learned and technical cultures could have happened only before the advent of professional engineering and outside of the context of powerful guild control, in a city that was expending construction and engineering efforts in many directions. Here I discuss one example of this interchange having to do with hydraulic engineering, specifically flood control.

The Tiber River, which flowed through the centre of Rome and provided essential water and other resources to the city, was prone to flooding. The disastrous flood of 1557 resulted in widespread destruction to the city and to its infrastructures such as sewers and bridges. It was neither the first nor the last flood of the unruly Tiber River, but it was a particularly severe one. Because of its severity and also perhaps because of the particular era in which it occurred, one result was an unusual number of writings by both practitioners and learned men that treated the problem of flooding from a variety of points of view and suggested diverse solutions.[52]

The physician Andrea Bacci spent the years from 1558 to his death in 1600 concerned with the flooding of the Tiber. He wrote his first treatise on the subject in 1558, and then continued to expand and revise it. There is an enlarged revision of 1576; a manuscript tract dedicated to Clement VIII, who became pope in 1592, written in the flyleaves of a copy of the 1576 edition in the Vatican library; and there is another expanded revision of 1599. Bacci had an ongoing interest in natural philosophical issues such as the nature of water and the causes of flooding, which included reflections on Aristotelian texts such as the *Meteorology*. He also provides recommendations for flood prevention in Rome that amount to what he considers a return to ancient Roman river management practices – fortify and augment the banks of the river, lower the riverbed to its ancient level, clean the drains and sewers, and appoint a caretaker of the rivers.[53]

The military engineer Antonio Trevisi arrived in Rome in 1559, and he soon brought out two publications that pertained to flooding. The first, in 1560, treated the flooding of the Tiber River. Trevisi dedicated it to Federico Borromeo (1535–62), the nephew of Pope Pius IV (r. 1559–65). He begins his treatise not with the issue at hand, but with a description of the Aristotelian cosmos, the kinds of waters on earth and the nature of water itself. In these discussions he follows Aristotle and is probably relying on Bacci's treatise published two years before. Trevisi does offer his plan to prevent flooding in one chapter of the treatise but ends with a chapter that consists of a dialogue between a master and an apprentice. Their topic of conversation is not flood control, but how to raise ships from the bottom of a lake. From the mid-fifteenth century the subject had been the focus of intense interest on the part of humanists and engineers, especially because two ancient ships had been discovered at the bottom of Lake Nemi to the south of Rome.[54] Thus did Trevisi present his engineering proposal surrounded by natural philosophical learning on the one hand, and a dialogue on a topic of humanist and engineering interest on the other.

Trevisi's second publication was the republication of a map of Rome originally created by a military engineer, Leonardo Bufalini (d. 1552), and first published in 1551. Trevisi's version, published in 1560, seems to have been the same as Bufalini's except that he added letters to the bottom addressed to the Conservators of Rome (the three men who led the communal government), to virtuous architects, to Carlo Borromeo (1538–84), brother of Federico and nephew to the pope and to readers. In the letters Trevisi urged his plan for flood control, which involved construction of a huge trench starting below Ponte Milvio and running through Prati (which was then relatively uninhabited) to a low-lying area between the Vatican and Trastevere called the Valle Inferno. Some aspects of Trevisi's proposal were carried out by Pius IV in the early 1560s, including the construction of large trenches around Castel San Angelo, which in part remain.[55]

Other writings on Tiber River flooding included a small tract by the magistrate Luca Peto (1512–81). Peto was a jurist who wrote the revised law code of Rome, published in 1580. He was also a magistrate who aided the completion of the repair of an ancient aqueduct, the Acqua Vergine, and he wrote a treatise on the weights and measures of the ancient Greeks and Romans. Concerning Tiber River flooding, he urged that the number of arches on the bridges be reduced and that the mills on the river be removed.[56]

As the examples of Trevisi, Bacci and Peto show, writers on the flooding of the Tiber dealt with the history of flooding, natural philosophical issues of the nature of water and the nature of flooding in diverse areas, and they offered practical engineering solutions. Whether the authors were practitioners like Trevisi or university-educated men like Bacci and Peto, their writings reveal an interest in both technical and practical issues and in history, natural philosophy and other aspects of learned culture.

CONCLUSION

The proliferation of trading zones between skilled artisans and learned men in the sixteenth century helped influence an approach to the investigation of the natural world that valued hands-on experience, accurate measurement and empirical approaches. This essay has treated several examples of arenas that became important trading zones – arsenals, mines and ore-processing sites and a capital city. Such trading zones developed because guns and fortification, mines and metals and vital and magnificent urban centres came to be central to the economic power and political authority of princes and oligarchs.

The development of such trading zones was accompanied by the proliferation of books on technological subjects, books written both by those trained in workshops and those trained in universities. It was in the context both of face-to-face conversations and investigations, and of writing and reading such books, that the skilled acquired learning and the learned acquired skill. The two categories overlapped and the distinction became blurred in certain spheres and arenas. This blurring of two separate realms did not occur universally through all ranks of society, nor did it change the hierarchical social and political structure of that society. Shoemakers and university professors still lived and worked worlds apart in the late sixteenth century, as they had in the twelfth. Still, the types of practitioners most often engaged in trading zones – painters, sculptors, engineer/architects and navigators, for example – did enjoy rising status in these centuries.

Many 'trading zones' developed and often were situated close to elite individuals and the essential interests of powerful rulers and states. This proximity to centres of power meant that the empirical values promoted and utilized in such trading zones gained general currency. Further, these powerful rulers, princes and oligarchs caused the built landscape to be visibly transformed with magnificent palaces, churches, public buildings and redesigned cities. Elites were themselves increasingly surrounded by luxurious goods, ornaments including paintings and sculptures in the new style and lavish apparel. Trading zones framed many of the activities that brought about these changes.

How precisely did the fifteenth- and sixteenth-century proliferation of trading zones influence the rise of the new sciences? Or, to put it another way, what ultimately became of trading zones in terms of their significance for those sciences? The answer is suggested by some of the studies in a recent collection, *The Mindful Hand*, whose editors argue that the imposition of divisions between handwork and intellectual work, between theory and practice, and other such dichotomies, which often frame accounts of the early modern sciences, is distorting. For example, in a fine study of seventeenth-century dioptrics, Fokko Dijksterhuis shows that theoretical, mathematical and constructive aspects of the study of refraction and the making of telescopes were fully integrated enterprises. Rather than being a separate activity (as it has traditionally been represented), the construction of accurate telescopes was as important and integral to the discipline of dioptrics as its theoretical and mathematical components, and all three went hand in hand.[57]

My view is that this integration of theoretical and practical components is the end result of a historical development – in dioptrics as well as in many of the other new sciences of the seventeenth century. Trading zones as arenas of influence represent a time-limited development. They become far less important as the new sciences develop in all their diversity and themselves incorporate the components of skill, theory and mathematics into their varied investigations of the natural world.

Notes

* This paper began as part of the Horning Visiting Scholar series of public lectures that I gave at Oregon State University in April 2010 that have been published as Pamela O. Long, *Artisan/ Practitioners and the Rise of the New Sciences, 1400–1600* (Corvallis, OR, 2011). A different version of the paper was presented at the workshop, 'Conceptualising the Production and Diffusion of Useful and Reliable Knowledge in Early Modern Europe', at the London School of Economics in January 2011. I thank Anita Guerrini and David Luft for inviting me to give the initial lecture series in Oregon, Patrick O'Brien and Simona Valeriani for inviting me to the London workshop and the audiences and participants in both venues for lively and valuable discussions.

1. See esp. Edgar Zilsel, *The Social Origins of Modern Science*, ed. Diederick Raven, Wolfgang Krohn and Robert S. Cohen (Dordrecht, 2000). See also Christian M. Götz and Thomas Pankratz, 'Edgar Zilsels Wirken im Rahmen der wiener Volksbildung und Lehrerfortbildung', in *Wien-Berlin-Prag: Der Aufstieg der wissenschaftlichen Philosophie: Zentenarien: Rudolf Carnap, Hans Reichenbach, Edgar Zilsel*, eds Rudolf Haller and Friedrich Stadler (Vienna, 1993), 467–73; Nicholas Jardine, 'Essay Review: Zilsel's Dilemma', *Annals of Science*, 2003, 60: 85–94; Wolfgang Krohn and Diederick Raven, 'The "Zilsel Thesis" in the Context of Edgar Zilsel's Research Programme', *Social Studies of Science*, 2000, 30: 925–33; Diederick Raven, 'Edgar Zilsel's Research Programme: Unity of Science as an Empirical Problem', in *The Vienna Circle and Logical Empiricism: Re-evaluation and Future Perspectives*, ed. Friedrich Stadler (Dordrecht, 2003), 225–34 and Monica Wulz, 'Collective Cognitive Processes around 1930: Edgar Zilsel's Epistemology of Mass Phenomena', http://philsci-archive.pitt.edu/archive/00004740/ (accessed 15 July 2010).

2. See esp. Jole Agrimi and Chiara Crisciani, 'Per una ricerca su *experimentum-experimenta*: Reflessione epistemologica e tradizione medica (secoli XIII–XV)', in *Presenza del lessico greco e latino nelle lingue contemporanee*, eds Pietro Janni and Innocenzo Mazzini (Macerata, 1990), 9–49; Peter Dear, 'The Meanings of Experience', in *The Cambridge History of Science*, vol. 3: *Early Modern Science*, eds Katharine Park and Lorraine Daston (Cambridge, 2008), 106–31; G. E. R. Lloyd, *Magic, Reason, and Experience: Studies in the Origin and Development of Greek Science* (Cambridge, 1979); and G. E. R. Lloyd, 'Experiment in Early Greek Philosophy and Medicine', in G. E. R. Lloyd, *Methods and Problems of Greek Science: Selected Papers* (Cambridge, 1991), 70–99; Heinrich von Staden, 'Physis and Technē in Greek Medicine', and Mark J. Schiefsky, 'Art and Nature in Ancient Mechanics', both in *The Artificial and the Natural: An Evolving Polarity*, eds Bernadette Bensaude-Vincent and William R. Newman (Cambridge, MA, 2007), 21–49 and 67–108, respectively; William R. Newman, *Promethean Ambitions: Alchemy and the Quest to Perfect Nature* (Chicago, 2004), 34–114; and William R. Newman, 'Technology and Alchemical Debate in the Late Middle Ages', *Isis*, 1989, 80: 423–45.

3. The foundational study is Charles B. Schmitt, *Aristotle and the Renaissance* (Cambridge, MA, 1983). For Aristotelianism in the medieval universities, see esp. Edward Grant, *The Foundations of Modern Science in the Middle Ages: Their Religious, Institutional, and Intellectual Contexts* (Cambridge, 1996), 33–53; and Paul F. Grendler, *The Universities of the Italian Renaissance* (Baltimore, 2002). See also Ann Blair, 'Natural Philosophy', in Park and Daston, eds., *op. cit.* (2), 365–406, esp. 372–9, who emphasizes innovations in Aristotelian natural philosophy during the Renaissance.

4. For an introduction to the large literature on humanism and the issues surrounding it, see esp. Christopher S. Celenza, *The Lost Italian Renaissance: Humanists, Historians, and Latin's Legacy* (Baltimore, 2004); Jill Kraye, ed., *The Cambridge Companion to Renaissance Humanism* (Cambridge, 1996); Albert Rabil, Jr, ed., *Renaissance Humanism: Foundations, Forms, and Legacy*, 3 vols. (Philadelphia, 1988); and Ronald G. Witt, *In the Footsteps of the Ancients: The Origins of Humanism from Lovato to Bruni* (Leiden, 2000). For humanism in the universities, see esp. Grendler, *op. cit. The Universities of the Italian Renaissance* (3), 199–248.

5. For antiquarian interest in physical objects, see esp. J. Fejfer, T. Fischer-Hansen and A. Rathje, eds, *The Rediscovery of Antiquity: The Role of the Artist* (Copenhagen, 2003); Philip J. Jacks, *The Antiquarian and the Myth of Antiquity: The Origins of Rome in Renaissance Thought* (Cambridge, 1993); Arnaldo Momigliano, 'Ancient History and the Antiquarian', *Journal of the Warburg and Courtauld Institutes*, 1950, 13: 285–315; Momigliano, 'The Rise of Antiquarian Research', in *The Classical Foundations of Modern Historiography*, Momigliano (Berkeley, 1990), 54–79; Alain Schnapp, *The Discovery of the Past*, trans. I. Kinnes and G. Varndell (New York, 1997); and Roberto Weiss, *The Renaissance Discovery of Classical Antiquity*, 2nd edn (Oxford, 1988).

6. Vitruvius, *On Architecture*, ed. and trans. Frank Granger, 2 vols, Loeb (Cambridge, MA, 1931–4). For a more recent English translation of the text and commentary with helpful drawings, see Vitruvius, *Ten Books on Architecture*, eds Ingrid D. Rowland and Thomas Noble Howe (Cambridge, 1999). A recent study and interpretation that places the work within the context of the Roman Empire is Indra Kagis McEwen, *Vitruvius: Writing the Body of Architecture* (Cambridge, MA, 2003). An erudite synthetic account of Vitruvian influence and architectural writing in the Renaissance is Alina A. Payne, *The Architectural Treatise in the Italian Renaissance: Architectural Invention, Ornament, and Literary Culture* (Cambridge, 1999); and see Pamela O. Long, *Artisan/Practitioners and the Rise of the New Sciences, 1400–1600* (Corvallis, OR, 2011), esp. chapter 3.

7. See Long, *op. cit.* (6), esp. chapters 3 and 4 for discussions and further bibliography.

8. See esp. Samuel Y. Edgerton, Jr, *The Renaissance Rediscovery of Linear Perspective* (New York, 1975); Martin Kemp, *The Science of Art: Optical Themes in Western Art from Brunelleschi to Seurat* (New Haven, CT, 1990); and Kim H. Veltman and Kenneth D. Keele, *Linear Perspective and the Visual Dimensions of Science and Art* (Munich, [?1986]). And see also the important study by Stuart Clark, *Vanities of the Eye: Vision in Early Modern European Culture* (Oxford, 2007).

9. See esp. Pamela O. Long, *Openness, Secrecy, Authorship: Technical Arts and the Culture of Knowledge from Antiquity to the Renaissance* (Baltimore, 2001); and Pamela H. Smith, *The Body of the Artisan: Art and Experience in the Scientific Revolution* (Chicago, 2004).

10. See esp. Horst Bredekamp, *The Lure of Antiquity and the Cult of the Machine*, trans. Allison Brown (Princeton, 1995); Luisa Dolza, 'Theatrum Machinarum: Utilitas et Delectation', in *The Power of Images in Early Modern Science*, eds J. Renn, W. Lefèvre, and U. Schoepflin (Bâle, 2003), 89–106; Daniela Lamberini, *Il Sanmarino: Giovan Battista Belluzzi, Architetto militare e trattatista del cinquecento* (Florence, 2007); Lamberini, *Il principe difeso: Vita e opera di Bernardo Puccini* (Florence, 1990); Wolfgang Lefèvre, ed., *Picturing Machines, 1400–1700* (Cambridge, MA, 2004); Rainer Leng, *Ars belli: Deutsche taktische und kriegstechnische Bilderhandschriften und Traktate im 15. und 16. Jahrhundert*, 2 vols. (Wiesbaden, 2002); Long, *op.cit.* (9); Marcus Popplow, *Neu, nützlich und erfinungsreich: Die Idealisierung von Technik in der frühen Neuzeit* (Münster, 1998); and Jonathan Sawday, *Engines of the Imagination: Renaissance Culture and the Rise of the Machine* (London, 2007).

11. For an excellent recent discussion, see Cesare S. Maffioli, *La via delle acque (1500–1700): Appropriazione delle arti e trasformazione delle matematiche* (Florence, 2010).

12. Peter Galison, *Image and Logic: A Material Culture of Microphysics* (Chicago, 1997), 781–844; Peter Galison, 'Computer Simulations and the Trading Zone', in *The Disunity of Science: Boundaries, Contexts, and Power*, eds Peter Galison and David J. Stump (Stanford, CA, 1996), 118–57; and Peter Galison, 'Trading with the Enemy', in *Trading Zones and Interactional Expertise*, ed. Michael E. Gorman (Cambridge, MA, 2010), 25–52.

13. For a study of expertise in these centuries, see Eric H. Ash, *Power, Knowledge, and Expertise in Elizabethan England* (Baltimore, 2004); and Ash, ed. *Expertise: Practical Knowledge and the Early Modern State, Osiris*, 2d ser., 2010, 25.

14. For discussions of patronage in the history of science, see esp. Bruce T. Moran, ed., *Patronage and Institutions: Science, Technology, and Medicine at the European Court, 1500–1750* (Rochester, NY, 1991); and Mario Biagioli, *Galileo Courtier: The Practice of Science in the Culture of Absolutism* (Chicago, 1993).

15. Marcel Mauss, *The Gift: Form and Reason for Exchange in Archaic Societies*, trans. W. D. Halls (New York, 1990). See also Pierre Bourdieu, *Outline of a Theory of Practice*, trans. Richard Nice (Cambridge, 1977), esp. 4–5, which points out that if subjective gift giving were understood in the way Mauss describes it objectively, the practice would fall apart. See also Paula Findlen, 'The Economy of Scientific Exchange in Early Modern Italy', in Moran, ed., *op. cit.* (14), 5–24.

16. To say that the individuals from diverse backgrounds came to lose some of their differences is not to suggest that they became the same. Although there are some instances where it is impossible to know which background a particular person came from, usually an individual maintained

his own identity while adopting some of the values of the other group. For studies of some of the trading zones mentioned here, see Bruce T. Moran, 'Courts and Academies', and Adrian Johns, 'Coffeehouses and Print Shops', in *The Cambridge History of Science*, Park and Daston, eds., *op. cit.* (2), 251–71 and 320–40, respectively; and Rob Iliffe, 'Material Doubts: Hooke, Artisan Culture, and the Exchange of Information in 1670s London', *BJHS*, 1995, 28: 285–318. For instrument makers' shops, see James A. Bennett, 'Shopping for Instruments in Paris and London', in *Merchants and Marvels: Commerce, Science, and Art in Early Modern Europe*, eds Pamela H. Smith and Paula Findlen (New York, 2002), 370–95.

   17. See Kelly DeVries, 'Sites of Military Science and Technology', in Park and Daston, eds. *op. cit.* (2), 306–19. For arsenals, see esp. Ennio Concina, ed., *Arsenali e città nell'occidente europeo* (Rome, 1987); and Ennio Concina, *L'Arsenale della Repubblica di Venezia* (Milan, 1984). For writings, see Maurice J. D. Cockle, *A Bibliography of Military Books up to 1642*, 2nd edn (London, 1957); Rainer Leng, *Ars belli: Deutsche taktische und kriegstechnische Bilderhandschriften und Traktate im 15. und 16. Jahrhundert*, 2 vols. (Wiesbaden, 2002); and Martha D. Pollak, *Military Architecture, Cartography, and the Representation of the Early Modern European City: A Checklist of Treatises on Fortification in the Newberry Library* (Chicago, 1991).

   18. Kelly DeVries, *Medieval Military Technology* (Peterborough, ON, 1992), 143–68; Bert S. Hall, *Weapons and Warfare in Renaissance Europe* (Baltimore, 1997), 105–200; and Volker Schmidtchen, *Bombarden, Befestigungen, Büchsenmeister: Von den ersten Mauerbrechern des Spätmittelalters zur Belagerungsartillerie der Renaissance* (Düsseldorf, 1977), 1–42.

   19. See Hall, *op. cit.* (18), 41–104; and Schmidtchen, *op. cit.* (18), 102–19.

   20. See Erich Egg, *Das Handwerk der Uhr- und der Büchsenmacher in Tirol* (Innsbruck, 1982), 183–201; and Erich Egg, *Der Tiroler Geschützguss, 1400–1600* (Innsbruck, 1961), esp. 95–162.

   21. Egg, *op. cit.* (20, *Der Tiroler Geschützguss); Erich Egg, 'From the Beginning to the Battle of Marignano – 1515', in *Guns: An Illustrated History of Artillery*, ed. Joseph Jobé (Greenwich, CT, 1971), 9–36; Schmidtchen, *op. cit.* (18), 83–94.

   22. Erich Egg, 'From Marignano to the Thirty Years' War, 1515–1648', in Jobé, ed., *op.cit.* (21), 37–54; and David Goodman, *Power and Penury: Government, Technology, and Science in Philip II's Spain* (Cambridge, 1988), 88–150. For Hogge and the English context, see Edmund B. Teesdale, *Gunfounding in the Weald in the Sixteenth Century* (London, 1991); and Edmund B. Teesdale, *The Queen's Gunstonemaker: Being an Account of Ralph Hogge, Elizabethan Ironmaster and Gunfounder* (Seaford, England, 1984). For an introduction to the work of Georg Hartmann, see John P. Lamprey, 'An Examination of Two Groups of Georg Hartmann Sixteenth-century Astrolabes and the Tables Used in their Manufacture', *Annals of Science*, 1997, 54: 111–42.

   23. Goodman, *op. cit.* (22), 88–108; David Goodman, *Spanish Naval Power, 1589–1665: Reconstruction and Defeat* (Cambridge, 1997); and Carla Rahn Phillips, *Six Galleons for the King of Spain: Imperial Defense in the Early Seventeenth Century* (Baltimore, 1986). For a classic account of the relationships of artillery and ships in the Mediterranean, see John Francis Guilmartin, Jr., *Gunpowder and Galleys: Changing Technology and Mediterranean Warfare at Sea in the Sixteenth Century* (Cambridge, 1974). For an excellent account of Spanish efforts to acquire and monopolize new technical and scientific knowledge, see Marìa M. Portuondo, *Secret Science: Spanish Cosmography and the New World* (Chicago, 2009).

   24. A. Rupert Hall's view that there was no connection between scientific ballistics and the practices of gunners has been effectively challenged by Frances Willmoth, who shows that the ordnance office played an important role in sustaining traditions of practical mathematics and mechanics, which included studies of ballistics. See A. Rupert Hall, *Ballistics in the Seventeenth Century: A Study in the Relations of Science and War with Reference Principally to England* (Cambridge, 1952); Richard W. Stewart, *The English Ordnance Office, 1585–1625: A Case Study in Bureaucracy* (Woodbridge, Suffolk, 1996); and Frances Willmoth, *Sir Jonas Moore: Practical Mathematics and Restorations Science* (Woodbridge, Suffolk, 1993); and for Tudor fortification, Steven A. Walton, 'State Building through Building for the State: Foreign and Domestic Expertise in Tudor Fortification,' in Ash, ed. *op. cit.* (12, *Expertise)*, 66–84. See also Steven Johnston, 'Making Mathematical Practice: Gentlemen, Practitioners, and Artisans in Elizabethan England' (PhD diss., Cambridge University, 1994), www.mhs.ox.ac.uk/staff/saj/thesis/abstract.htm (accessed 17 May 2011), which contains much about artillery and fortification as well as other mathematical topics; and see Anthony Gerbino and Stephen Johnston, *Compass and Rule: Architecture as Mathematical Practice in England* (Oxford, 2009).

25. See esp. Giorgio Bellavitis, *L'Arsenale di Venezia: Storia di una grande struttura urbana* (Venice, 1983); Ennio Concina, *L'Arsenale della Repubblica di Venezia: Tecniche e istituzioni dal Medioevo all'età moderna* (Milan, 1984); Robert C. Davis, *Shipbuilders of the Venetian Arsenal: Workers and Workplace in the Preindustrial City* (Baltimore, 1991); and Franco Rossi, 'L'Arsenale: I quadri direttivi', in *Storia di Venezia: Dalle origini alla caduta della Serenissima*, vol. 5: *Il Rinascimento: Società ed economia*, ed. Alberto Tenenti and Ugo Tucci (Rome, 1996), 593–639.

26. Mauro Bondioli, 'Early Shipbuilding Records and the Book of Michael of Rhodes', in *The Book of Michael of Rhodes: A Fifteenth-Century Maritime Manuscript*, 3 vols, eds Pamela O. Long, David McGee and Alan M. Stahl (Cambridge, MA, 2009), 3: 243–80, esp. 271–80; and Frederic Chapin Lane, *Venetian Ships and Shipbuilders of the Renaissance* (Baltimore, 1934), 56–9.

27. Long, McGee and Stahl, eds, *op. cit.* (26), 1: 211–17 and 2: 272–81, for Michael's service record of his voyages. Based on his service record and other archival documents, Alan M. Stahl has written a detailed biography: 'Michael of Rhodes: Mariner in Service to Venice', in Long, McGee and Stahl, eds, *op. cit.* (26), 3: 35–98.

28. Raffaella Franci, 'Mathematics in the Manuscript of Michael of Rhodes', in Long, McGee and Stahl, eds, *op. cit.* (26), 3: 115–46; Franci shows that Michael was a good mathematician and worked the problems himself.

29. Piero Falchetta, 'The Portolan of Michael of Rhodes', in Long, McGee, and Stahl, eds, *op. cit.* (26), 3: 193–210. Falchetta discusses the errors in the portolan and suggests that it was included not as a practical guide for navigators but to impress noble patrons and other non-skilled elite persons.

30. Dieter Blume, 'The Use of Visual Images by Michael of Rhodes: Astrology, Christian Faith, and Practical Knowledge', in Long, McGee, and Stahl, eds, *op. cit.* (26), 3: 147–91.

31. Faith Wallis, 'Michael of Rhodes and Time Reckoning: Calendar, Almanac, Prognostication', in Long, McGee, and Stahl, eds, *op. cit.* (26), 3: 281–319.

32. BlumeHutchins (30), 3: 177, suggests the context of reversal in a hierarchical society in which Michael created his image, a subversion of the heraldic code.

33. David McGee, 'The Shipbuilding Text of Michael of Rhodes', in Long, McGee, and Stahl, eds, *op. cit.* (26), 3: 211–41 and Bondioli, *op. cit.* (26).

34. Falchetta, *op. cit.* (29), 3: 193–210, shows that the portolan contains numerous errors and that it could hardly have been meant as a guide for practical navigation. What he writes concerning portolan texts also could apply also to other parts of Michael's book: 'They [portolans] were no longer necessary or at any rate useful instruments for going to sea. Rather they were texts distinguished by a certain degree of autonomy, whose contents only have the appearance of being technical. In the final analysis we can assert that these texts no longer maintained an instrumental function – or rather, their instrumental function seems to be much less significant than the new function they assumed, which belonged primarily within the symbolic sphere. They manifest both the transformation of the epistemological framework of knowledge related to navigation as well as the transformation of the more general system of cultural values. Thus they bring into focus, even within the maritime world, the ever-increasing value of the *libro* as testimony – as well as means – of knowledge' (210).

35. McGee, *op. cit.* (33), 237–41.

36. For more details, see Pamela O. Long, 'Introduction: The World of Michael of Rhodes, Venetian Mariner', in Long, McGee, and Stahl, eds, *op. cit.* (26), 3: 1–33, esp. 15–20 and 30–1.

37. Nicholas of Cusa, *Opera omnia*, vol. 5: *Idiota: De sapientia, de mente,de staticis experimentis*, rev. edn, ed. Renata Steiger et al. from the edition of Ludwig Baur (Hamburg, 1983). There is an anonymous English translation, *The Idiot in Four Books* (London, 1650); and a more recent English translation of *De Mente* – Nicholas of Cusa, *Idiota de Mente: The Layman: About Mind*, trans. Clyde Lee Miller (New York, 1979).

38. See Ennio Concina, *Navis: L'umanismo sul mare (1470–1740)* (Turin, 1990); and Lane, *op. cit.* (26), 56–9, 64–71. For Vettor Vausto, see F. Piovan, 'Fausto, Vittore', *Dizionario biografico degli Italiani* (Rome, 1960–), 45: 398–401; and N. G. Wilson, 'Vettor Fausto, Professor of Greek and Naval Architect', in *The Uses of Greek and Latin*, eds A. C. Dionisotti, Anthony Grafton and Jill Kraye (London, 1988), 89–95.

39. See Concina, *op. cit.* (38, *Navis*); Lane, *op. cit.* (26), 64–71. For Galileo, the arsenal, and the military compass, see Galileo Galilei, *Operations of the Geometric and Military Compass, 1606*, trans. Stillman Drake (Washington, DC, 1978). And see Jürgen Renn and Matteo Valleriani, 'Galileo and

the Challenge of the Arsenal', *Nuncius*, 2001, 16, 481–503; and Matteo Valleriani, *Galileo Engineer* (Dordrecht, 2010), 27–38 (on the compass), 117–53 (on Galileo and the arsenal).

40. Vannoccio Biringuccio, *De la pirotechnia, 1540*, ed. Adriano Carugo (Milan, 1977); and an English translation, Vannoccio Biringuccio, *The Pirotechnia of Vannoccio Biringuccio: The Classic Sixteenth-Century Treatise on Metals and Metallurgy*, trans. and eds Cyril Stanley Smith and Martha Teach Gnudi, 2nd edn (1959; New York, 1990), 213–60 (bk. 6, 1–11). See also Andrea Bernardoni, *La conoscenza del fare: Ingegneria, arte, scienza nel De la pirotechnia di Vannoccio Biringuccio* (Rome, 2011).

41. Niccolò Tartaglia, *Nova scientia inventa da Nicolo Tartalea B.* (Venice, 1537); and Niccolò Tartaglia, *Quesiti et inventioni diverse de Nicolo Tartalea Brisciano* (Venice, 1546). And see Gerhard Arend, *Die Mechanik des Niccolò Tartaglia im Kontext der zeitgenössischen Erkenntnis- und Wissenschaftstheorie* (Munich, 1998); Serafina Cuomo, 'Shooting by the Book: Notes on Niccolò Tartaglia's "Nova Scientia"', *History of Science*, 1997, 35: 155–88; and Mary J. Henninger-Voss, 'How the "New Science" of Cannons Shook Up the Aristotelian Cosmos', *Journal of the History of Ideas*, 2002, 63: 371–97.

42. John U. Nef, 'Mining and Metallurgy in Medieval Civilisation', in *The Cambridge Economic History of Europe, vol. 2: Trade and Industry in the Middle Ages*, eds M. M. Postan and Edward Miller, assisted by Cynthia Postan, 2nd edn. (Cambridge, 1987), 691–761, 933–40; and see Ian Blanchard, *Mining, Metallurgy and Minting in the Middle Ages*, 3 vols. (Stuttgart: F. Steiner, 2001–5), vols 2 and 3. Mining scholarship includes numerous archival-based studies of local regions. See, for example, Angelika Westermann, *Entwicklungsprobleme der Vorderösterreichischen Montanwirtschaft im 16. Jahrhundert: Eine verwaltungs', rechts-, wirtschafts-, und sozialgeschichtliche Studie als Vobereitung für einen multiperspektivischen Geschichtsunterricht* (Idstein, 1993); and Catherine Verna, *Les mines et les forges des Cisterciens en Champagne méridionale et en Bourgogne du nord, XIIe–XVe siècle* (Paris, 1995).

43. Nef, *op. cit.* (42), 723–46. For Agricola, see Georg Agricola, *De re metallica libri XII* (Basel, 1556); and the English translation with extensive technical notes, Agricola, *De re metallica*, trans. Herbert Clark Hoover and Lou Henry Hoover (1912; New York, 1950).

44. Nef, *op. cit.* (42), 723–46; and Blanchard, *op. cit.* (42), 3: 1071–4. For coal production, see esp. Paul Benoit and Catherine Verna, eds., *Le Charbon de terre en Europe occidentale avant l'usage industriel du coke*, Proceedings of the XXth International Congress of History of Science (Liège, 20–26 July 1997) (Turnhout, Belgium, 1999).

45. Philippe Braunstein, 'Innovations in Mining and Metal Production in Europe in the Late Middle Ages,' *Journal of Economic History*, 1983, 12: 573–91; and Hermann Kellenbenz, *The Rise of the European Economy: An Economic History of Continental Europe from the Fifteenth to the Eighteenth Century*, ed. Gerhard Benecke (London, 1976), 85–8.

46. Braunstein, *op. cit.* (45), 587–91.

47. For these writings and further bibliography, see Pamela O. Long, 'The Openness of Knowledge: An Ideal and Its Context in 16th-Century Writings on Mining and Metallurgy', *Technology and Culture*, 1991, 32: 318–55; and see Bernardoni, *op. cit.* (40).

48. See Long, *op. cit.* (47), Long, *op. cit.* (9), 176–91, and Wolfgang Lefèvre, 'Picturing the World of Mining in the Renaissance: The Schwazer Berguch (1556)', Preprint 407, Max-Planck-Institut für Wissenschaftsgeschichte, 2010, www.mpiwg-berlin.mpg.de/en/forschung/Preprints/P407. PDF. For Biringuccio, see note 40.

49. A good introduction to a large literature with reference to three other cities – Antwerp, Amsterdam and London – are the articles in Patrick O'Brien, Derek Keene, Marjolein 't Hart and Herman van der Wee, eds, *Urban Achievement in Early Modern Europe: Golden Ages in Antwerp, Amsterdam and London* (Cambridge, 2001).

50. For hydraulic projects, see David Karmon, 'Restoring the Ancient Water Supply System in Renaissance Rome: The Popes, the Civic Administration, and the Acqua Vergine', *Aqua urbis Romae: The Waters of the City of Rome*, www.iath.virginia.edu/waters (accessed 19 May 2011); Pamela O. Long, 'Hydraulic Engineering and the Study of Antiquity: Rome, 1557–70', *Renaissance Quarterly*, 2008, 61: 1098–138; and Katherine Wentworth Rinne, *The Waters of Rome: Aqueducts, Fountains, and the Birth of the Baroque City* (New Haven, CT, 2010). For the obelisks, see Brian A. Curran, Anthony Grafton, Pamela O. Long and Benjamin Weiss, *Obelisk: A History* (Cambridge, MA, 2009).

51. See especially the essays in Antonella Romano, ed., *Rome et la science moderne entre Renaissance et Lumières* (Rome, 2008); and Maria Pia Donato and Jill Kraye, eds, *Conflicting Duties: Science, Medicine, and Religion in Rome, 1550–1750* (London, 2009).

52. Long, *op. cit.* (50), 1101–3.

53. Ibid., 1103–9. For Bacci's flood writings, see Andrea Bacci, *Del Tevere: Della Natura et bonta dell'Acque e Delle Inondationi Libri II* (Rome, 1558); Andrea Bacci, *Del Tevere di m. Andrea Bacci medico et filosofo, libri tre* (Venice, 1576); and Andrea Bacci, *Del Tevere libro quarto* (Rome, 1599). The handwritten tract is in the flyleaves of the 1976 edition of *Del Tevere*, in the Vatican Library in Vatican City: BAV, shelf no. Aldine II 98.

54. Antonio Trevisi, *Fondamento del edifitio nel quale si tratta con la santita de N.S. Pio Papa IIII Sopra la innondatione del Fiume* (Rome, 1560). For raising the ancient ship, see esp. Concina, *op. cit.* (38), 4–21. For Alberti's attempt to raise the ship, see esp. Anthony Grafton, *Leon Battista Alberti: Master Builder of the Italian Renaissance* (New York, 2000), 248–53.

55. See Long, *op. cit.* (46, 'Hydraulic Engineering'), 1113–6; and Jessica Maier, 'Mapping Past and Present: Leonardo Bufalini's Plan of Rome (1551)', *Imago Mundi*, 2007, 59: 1–23.

56. Long, *op. cit.* (50, 'Hydraulic Engineering'), 1119–23; Luca Peto, *Discorso di Luca Peto intorno alla cagione della Eccessiva Inondatione del Tevere in Roma, et modo in parte di soccorrervi* (Rome, 1573).

57. Lissa Roberts and Simon Schaffer, 'Preface' and Fokko Jan Dijksterhuis, 'Constructive Thinking: A Case for Dioptrics', in *The Mindful Hand: Inquiry and Invention from the Late Renaissance to Early Industrialisation*, eds Lissa Roberts, Simon Schaffer and Peter Dear (Amsterdam, 2007), xiii–xxvii and 58–82, respectively.

Three-dimensional Models as 'In-between-objects' – the Creation of In-between Knowledge in Early Modern Architectural Practice

SIMONA VALERIANI
London School of Economics

INTRODUCTION

The coming together of two kinds of knowledge – the theoretical and the experiential – was an important factor in the emergence of a new culture for investigating nature that underpinned the development of the new empirical sciences in Early Modern Europe. The sharing of both working locations and practices by people with conceptual and applied skill sets allowed for the exchange of their factual and methodological expertise and their knowledge creation practices, facilitating the development of new ways of investigating nature and creating knowledge about natural phenomena. This theme has been elaborated in recent years under different labels such as the 'Mindful Hand'[1] and the 'Enlightened Economy'[2] as well as, more latterly, in Pamela Long's development of the concept of 'Trading Zones'.[3]

The argument put forward in this chapter is that a range of 'in-between objects' played an important role in the coming together of such categories as theory/praxis, intellectuals/artisans, speculative knowledge/skill which had been seen as distinct in the Middle Ages. We can give such artefacts as maps, scientific instruments, technical drawings, three-dimensional models, etc. the label 'in between objects' – and argue that they were important *loci* where practically minded intellectuals and speculating artisans, navigators, geographers, etc. could meet and share their different 'knowledges'.[4] In so doing they created something new that no one group could have produced independently.[5] While, obviously, these objects already existed and were in use before the Early Modern times, their importance – in both general terms, and specifically their significance as instruments for knowledge production – increased in the period under consideration.

Analysing the role(s) played by such objects can help us understand how the ways in which knowledge was created and accredited changed in Early Modern Europe. The relationship between learned knowledge and knowledge acquired by doing appears to have varied constantly during this period, and in a somewhat contradictory fashion: while the degree of usefulness attributed to the kind of knowledge held by practitioners was rising, at the same time a process of codification and 'scientification' of knowledge was tending to marginalize such skills, and underline instead the importance of theoretical knowledge (and so also of those who held it). In the field of architecture in particular – where for centuries reliability had been connected with the practical expertise developed via trial and error over generations – the seventeenth century sees attempts to explain, for example, stability and strength in scientific (i.e. theoretical) terms. While these efforts did not bear fruit until the late eighteenth century, they had begun to influence the ways in which reliability of knowledge was judged much earlier, causing a shift towards relying on theoretical knowledge (and its holders) for solutions to technical problems.[6]

Among the range of in-between objects mentioned above, this chapter focuses on the uses of three-dimensional models,[7] showing how they mediated between different kinds of expertise to produce new knowledge which was 'in-between' social groups, epistemic traditions, abstraction and materiality – and between what was already known and what was still to be found out. The role played by models in science has become a more prominent topic of discussion in the history and philosophy of science over recent decades. The collection of essays edited by Morgan and Morrison,[8] for example, explicitly addresses how models act as instruments that mediate between theories and the world of practice. While the collection offers interesting theoretical insights into these issues, its main focus is on how models are used in modern science – particularly physics, mathematics and economics – and three-dimensional models are not prominent. Other attempts have been made to look specifically into three-dimensional models, with particular attention to the period from the eighteenth century onwards.[9] The emphasis in such literature has been mostly on models as teaching instruments and as demonstration objects, for mediating between teachers and students, scientists and the public, artists and patrons, etc. – in such cases we could say models function as 'rhetorical devices'. The aim here is instead to elucidate how three-dimensional models (together with other in-between objects not discussed here) were instrumental in fostering a new way of investigating nature that emerged in Early Modern Europe. We examine in more detail how three-dimensional models sometimes functioned as in-between objects – in embodying existing knowledge coming from different 'sources' – but in other cases went further, to become instruments for the production of new knowledge, achieved by merging different kinds of skills and knowledge.

To achieve this aim, we focus on the field of architecture and the role three-dimensional models played in that context in the Early Modern period. Architecture – a discipline at the intersection between science, art and skill – seems a good field to focus on, and is one in which three-dimensional models not only have a long tradition but also seem to develop in new ways in the period under consideration. As in the case of the history of science noted above, the extant literature on architectural models also concentrates mainly on presentation models, intended to visualize a proposed building in three dimensions to assist the architect in securing a commission from a patron, or in discussing project details; or to reproduce an extant building for teaching or public relations purposes. Despite the merits of this literature, there is more to investigate and understand about how the process of producing three-dimensional models helped mediate between different 'knowledges' and led to the production of new knowledge (Table 3.1).

After giving an overview of the different functions of models in architectural practice, the chapter describes the historical development of the use of three-dimensional models in architecture. The focus will be first on the classic literature and its interpretation by the leading Italian architects of the Renaissance, which was hugely influential, both internationally and for generations to come. As (in many respects) England is seen as one of the key locations for the development of the new culture of natural enquiry and knowledge formation in Early Modern times, the investigation then shifts towards how three-dimensional models were used in the English context. To make the discussion more concrete and focused, a case study considers the activities of Sir Christopher Wren, as situated in the contemporary 'scientific' and architectural context.[10] The chapter closes with some general notes on models as examples of 'in-between' knowledge.

THREE-DIMENSIONAL MODELS IN ARCHITECTURE

The most prominent variant of architectural models are the much studied 'presentation models' described earlier, whose richness and artistic value mean they were often retained after the associated architectural works have been completed and so, in many cases, remain for posterity. However, it is important to realize that models also had a number of other functions (Table 3.1). Working models were used to develop solutions for stylistic and technical problems that arose during construction. Perhaps the use of models cited most often in the historical literature was to calculate the quantities of materials needed for

Table 3.1 Three-dimensional models: their functions in architectural practice and their relationship to knowledge

Relationship to knowledge	Practical functions			
Rhetoric device	Presentation models	Models for communicating technical ideas	Teaching models	
Embodying different kinds of knowledge/skill	Models as contractual basis			Models as devices for calculating materials and labour
Creating new (in-between) knowledge	Working Models			

construction and the kinds and numbers of craftsmen required, and a similar important function saw them used in a legal sense, as part of contractual stipulations, documenting all the details of the structure to be built against which the finished building could be checked. Thus models could be made to communicate technical ideas between architects and patrons or between architects and craftsmen; to develop technical solutions; to help plan, monitor and measure actual works; to document successful solutions in concrete form, which could function equally eloquently as demonstrations of architects' creativity or as teaching aids.

Three-dimensional miniatures of buildings were used in many early civilizations – and can be traced back to ancient Egypt – but it seems the objects that have come down to us from such periods should generally be understood as architectural representations designed for religious purposes (such as votive objects and grave furniture), and only unusually as aids to building processes.[11] The use of three-dimensional models in architectural projects in the European context is mentioned in some Greek sources,[12] as well as in the only architectural treatise that remains from antiquity – Vitruvius' *De architectura* (first century BC). However he does not include models in his descriptions of the design process, and only mentions them explicitly when discussing the construction of machines.[13] So the ancient world seems to have used models but not to have assigned them prominent roles – at least from a methodological and theoretical point of view.

Examples of models used for design and construction can be dated to the Middle Ages, but how widely they were used in architectural practice is open to discussion.[14] A significant increase in the importance of models can be observed during the Renaissance period, starting in Tuscany in the 1350s and spreading quickly throughout Europe.[15] The first building for which we have abundant evidence of their use is S. Maria del Fiore in Florence, where wood and brick models were produced as aids to the construction process,[16] as they were for the construction of S. Petronio at Bologna, which started in 1390. In contrast, the design and construction process of Milan's late gothic cathedral was conducted without the use of models while Northern experts were in charge, but in the 20 years after the project was taken over by Italian masters (in 1468) as many as eleven models were constructed.[17]

It has been argued that Italian models from the fifteenth century represent a way for building designers to present their ideas and claim intellectual property rights over them in a form that could be widely understood, even by illiterate people. These building 'designers' – the profession and thus the label 'architect' had not yet really been developed – also used models which were often rather sketchy (and were sometimes backed up by secrecy agreements[18]) effectively to conceal some important details of their 'invention': the individual who most obviously represented this attitude was Filippo Brunelleschi (1377–1446), who often built his own models.[19]

Over the fifteenth and sixteenth centuries, as Italian architects gradually detached themselves from construction sites and became more closely connected with princes and courts, models evolved into instruments to communicate the architect's instructions to the workforce more precisely and more robustly. This progress in the use and understanding of models reverberates through Renaissance architectural writings: thus, while Leon Battista Alberti (1404–72) devotes several pages of his *De Re Aedificatoria* (which influenced future generations of architects over some centuries to come) to models, he makes no mention of them in the section dedicated to conceiving new buildings,[20] where (following Vitruvius) the building design process is associated instead with mental activities that are 'fixed' in drawings (book I, *De Lineamentis*).

> It is possible to project whole forms in the mind without recourse to the material by designating and determining a fixed orientation and conjunction for the various lines and angles. Since that is the case let lineaments be the precise and correct outline, conceived in the mind . . . and perfected in the learned intellect and imagination.[21]

Aberti considered ideas as being a superior part of the invention process to the realm of materiality, where models belonged – but he did not denigrate their use, which he discusses over several pages at the start of book II (devoted to materials) and which he clearly recognizes as useful for more practical purposes:

> I would always commend the time-honoured custom . . . of preparing models of wood or any other material. These will enable us to weigh up repeatedly and examine, with the advice of experts, the work as a whole and the individual dimensions of all the parts and, before continuing any further, the likely trouble and expense.[22]

As Werner Oechslin has discussed in detail, Alberti described models with the double term '*modulis atque exemplaribus*' (referring to their relevance to both the theoretical/mental and material spheres), which aligns with this chapter's arguments of their important status as functioning 'in-between' theory and praxis.[23]

An alternative tradition to that of Alberti – for whom the creative process happens essentially in the mind, and the model is little more than a mere representation of what the mind has already conceived – is embodied by such figures as Michelangelo Buonarroti (1475–1564). In this conception, the creator's invention happens via the materiality of the model itself: Michelangelo made extensive use of a range of models throughout his design processes, from clay models to work out general ideas, to wooden models to present designs to his patrons, to *modelli al vero* (large scale models – sometimes even 1:1) used on building sites to communicate with his workforce.[24]

From the late fifteenth century, Italy saw the increasing use of models as experimental instruments through which building construction details and potential problems that were not revealed by drawings or small models could be investigated. The importance of models as designing tools became very evident in the Veneto (the region around Venice), where, in particular, they became indispensable mediation and communication tools between architects, princes, generals and military engineers who increasingly made models of fortifications that included both the building concerned as well as the surrounding area, enabling experiments about distances, shooting trajectories, etc. in which the various kinds of knowledge held by the different actors could be merged.[25] So it is no surprise that models figure explicitly for the first time (alongside quills and ink) as architect's tools in *L'Idea dell'Architettura Universale* (1615), an architectural treatise by the Venetian Vincenzo Scamozzi (1552–1616), where the three-dimensional model becomes (even more explicit than in Alberti's work) an 'in-between object', where theory and praxis are mixed.[26]

We now consider how the influential Italian architectural tradition (both in writings and in building practice) was taken up in England in the seventeenth century, and what place three-dimensional models occupied in this cultural context. Models were used increasingly in English architectural practice from the late seventeenth century onwards. J. Wilton-Ely notes that one of the earliest references to architectural models in England concerns the French joiner Adrian Gaunt, who (in 1567) produced a model for the construction of the Elizabethan Country house at Longleat.[27] Models are also mentioned in such early English architectural writings as Wotton's *Elements of architecture* (1624),[28] Sir Roger Pratt's notes on architecture[29] and in Sir Balthazar Gerbier's very popular publication *Counsel and Advice to all Builders* (1664). These authors all follow Alberti in recommending making models before construction starts, to avoid mistakes and costly alterations later on; they also make it clear that models are meant to help solve problems of proportions and general design, as well as to expose potential technical difficulties. A work summarizing the knowledge of the time – Chamber's *Cyclopædia* (compiled between ca. 1680 and 1740) – also lists the term 'model', relating it *in primis* to three-dimensional architectural models:

> MODEL is particularly used in Building . . . in order for the better Conducing and Executing of some great Work, and to give an Idea of the Effect it will have in Large. In all large buildings, it is much the surest way to make a Model in Relievo and not to trust to a bare Design, or Draught.[30]

Wilton-Ely has further suggested a link between the introduction of models into English architectural practice and the adoption of a new, more elaborate architectural style,[31] and it seems clear this was an important aspect, both because the new style required more 'explanation', but also because it coincided (at least in part) with a new understanding of the role of the architect and of how design and building processes should be organized.

A CASE STUDY: CHRISTOPHER WREN'S USE OF MODELS

Models in the Construction of St Paul's Cathedral

The current fabric of St Paul's Cathedral in London is the result of the design efforts of Sir Christopher Wren (1632–1723) and his collaborators.[32] A medieval antecedent had stood on the same site, which had been recognized as being in need of restoration and of modernization even before the Great Fire of London (1666).[33] Soon after the fire it was decided to pull down the medieval cathedral's burnt out remains and start constructing a new one. In 1668 Christopher Wren (who had been appointed in 1666 as commissioner for the rebuilding of London,[34] and became surveyor of the King's works in 1669) was asked to produce a design: the cathedral was completed in 1710 and Wren's longevity allowed him to follow its construction through to completion.

As perhaps the most significant English architectural achievement of its age, St Paul's cathedral has been the subject of voluminous scholarship, analysing many different facets of its erection, which is very well documented in its surviving building accounts.[35] Rather than focusing on the well-known presentation models (see Figures 3.1 and 3.2),[36] this chapter concentrates instead on the (so far neglected) three-dimensional models that were actually used in the cathedral's construction. The accounts record the use of at least 70 models: the exact number is difficult to determine – while some entries are very specific (noting both the model's purpose and the materials used), others are much vaguer, only detailing payments to craftsmen for models made over certain periods. (An additional difficulty is that, in the seventeenth century, the term 'model' was also sometimes used for drawings and other building aids, such as moulds.)

Wren and his collaborators evidently used a large number of 'working models' to try out and develop their ideas.[37] In some cases these were commissioned to joiners, and seem to fall into the category of 'design-models', mainly concerned with stylistic issues. In other cases they were made by carpenters or

Figure 3.1 The so-called First Model for the reconstruction of St Paul's cathedral (1669–70), from Keen et al. 2004, 187

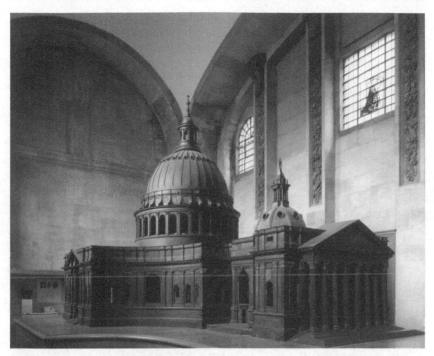

Figure 3.2 The so-called Great Model for the reconstruction of St Paul's Cathedral (1673–74), from Keen et al. 2004, 190

masons, and clearly related to construction details: these seem to have been instruments by which craftsmen and the architect solved technical problems together,[38] and were sometimes even made from the same materials they intended to use in the final structure.

The models made for St Paul's dome are good examples of this latter type of use. The dome is, famously, the most daring part of the cathedral's architecture, and many historians have commented on its genesis. Analysing the models Wren commissioned during its construction helps to shed light on the roles of both theoretical reflections and skill in its design process.[39] Between 1684 and 1689 a series of models were made for the 'tribune' of the dome, and masons were commissioned to produce models for the dome itself between 1690 and 1695, which – judging from the brief descriptions in the accounts – were progressively more detailed attempts to work out the final solution for its construction. Thus the mason Eduard Strong was paid in January–February 1690/91 for a 'Modell for ¼ part of dome'[40] and in April 1691 'For making part of a Modell in small Stones for part of the Dome',[41] which seems to have been used to work out how the proposed structure could actually be built in stone, with the mason's expertise being called on to develop the architectural idea in detail. In June 1694 the same Edward Strong was paid for 'making a large Modell of a 1/8th of the Great Dome'.[42] The fact that an increasingly small part of the dome was modelled, and that a carver was involved, testifies to increasing degrees of detail. At roughly the same time new designs for the dome – for which drawings survive (see Figure 3.3) – were made by Wren's assistant, Nicholas Hawksmoor (1661–1736).[43] This shows how, at key moments, the design process was being developed by the joint efforts of architects at their drawing tables and craftsmen making models, the two sharing their skills in a two-way process with the model as an 'in-between' object, in whose production

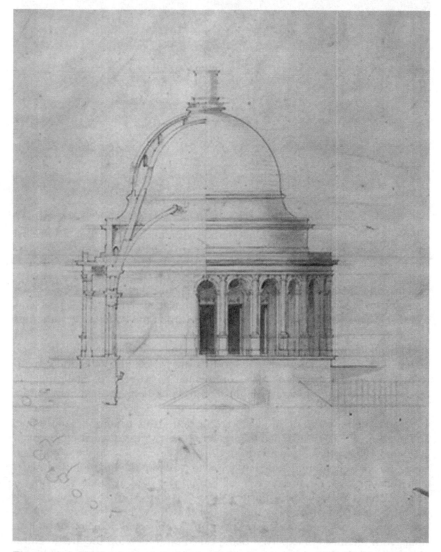

Figure 3.3 N. Hawksmoor, design for St Paul's dome, ca. 1693–95, from Higgott 2009, 165

two ways of 'knowing' met and combined. We could argue, therefore, that the opinion so often voiced in the literature – that the use of architectural models was a one-way process in which architects instructed their craftsmen – requires some revision.

So far, we have concentrated on the use of models for presentation to patrons and as working models whose purpose is to help develop solutions for stylistic and technical problems. Two other uses for models can be read from the St Paul's building accounts. First is the communication of technical ideas – one example of which is a transportable model of the roof trusses built in 1692 by a joiner together with 'a box to put it in'.[44] This was probably a sort of suitcase and indicates Wren's intention to use this model as a reference to be taken to other building sites, to make patrons and carpenters aware of the specifics of what was an innovative structure for England at the time.[45] A further use of models was as part of construction contracts, where the model had a legal status and function: we can find several instances in the St Paul's accounts where craftsmen's contracts refer specifically to models which define how work needs to be carried out – as, for example:

> July 18th 1705: Agreed with John Longland & Richard Jennings, Carpenters, and the Survivor of them, for framing, rasing, & finishing the great Roof of the West End of St Paul's Cathedral fit for the Plummer . . . according to the Modell Produced & approved for that purpose.[46]

This use of models was not peculiar to St Paul's, but is also documented in other sources, including, for example, Pratt's notes on architecture mentioned above.[47]

Wren's Structural Models: Between Mathematics and Rules of the Art

Writing to the commission for the rebuilding of St Paul's, Wren argued for the use of models 'for the encouragement and satisfaction of benefactors that comprehend not designs and drafts on paper as well as for the inferior artificers' clearer intelligence of their business',[48] placing himself in a tradition in which the architect – clearly situated 'above' craftsmen – uses models to communicate his ideas to patrons and workforces. Nonetheless, the data from the St Paul's building accounts seems to suggest that models were much more polyvalent instruments in Wren's actual practice, and he used them as experimental devices to work out – with the help of the craftsmen's skills – the designs of complicated building elements and how they could be realized in stone and brick.[49]

Wren also used architectural models to help solve structural problems. Apart from St Paul's and its dome, the (now lost) model of the famous roof structure of the Sheldonian Theatre (presented to the Royal Society in 1663) testifies to this kind of use, as does the (ca. 1662) model for Pembroke College Chapel, Cambridge, constructed in 1665, which again shows details of a roof structure that was innovative for England at the time. Other examples include Wren's suggestions for the repair of Westminster Abbey, which allows us to look in more detail at Wren's 'mathematical' approach to architecture. By way of introduction, it should be noted that Wren had been already called in as a consultant on the repair of Gothic buildings in previous circumstances, most notably at Old St Paul's[50] and at Salisbury cathedral,[51] where he had discussed problems of stability and of resistance to weight that had caused damage in the tower and the crossing. Wren's writings on Westminster Abbey show the further development of such theoretical considerations about the 'statics' of gothic cathedrals, and in particular on the roles of buttresses, towers and spires:

> I conceive the Architect knew very well, that the four Pillars above the Intersection of the Cross-nave would not prove sufficient Butment . . . unless they were much bigger than the other Pillars . . . but tho' they could not be made bigger, yet they could be made heavier to stand against the Pressure, which may prove an Equivalent.
>
> And this is the Reason why in all Gothick Fabricks of this Form, the Architects were wont to build Towers or Steeples in the Middle, not only for ornament, but to confirm the middle Pillars against the Thrust.[52]

Wren explains this conclusion by adding a drawing (Figure 3.4) to his report, and his accompanying text is fashioned like a geometrical demonstration: 'Let ABC be an arch resting at C, against an immovable wall K M, but at A upon a pillar AD, so small as to be unable to be a sufficient Butment to the Pressure of the Arch AB. . . .'

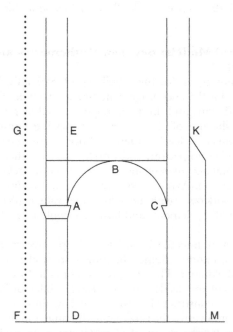

Figure 3.4 C. Wren's sketch showing the 'criteria of stability' of gothic architecture (Wren 1750, 301).

As the steeple in the middle of Westminster Abbey had never been built (Figure 3.5), the pillars at the crossing were bent inward, causing the walls above to crack, so Wren suggested first restoring the pillars 'which I have considered how to perform and represented in a Model'.[53] Unfortunately this model has not come down to us, although we do have the 'presentation model' (Figure 3.6) Wren prepared to show how the construction of the church should have been finished by adding a steeple. Wren argued that this had been the original architect's intention and – as he 'demonstrated' in his sketch and accompanying text – would have ensured the crossing's stability.

The mathematical and mechanical knowledge available to architects in the seventeenth century provided no proper theory that could explain or predict the stability of the gothic structures Wren was repairing, nor of St Paul's dome. But Wren was certainly one of the scholars of the time who were engaged in advancing this knowledge, and in trying to apply what theoretical ideas were available.[54] His structural models were objects that we can say stood 'in-between' already existing knowledge and the new knowledge that was being created: and they also stand as objects that combined Wren's theoretical approach and knowledge with the skills and knowledge of the master craftsmen giving a material form to his ideas and making them feasible.

While this use of models particularly reflects Wren's 'mechanical' interests, his use of models to solve structural problems can be situated in a long tradition (to choose just one example, see Brunelleschi's models for the dome of S. Maria del Fiore). The question of the suitability of models to work out the size of structural elements to ensure the stability of a proposed building had been at the center of a long and significant scientific-technological debate about scaling up, which had been discussed in several extant architectural works. Vitruvius had touched on the topic, noting the failure of

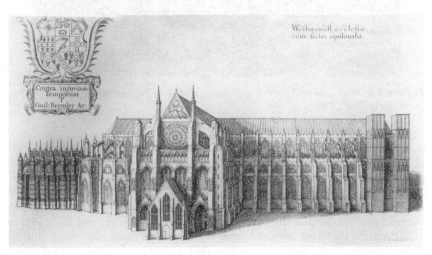

Figure 3.5 Westminster Abbey's North front before the addition of the steeple (Engraving by W. Hollar, c. 1654).

Figure 3.6 Wren's Model for the spire to be added to Westminster Abbey (c. 1720), from Cocke 1995, 131.

some machines that had been built by scaling-up perfectly functioning models: Alberti, on the other hand, insisted on the universality of the laws of proportions that should enable deriving the real object from a smaller version. Other Renaissance authorities – such as Andrea Palladio (1508–80)[55] and Daniele Barbaro (1515–70)[56] – had also maintained that models could be used to work out the size of elements for real buildings, and that failures of structures that had been enlarged from models must have been due to imperfections in the materials used, rather than to any fundamental problems of scaling.

Several scholars investigated the scaling problem in the sixteenth and seventeenth centuries. The debate was famously taken up by Galileo Galilei, in his *Discorsi e dimostrazioni matematiche* (1638), where he criticizes the use of models for such purposes. Galileo was (in his own words) founding a 'new science' concerned with the strength of materials and (in common with other contemporary writers) made early attempts to distinguish failures due to insufficient material strengths (possibly associated with incorrect dimensioning from scaling up) and those derived from matters of stability inherent in the original designs.[57] We now know that models are quite useful for simulating stability, but are much less help in calculating the minimum sizes of structural elements to predict their strength.[58]

Wren's interest in architecture developed after he had already established his scholarship in other branches of knowledge. He used three-dimensional models – particularly in astronomy[59] and in anatomy,[60] but also in optics – for both research and demonstration purposes. These experiences in other branches of knowledge influenced how he went about developing his design for St Paul's, and more generally how he approached the many problems that confronted him during his long career as surveyor of the King's works and consultant on architectural and structural matters. His 'experimental' use of models in architecture seems to relate both to his previous experiences in other fields and to his broad scientific and methodological interests – but it should also be noted that his approach aligned with the long theoretical and practical traditions that had developed in Italy since the late fourteenth century, of which Wren – an extremely erudite man – was surely aware. Perhaps unusually for his English milieu – and also, probably, made possible by the extraordinary architectural opportunities created by the Great Fire – his architectural activities fit extremely well with the 'cutting edge' of European advances in architecture and in scientific discourse.

The spread of three-dimensional models from Italy to the rest of Europe from the fifteenth century onwards was an important step in a more general development that saw the growth of standardized 'instruments' – both formal and technical – for managing design processes and improving communication between different types of actors, within whose individual fields professionalization and specialization was also emerging. It has been suggested that models became more important when the design process and the supervision of works on building sites became fragmented activities, shared between different actors.[61] The seventeenth century saw the development – particularly in France – of new techniques and a new 'language' for technical and architectural drawings,[62] a phenomenon that related to many other disciplines besides architecture. The models and drawings Wren made in medicine and astronomy – for example – became exemplary 'instruments' of the new way of 'doing' science. For Scamozzi, models were 'sensual demonstrations'[63] – for Ephraim Chambers, drawings equated to 'geometrical demonstrations':[64] both saw them as instruments to produce knowledge. Given that architecture can be seen as the activity 'par excellence' between 'science' and the mechanical arts, it is no surprise that the increasing importance of such tools became particularly evident in this field.

CONCLUSIONS: MODELS EMBODYING AND CREATING IN-BETWEEN KNOWLEDGE

The European Early Modern period is characterized by the development of a number of artefacts including, for example, such objects as classical scientific instruments (much discussed), maps, models and drawings that served to conjoin different knowledge systems. This chapter has focused on three-dimensional models and shown how, in many respects, they were used – and at the time consciously conceived – as 'in-between objects'. They may either 'simply' embody different kinds of knowledge in one object, or (in a more complex sense) combine different kinds of knowledge and skill in such a way that their creation actually generates new, 'in-between', knowledge (Table 5.1). They may be situated between different social groups, mediating between patrons and architects, architects and craftsman, etc., and can also function 'in-between' generalization and specificity, abstraction and materiality (as exemplified in their role as the basis of contracts) or – in a wider sense – between the general rules of the art and the specificity of each site; in-between past and future, between the security of proven solutions and the hope of further innovation; and as objects in-between theory and praxis.

In this last respect we can observe a dichotomy. The Renaissance sees an upsurge in the use of models as 'sensory demonstrations' (as Scamozzi put it) and elevation of their status to that of official experimental instruments in the creative enterprise of architecture. Thus they outgrow their former role (as expressions of an inferior *techne*) and become acknowledged as mediating instruments between two spheres – theory and praxis – that had hitherto been recognized as being fundamentally distinct. On the other hand, with the development of architects' new awareness of themselves as artists and intellectuals, more detached from materiality and the building site than their medieval predecessors, the model becomes a boundary object. Disregarding the actual genesis and use of models in the building process, architects tend to portray themselves as using models to instruct 'inferior artificers' and describe the knowledge flows associated with models as being unidirectional. So, while models are *loci* where mind and hand come together, and where substantial knowledge is exchanged between actors with different backgrounds and from different epistemic traditions – and where, at times, new knowledge is produced – increasingly self-conscious architects are now adopting them as boundary markers which set them apart as creative beings, above those who merely enact their designs.

ACKNOWLEDGEMENTS

The research that enabled the development of this chapter received funding from the European Research Council under the European Union's Seventh Framework Programme (FP7/2007–2013)/ERC grant agreement No. 230326), as part of the URKEW Project. Without the generous support of the ERC and of the Project's PI, Patrick O'Brien, this chapter could not have been written. Earlier work that fed into this study had been carried out while I was funded by the Leverhulme Trust and ESRC as part of the project: 'The nature of evidence. How Well Do Facts Travel?'. My thanks go to the funding bodies and to Mary S. Morgan, who encouraged me and gave me the opportunity to freely explore new topics as well as read through earlier versions of this chapter.

I am very grateful to all the colleagues with whom I discussed the materials of this chapter, and I particularly wish to thank, Maarten Prak and Patrick Wallis for reading earlier versions of this chapter and giving thought-provoking and very helpful comments, and Jon Morgan of Paraphrase for his editorial help.

Notes

1. Roberts et al. 2007.
2. Mokyr 2010.
3. Long 2011, see also Pamela Long's chapter in this volume. Other scholars have considered this topic in recent years, see for example the recent Maffioli 2010.
4. For a discussion of the role of models during the Enlightenment, particularly for machines and ships, see Fox 2010.
5. Of course – despite their distinctiveness – these two categories have never been completely separated. For the thesis that in a number of cases in the Renaissance they become more and more blurred, see P. O. Long 2011.
6. As an example, see Carlo Fontana's *Templum vaticanum et ipsius origo* (1694) where the author, in the section devoted to the construction of roofs inserts chapter XII, *Causa perché sia necessaria l'ordinazione delli Tetti dalli Professori* (*Reasons why it is necessary that roofs are designed by professors*), where he criticizes practitioners (*Mecanici*), who act only on the basis of experience (*ordinano, & operano alla cieca, solo da una mera pratica,* Fontana 1694, 101).
7. Three-dimensional models were obviously used in many other areas – such as shipbuilding or in scientific enterprises such as astronomy and medicine – but these are outside the focus of this chapter.
8. Morgan and Morrison 1999.
9. Chadarevian and Hopwood 2004.
10. On the link between Wren's architecture and the Baconian programme see Li 2000, 2007.
11. For an example of models of architectural elements such as columns produced in Imperial Egypt in the context of building practice, see Feuerbach forthcoming.
12. Aristotle mentions models used to decide between different proposed buildings: for this and other references from ancient Greece see Di Pasquale 1996, 77–8.
13. Vitruvius 2009, Book 10, Ch. XVI.5, 317. In some translations, models are mentioned in book I, Chapter I (the education of the architect) as ways of representing the design, but it is most probable that what was meant there were drawings. For a discussion of the use of models in the design process in antiquity see Scolari 1988, 16 and footnotes 1–5, pages 29–31, and more detailed information in Centre de Cultura Contemporania de Barcelona 1997. Two recent conferences have been devoted to models, including examples from antiquity: *Models and Architecture*, International Conference, Architekturmuseum Munich, 6–8 November 2009; *The Model: A Tool in the Architectural Project*, École de Chaillot and Musée des Monuments Français, Paris, 20–1 May 2011 (proceedings forthcoming).
14. An example of the use of models in medieval times can be found in connection with the design and construction of the roof of Westminster Hall by Hugh Herland, master carpenter to Richard II, see: Waldram 1935. For a discussion of the use of drawings in English medieval architectural practice see Pacey 2007, and for an analysis of Italian practice see Borgherini 2001. Di Pasquale 1996, 76 believes that models must have been in use in medieval Italy.
15. Scolari 1988, 16 mentions a model for the Abbey of Saint-Germain d'Auxerre from the eleventh century, as the earliest known example. For Italian models from late Middle Ages and Renaissance, see Lepik 1994, Millon and Lampugnani 1994 (published in conjunction with the exhibition held in Venice, Palazzo Grassi) and Evers 1996; see Harvey 1972 for models in English and French architecture; for the use of models in German countries see Reuter and Beckenhagen 1994; and for European baroque models see also Milton 1999 (Catalogue of an exhibition organized by the Palazzo Grassi and held at the Stupinigi Hunting Lodge, Turin).

16. Pacciani 1987, 9.

17. Ibid., 9.

18. Scolari 1988, 18.

19. During the Renaissance the concept that the designing process was a mental/intellectual activity separated from the manual labour of the craftsmen became more explicit and dominant. European figures that mark the history of architecture in this respect are Filippo Brunelleschi (1377–1446) in Italy, Philibert De L'Orme in France (ca. 1514–1570) and Juan de Herrera (1530–97) in Spain. For De L'Orme, see P. Potié 1996.

20. Alberti [1486]. The manuscript was finished by 1450 but the book was not printed until 1486, after Alberti's death.

21. Alberti 1988 [1486], 7.

22. Ibid., 33–4.

23. Oechslin 1996, 44–6.

24. Mussolin 2006.

25. Scolari 1988, 24–6.

26. Oechslin 1996, 47.

27. Wilton-Ely 1967, 27. For a discussion of later examples, see Wilton-Ely 1968.

28. Wotton, 1624, 65–6.

29. Gunther 1928, the notes were written by Pratt in the 1660s.

30. Chambers 1740, 565.

31. Wilton Ely 1967, 28.

32. Edward Woodroofe was his assistant and John Tillison his Clerk of Works, while Nicholas Hawksmoor joined the team later.

33. In the 1620s a porch designed by Inigo Jones in Renaissance style had been added to the façade as an attempt to remedy what was perceived as the poor appearance of the building.

34. Together with Robert Hook, Hugh May, Robert Pratt, Edward Jerman and Peter Mills.

35. Just to mention recent publications: Keen et al. 2004, specifically on the building process, see Campbell 2007.

36. For a discussion of the so-called First Model and Great Model and a description of their genesis and architectural significance see Higgott 2004, 186–9. For a detailed description of the models used in St Paul's, see Valeriani forthcoming.

37. In the case of complex structures, the presentation model and the technical model can coincide, as the architect might want to impress the patron with his innovative techniques, or need to convince his audience of the feasibility of what he is proposing. See for example Brunelleschi and the masonry model of the Florentine dome built in 1418 without centring (Guasti 185, 7 Docs. 18, 43; quoted after Prager and Scaglia 1970, 30).

38. A good example is the entry in September 1705 'E.S. a Mason 19 days. Making a Modell for securing the Work from wet at ye top of ye Lead Pipes at 2s 6d. £2.7.6', Wren Society (from now on cited as WS), vol. XV, 128.

39. Information on the production of these models can also inform the discussion on the possible French inspiration for St Paul's dome (Summerson 1990).

40. WS XV, 80.

41. Ibid., 85.

42. Ibid., 134.

43. G. Higgot discusses two sets of drawings made in 1690–1 and 1693–5 (Higgot 2009, 164 and fig. 87; 165 and fig. 152). Discussing the two cone-like structures in the dome, he notes that 'Wren arrived at their profiles, buttressing and reinforcements experimentally, aided by his master mason Edward Strong' (Higgot 2009, 164). A model 'of Legg of Dome on Inside thereof' was paid for in August 1692 (WS, XIV, 99). The construction of the dome above the great arches started in January–February 1695 (WS, XV, 6). After starting his career as Wren's assistant N. Hawksmoor became an important architect in his own right; for a relatively recent monograph on him, see Hart 2002.

44. WS, XIV, 100.

45. By 1692 many of Wren's city churches were already complete, or construction was advanced. An exception is, for example, St Vedast Foster Lane (roof built in 1696–9): here the roof was built by the carpenter John Longland, so that the model would have been useful more to the patrons than to the craftsmen. Another Wren building that uses king post trusses is All Souls

College, Oxford (1721, carpenter unknown). For a discussion of the use of king post trusses by Wren and the likely classical models he referred to, see Valeriani 2011, 2006.

46. WS, XVI, 28. Other examples are traceable in St Paul's records. A similar instance (connected with Wren) is to be found in the documentation of the repairs to Westminster Abbey: 'Ordered that the Dome be repaired to the top of the old Roof by the Workmen according to Model now laid before the Committee by the several workmen and Estimates by them given in' ('Fabrick Orders', 15April 1726). Note that here the workmen themselves are producing and presenting the models.

47. Gunther 1928, 22.

48. Wren, Report on the repairs to St Paul's Cathedral, in Wren 1750, 277.

49. The use of models to work out the shape of each stone composing a vault is particularly evident in the case of complicated geometries, and in particular characterizes the French stereotomic tradition.

50. Wren's report on the state of the church and the necessary intervention is published in Wren 1750, 274–7.

51. Wren's report on the state of the church and the necessary intervention is published in Wren 1750, 303–8.

52. Wren 1750, 300–1.

53. 'The architect . . . wisely considered that if he tied these Arches every Way with Iron . . . this might serve the Turn till he built the Tower to make all secure. These Irons . . . have been stolen away and this is the reason for the four Pillars being bent inward . . .; but nothing can be amended, till first the Pillars are restored, which I have considered how to perform and represented in a Model' (Wren 1750, 301).

54. For the latest discussion (and references to earlier works) of the influence of mathematical considerations on the best shape for a dome (Hooke's hanging-chain principle) on Wren's design for St Paul's dome, see Higgot 2009.

55. Palladio, 1570, III. 18.

56. Barbaro [1556] 1987, 128–9.

57. For a discussion of the Renaissance writings on the problem of proportions and the strength of materials – also before Galileo – see Valleriani 2009.

58. Di Pasquale 1988. For a discussion of the suitability of models to simulate stability and not to predict strength see also Heyman 1968.

59. By the 1650s Wren had already produced his *Panorganum Astronicum* – a model of the earth, sun and moon showing their periodic relationships. After observing Saturn and developing his theory of its rings (1654–9), he made a model of both planet and rings in 1659 to accompany his lectures on the topic. But his most famous astronomical model was the lunar globe he presented to King Charles in 1661. Wren's use of models in astronomy is therefore related to didactic and demonstration purposes: they are a means to show his theories or are produced as precious gifts for potential patrons. The production of astronomical models has a very long tradition that goes back millennia. Closer to Wren's own times we see Galileo using a model of the moon as an 'experimental object' to study the possible origin of the shadows visible on the lunar surface through the telescope, as he notes in his *Dialogo*, see Wallace 2003, 113.

60. Wren used models as didactical aids (he probably produced anatomical pasteboard models to illustrate Sir Charles Scarburgh's lectures at Surgeons' Hall, see Gerbino and Johnston 2009, 85, which points to Bennett 1976) but (probably) also as a way of fixing the observations made on corpses and to give material form to his theories about the mechanical functioning of body parts.

61. B. Contardi 1991, 10–11. This might be an element that influenced the way models were used at St Paul's but it does not seem a central point as – despite his many commitments – Wren was present at St Paul's regularly.

62. This also influenced the innovative way in which the design process was organized at St Paul's. For a discussion of the use of drawings at St Paul's see Gerbino, Johnston 2009, 97–110.

63. '*Il Modello è parte che viene dimostrata sensibilmente, & in atto*' Scamozzi 1615, Parte Prima, Libro Primo, Cap. XV, 51.

64. Chambers 1728, 521, discussing the term 'mechanics': 'it is frequently found helpful to decipher, or picture out in Diagrams, whatsoever is under consideration, as it is customary in common Geometrical Demonstrations; and the Knowledge obtained by this Procedure, is called Mechanical Knowledge'.

References
Alberti, L. B. *De re aedificatoria. On the Art of Building in Ten Books,* translated by Joseph Rykwert, Robert Tavernor and Neil Leach (Cambridge, MA, 1988 [1486]).
Daniele Barbaro, *Dieci libri dell'architettura di M. Vitruvio* . . . (Milano, [1556] 1987).
Bennett, J. A. 'A Note on Theories of Respiration and Muscular Action in England c. 1660', *Medical History,* 1976, 20: 59–69.
Borgherini, M. *Disegno e progetto nel cantiere medievale* (Venezia, 2001).
Campbell, J. W. P. *Building St Paul's* (London, 2007).
Centre de Cultura Contemporania de Barcelona, *Las Casas del Alma. Maquetas Arquitectónicas de la Antigüedad (5500a.C./300 d.C)* (Barcelona, 1997).
Chadarevian, S. and Hopwood, N. (eds), *Models, the Third Dimension of Science* (Stanford, 2004).
Chambers, E. *Cyclopædia* (London, 1740).
Cocke, T. *900 Years: The Restorations of Westminster Abbey* (London, 1995).
Contardi, B. 'I modelli nel sistema della progettazione architettonica a Roma tra 1680 e 1750', in B. Contardi and G. Curcio (eds), *In Urbe Architectus. Modelli, Disegni, Misure. La professione dell'architetto. Roma, 1680–1750* (Roma, 1991), 9–22.
Di Pasquale, S. 'Leon Batista Alberti and the Art of Building', *Nexus II: Architecture and Mathematics* (1988), 115–25.
— *L'arte del Costruire tra conoscenza e scienza* (Veneza, 1996).
Evers, B. (ed.), *Architekturmodelle der Renaissance – die Harmonie des Bauens von Alberti bis Michelangelo* (München 1996).
Feuerbach, U. 'The Use of Models in Ancient Egypt', in Proceedings of the conference *The Model, a Tool in the Architectural Project,* published by Ecole de Chaillot, Cité de l'Architecture et du Patrimoine, Editions Lieux Dits (forthcoming).
Fontana, C. *Templum vaticanum et ipsius origo. Cum Aedificiis maximè conspicuis antiquitùs, & recèns ibidem constitutis; editum ab Equite Carolo Fontana Deputato celeberrimi ejusdem Templi Ministro, atque Architecto* (Roma, 1694).
Fox, C. *The Arts of Industry in the Age of Enlightment* (New Haven and London, 2010).
Guasti, C. *La cupola di S. Maria del Fiore* (Florence, 1857).
Gerbino, Stephen and Johnston, A. (eds), *Compass & Rule. Architecture as Mathematical Practice in England* (New Haven and London, 2009).
Gunther, R. T. *The Architecture of Sir Roger Pratt* (Oxford, 1928).
Hart, V. *Nicholas Hawksmoor: Rebuilding Ancient Wonders* (New Haven and London, 2002).
Harvey, J. *The Medieval Architect* (London, 1972).
Heyman, J. 'The Rubber Vaults of the Middle Ages and Other Matters', *Gazette des Beaux-Arts,* March 1968, 177–88.
Higgot, G. 'The Fabric to 1670', in Keen et al. 2004, 171–90.
— 'Geometry and Structure in the Dome of St Paul's Cathedral', in Gerbino and Johnston 2009, 155–72.

Keen, D., Burns, A. and Saint, A., *St Paul's. The Cathedral Church of London 604–2004* (New Haven and London, 2004).

Lepik, A. *Das Architekturmodell in Italien, 1335–1550*, Römische Studien der Bibliotheca Hertziana; 9 (Worms, 1994).

Li, S. 'Christopher Wren as a Baconian', *The Journal of Architecture*, 2000, 5: 235–66.

— *Power and Virtue: Architecture and Intellectual Change in England 1660–1730* (London and New York, 2007).

Long, P. O. *Artisan/Practitioners and the Rise of the New Sciences, 1400–1600* (Corvallis, OR, 2011).

Maffioli, C. S. *La via delle acque (1550–1700): Appropriazione delle arti e trasformazione delle mathematiche* (Firenze, 2010).

Millon, H. A. Magnago Lampugnani, V. (eds), *The Renaissance from Brunelleschi to Michelangelo: The Representation of Architecture* (London, 1994).

Milman, L. *Sir Christopher Wren* (London, 1908).

Milton, H. A. (ed.), *The Triumph of the Baroque: Architecture in Europe, 1600–1750* (Milano, 1999).

Mokyr, J. *The Enlightened Economy: An Economic History of Britain, 1700 1850* (New Haven and London, 2010).

Morgan, M. S. and Morrison, M. *Models as Mediators. Perspectives on Natural and Social Sciences* (Cambridge, 1999).

Mauro Mussolin, 'Forme in fieri. I modelli architettonici nella progettazione di Michelangelo', in C. Elam (ed.), *Michelangelo e il disegno di archittura* (Venezia, 2006), 95–111.

Newmann, C. 'Sir Charles Scarburgh', *British Medical Journal*, 1975, 3: 429–30.

Oechslin, W.,Das Architekturmodell zwischen Theorie und Praxis', in B. Evers (ed.), *Architekturmodelle der Renaissance* (München, 1996), 40–9.

Pacciani, R. 'I modelli lignei nella progettazione rinascimentale', *Rassegna*, anno IX, dicembre 1987, 32: 6–19.

Pacey, A. *Medieval Architectural Drawing: English Craftsmen's Methods and their Later Persistence (c.1200–1700)* (Stroud, 2007).

Palladio, A. *I Quattro Libri dell'Architettura* (Venezia, 1570).

Potié, P. *Philibert De L'Orme. Figures de la Pansée Constructive* (Marseille, 1996).

Prager, F. Scaglia, G. *Brunelleschi, Studies of his Technologies and Inventions* (Cambridge, MA, 1970).

Reuter, H. Berckenhagen, E. *Deutsche Architekturmodelle. Projekthilfe zwischen 1500 und 1900*, Jahresausgabe des Deutschen Vereins für Kunstwissenschaft (Berlin, 1994).

Roberts, L. Schaffer, S. Dear, P. (eds), *The Mindful Hand: Inquiry and Invention from the Late Renaissance to Early Industrialisation* (Amsterdam, 2007).

Scamozzi, Vincenzo, *L'idea Dell'Architettura Universale* (Venezia, 1615).

Scolari, Massimo, 'L'idea di modello', *Eidos,* June 1988, 2: 16–39.

Summerson, J. 'J. H. Mansart, Sir Christopher Wren and the dome of St Paul's Cathedral', *Burlington Magazine*, 1990, 132/1042: 32–6

Valeriani, S. 'Sir Christopher Wren and the use of models in the construction of St Paul's cathedral,' in Proceedings of the conference *The Model, a Tool in the Architectural Project*, published by Ecole de Chaillot, Cité de l'Architecture et du Patrimoine, Editions Lieux Dits (forthcoming).

— 'Facts and Building Artefacts: What Travels in Material Objects?' in P. Howlett and M. S. Morgan (eds), *How Well Do 'Facts' Travel?* (Cambridge, 2011), 43–71.

— 'The Roofs of Wren and Jones: A Seventeenth-Century Migration of Technical Knowledge from Italy to England', Working papers on The Nature of Evidence: How Well Do 'Facts' Travel?, 14/06, LSE, Department of Economic History.

Valleriani, M. 'The Transformation of Aristotle's *Mechanical Questions*: A Bridge Between the Italian Renaissance Architects and Galileo's First New Science', *Annals of Science*, 66/2: 183–208.

Vitruvius, M. *On Architecture*, translated by R. Schofield (London, 2009).

Waldram, P. J. 'Science and Architecture: Wren and Hooke', *Journal of the Royal Institute of British Architects*, 1935, 42/9: 558.

Wallace, W. A. 'Galileo's Jesuit Connections and Their influence on His Science' in: *Jesuit Science and the Republic of Letters*, M. Feingold (ed.) (Cambridge, MA, 2003), 99–126.

Wilton-Ely, J. 'The architectural Model', *Architectural Review*, July 1967, CXLI: 26–32.

— 'The architectural model: English baroque', *Apollo Magazine*, October 1968, 88: 250–59.

Wotton, H. *The Elements of Architecture . . . from the Best Authors and Examples* (London, 1624).

Wren, C. *Parentalia or Memoirs of the Family of the Wrens* (London, 1750).

Wren Society, vol. XIV (Oxford, 1937).

— vol. XV (Oxford, 1938).

— vol. XVI (Oxford, 1939).

The Circulation of Knowledge in Early Modern Europe: Embodiment, Mobility, Learning and Knowing

LISSA ROBERTS

University of Twente

Like many of his early eighteenth-century contemporaries, Daniel Defoe was interested in comparing Great Britain with the Netherlands. In an age of international competition for rapidly increasing maritime trade, he was happy to report that the River Thames 'from London-bridge to Blackwall, is one great Arsenal: nothing in the World can be like it'. And while Amsterdam's harbour was full of ships, Defoe undertook his own local London survey, counting some 'two thousand sail of all sort, not reckoning barges, lighters or pleasure boats or yachts'.[1] By the early 1700s, teeming ports such as London and Amsterdam overflowed with goods and the populations who built and manned the vessels by which they were imported and exported. But commercial accumulation and trade were not the only activities centred there. These sites were also dense with the production, accumulation and exchange of knowledge and skill – some domestic in origin, some imported along with the crews and cargoes that arrived daily from distant shores.

Historians have come to recognize such concentrated intermingling of material and commercial concerns with knowledge and ability as both commonplace and characteristic of significant portions of early-modern Europe. And while globally based maritime trade was a key site for this hybrid development, similar trends were equally manifest in market towns and cities across the continent, carried by the manufacture of and trade in commodities such as textiles, as well as the market for consumables ranging from medicines to alcoholic beverages. At the same time, both urban workshops and rural sites including mines and mills housed the productively entrepreneurial pairing of material and mechanical or chemical exploitation. Next to the eye-catching breakthroughs heralded by Europe's premier scientific societies and academies, a world of mundane work and exchange was thus responsible for much of the production, circulation and use of knowledge and skill related to European economic growth.

Contemporary endeavours such as Diderot and d'Alembert's *Encyclopédie* sought to capture and encourage this spread by bringing the 'arts' and 'sciences' together in a single publication. As the first lines of the entry for 'encyclopaedia', penned by Diderot, make clear, 'the purpose of an *encyclopaedia* is to collect knowledge disseminated around the globe'. The word 'encyclopaedia', we are told, is an amalgam of 'the Greek nouns κύκλος, *circle*, and παιδεία, *knowledge*', which suggests more than a simple compilation. Rather, by connecting information, ideas and images to form a carefully linked chain, the project's goal was 'to change the common way of thinking'. In this regard, Diderot's words resonate with recent discussions of the phrase 'circulation of knowledge' which are directed towards changing the common way of thinking about the history of science and technology. So too do they underscore the insights, limitations and challenges of the explanation for historical development which the phrase conveys.[2]

In this chapter I want to revisit the phrase 'circulation of knowledge' to explore how both its explanatory power and limitations can help us evaluatively appreciate the theme of this special issue. This involves examining what the focus on knowledge entails as we move through the cycle which 'circulation' suggests – production, translation, appropriation and use. Why privilege knowledge as that which circulates and what are the interpretative consequences of doing so? What does it mean in concrete historical terms to speak of the embodied movement and consumption of knowledge? And what of the historical narrative implied by this focus? Does it fit with what we know about the map of and interrelations among developments in commerce, culture, technology and natural inquiry?

Perhaps we can begin to recognize the complexities these questions raise by briefly returning to the *Encyclopédie*. As extensively documented by historian Robert Darnton and others, this groundbreaking compendium was itself a hybrid product of collaboration among entrepreneurs, authors (including some of the age's most well-known *philosophes*) and artisans.[3] This is not to say that entrepreneurs managed the business end of things while authors provided knowledgeable content and artisans saw the work physically through the press. Rather, we know for example that publishers – Andre Le Breton, who initiated and financed the original endeavour, as well as a number of pirates – and interaction with censors left an indelible mark on content, as did discussions between authors and their informants, along with extensive 'borrowing' from already published sources (both books and plates). Originally conceived as a commercial endeavour – the largest and probably most profitable publishing venture of the eighteenth century – the *Encyclopédie* can only be parsed into intellectual, technical and commercial components through an act of retrospective, artificial division.[4]

Another way to begin thinking about these issues is to consider how heterogeneous topics drawn from the 'arts' and 'sciences' were discussed and represented within the covers of a single publication which was organized alphabetically rather than topically. It would seem that orderly integration in this case could only be achieved through a process of translation which depicted the world of work and material production in the same manner as objects, natural phenomena and concepts. Static images and verbal descriptions were thus used to familiarize readers with the parts that composed the whole of various machines, inventions and crafts, substituting visual representation and discursive knowledge for hands-on productive experience. But this kind of passive armchair knowledge could hardly be expected to provide an effective substitute for experiential learning. We must understand Diderot's goal of 'changing the common way of thinking' as a political rather than practical one, especially when we consider that relatively little of the information about and representations of crafts found in the *Encyclopédie* was in fact cutting-edge; a good deal actually related to processes and apparatus in use during the late seventeenth and early eighteenth century. And, despite his claims to have visited numerous workshops to witness procedures first hand, it would appear that Diderot was less directly familiar with the arts of which he wrote than suggested.[5]

Considering the way in which the arts and artisanal practices were presented in the *Encyclopédie* brings with it the question of how readers interpreted what they found between its volumes' covers. Posed more generally, it raises the issue of cognition as an important element in the process of knowledge circulation, a theme which this chapter takes up in its second section. For now it is interesting to see how the encyclopaedist Diderot dealt with the issue. As early as the *Encyclopédie's* 'Prospectus' of 1750, he declared the insufficiency of discursive language to teach how the arts were carried out in a practical sense. 'It is handicraft which makes the artist, and it is not in Books that one can learn to manipulate . . . there are many things that one learns only in the shops'.[6]

As a philosophical author, dedicated populariser and (fine) art critic, nonetheless, Diderot repeatedly returned to the processes of human cognition in an attempt to understand and express how humans translate perceptions of heterogeneous sensations, along with verbal and visual representations, as they seek to grasp all they encounter. In his *Lettre sur les sourds et muets*, he described the human mind as 'a moving picture (*un tableau movant*) which we consistently try imitatively to paint'.[7] If our mind is thus a kind of movie theatre in which a reflection of the external world's rich heterogeneity continuously plays, so too does it actively attempt to capture that film by producing a stream of representative signs.

> We spend a great deal of time trying to recreate [the states of our mind] with fidelity. But it exists all at once and in its entirety; our spirit does not proceed bit by bit as does expression . . . The formation of language necessitated decomposition . . . Oh sir! How our understanding is modified by signs, and what a frozen copy of reality is the most animated discourse.[8]

No matter how much a reader or direct observer takes in, then, he or she remains twice removed from the external world: first by absorbing an internal image rather than the palpable fullness of what is being observed; second by being limited to discursive language as a means of reflective thought and expression. Returning to enlightenment projects such as the *Encyclopédie*, we see how even those who were most intimately involved recognized how much more was required to stimulate the spread of actively practical knowledge and skill.

The rest of this chapter takes up this challenge by focusing on two topics. First, by examining various forms of material embodiment, how might knowledge and skills of various sorts be said to have actually circulated in the context of early-modern Europe? And second, by reviewing recent discussions of cognition which seek to go beyond examinations of internal mental states by considering cognition as embodied in a (social) network, how can we account for the active reception and use of that which circulated? After having thus examined embodied knowledge and knowing, we consider what the consequences of privileging (useful and reliable) knowledge as the crucial motor of change are for our historical understanding of innovation and economic growth in early-modern Europe.

FROM 'PRODUCTION AND DIFFUSION' TO THE CIRCULATION OF EMBODIED KNOWLEDGE

Words bear telling histories. The pairing of 'production' and 'diffusion' with 'knowledge' and 'innovation', for example, is historically linked to the development of what is often referred to as the 'linear model'. Briefly schematized, the 'linear model' accounts for innovation by beginning with 'pure' or 'basic' (i.e. disinterested 'scientific') research, which spurs 'applied' research, industrial development and diffusion. Rooted initially in efforts by American university scientists to help secure their positions and funding from the early 1900s, the model was most fully fleshed out and propagated by industrialists, business school economists and statistics gathered by organizations such as the National Science Foundation (NSF) and Organisation for Economic Co-operation and Development (OECD) to track research productivity.[9]

Faith in the 'linear model' as much more than an effective rhetorical device has mercifully waned in academic circles, but it continues to loom spectre-like over discussions of the historical relations among science, technology and economic growth.[10] Recently, authors such as Robert Allen and Joel Mokyr have argued that the process of European industrialization was ultimately rooted in the concepts and culture of 'Newtonian science'.[11] It is true that much of this discussion replaces talk of 'pure' and 'applied' research with a focus on 'useful and reliable knowledge' (URK), but even the most careful of commentators find their analyses entangled in the – at least verbal – distinction between the production and 'justification' of knowledge, on one hand, and its application and diffusion, on the other.[12] Ian Inkster, for example, begins his historically rich review of the relation between '"useful and reliable knowledge" and material progress in Europe' auspiciously by arguing that '[d]iffusion, adaptation and application are feasible processes in which URK played a role, but there is no reason to believe that they were ever arrayed in a line'.[13] He refers the question of reliability, however, to the production of and/or critical passage of knowledge through institutional sites such as the Royal Society that were characterized – culturally, if not in fact – by their (stance of) gentlemanly disinterestedness.[14] Hence, to cite Inkster's prime example, the iconic steam engine owed its early development to 'the complex relationships between URK and technique' – a formula structured out of the distinction between knowledge production (URK being the product) and the means of its application (technique). Beginning with Denis Papin, he argues that the first included Papin's early formal knowledge training and association with the *Académie des Sciences* and the Royal Society, as well as with 'natural philosophers' such as Christiaan Huygens and Leibniz. So too did experimentation serve 'several purposes, but especially in satisfying expert audiences of reliability'.[15]

For better or worse, then, the production and 'justification' of knowledge continue often to be projected as separate and (at least culturally) prior to 'application' and 'diffusion' within the intertwined histories of innovation and economic growth. And even if it is no longer fashionable to refer historically to science – defined as essentially constituted by the process and products of 'pure' research – as the first stage of development, the culture and institutions of 'science' (or its supposed predecessor 'natural philosophy') continue to be seen as having played a primary role in producing and making acceptable the kinds of knowledge that were subsequently applied to material innovation and growth. One way of interpreting this historiographical move is to say that a shift has taken place from viewing technological (and economic) development as dependent on scientific theory – a view that fit well with the dominance of intellectual history of science during the 1950s and 1960s – to a view that links it dependently to science as a sociocultural institution. This is a move that fits nicely with changes in how many have come to analyse the history of science in the wake of studies such as Thomas Kuhn's epochal *Structure of Scientific Revolutions*, but it does not yet entail a full re-evaluation of the larger question of the complex and often hybrid relation among material and knowledge production, circulation and appropriation.

Elements for such a re-evaluation are present, however. These include a more indepth look at what makes knowledge mobile and how the means of its mobility, apprehension and appropriation determine its production, development and distribution. To treat the question of mobility, the rest of this section examines the concept of embodied knowledge. Then, as stated in the introduction, we turn in the next section to the question of how mobile knowledge is apprehended by focusing on concepts such as embodied cognition. And because a thorough re-evaluation requires us to take a step back and ask whether knowledge should in fact remain the privileged locus of such an investigation, this chapter ends by asking what other options might be considered.

Plato notwithstanding, knowledge cannot exist or travel on its own in our material world. It needs a physical carrier, whether a human, a book, an illustration, a machine or an instrument. That is, it needs to be embodied.[16] This is easy to admit, but what we sometimes forget is just how much embodiment matters. Not only does it afford knowledge mobility, it also has a formative or transformative impact on that which it embodies. As already previewed in this essay's introduction, a classic and essential example can be drawn from the work done by historians of the book. Thanks to historians such as Rogier Chartier, Robert Darnton and – in the history of science – Adrian Johns, we know that not only the form but also the content, meaning and significance of early-modern European books depended on printers, publishers, booksellers, owners, readers and the journeys that connected them at least as much as on the original intention of the books' authors.[17] The same can be said for other objects taken to embody knowledge. The history of scientific instruments, for example, is filled with cases such as the calorimeter which was first designed to measure the presence of the chemical substance caloric and to help ascertain elective affinities, and not only went through a number of design changes, but also came to serve very different experimental, rhetorical and pedagogical purposes than those first envisioned by its original designers Lavoisier and Laplace.[18] Likewise, artisanal productions can be and were sometimes historically asserted as embodying both the skill of their creator and knowledge about nature.[19]

As this last sentence implies, another way to describe embodiment's nature is to state that it is, in principle, multivalent. Thus a technical drawing, such as those found in Diderot's *Encyclopédie* or a map such as those printed in the seventeenth-century workshop of Jan Blaeu, embodied the ability to be appreciated in more than one way. Such drawings were viewed by some as representing the steps in a manufacturing process, the construction of industrial equipment or the geographical position of various locations. But they were also appreciated as embodying enviable engraving skill. On some occasions, these sorts of knowledge were ignored (especially when the sources of knowledge and skilful production were not European) and objects such as maps, engravings and books were seen as having had no more value than that their ownership represented a certain cultural *cachet*. They were thus simultaneously valuable as bearers of knowledge about a given subject; embodied evidence of artistic, printing or publishing knowledge and skill; and indicators of cultural sophistication.[20] This means that historians have to track the career of an object and the knowledge and skill it was taken to embody with thoroughness and care before being able to judge what it has to tell us about the utility, reliability or consequence of its circulation. The human embodiment of knowledge and skill is no exception; historical actors (like people today) brought together various diachronic and synchronic identities, which led them to share the knowledge and skill they possessed in various ways with various audiences.

Cultural historians have recently helped us to appreciate an important variation on this theme. Not only are objects, plants, animals and humans multivalent in the ways just described, the knowledge and skills they might be said to embody can be transplanted or re-presented in other media. This not only has an important impact on their meaning but also sends their embodied trajectories in new and sometimes surprisingly significant directions. While intermediality is usually discussed in relation to cultural production, there is no reason why the concept cannot be used as a way to interpret and understand the history of combined material and knowledge production and circulation. Historian Benjamin Schmidt, for example, has uncovered a number of fascinating early-modern European cases in which the same culturally significant images could be found on the border of a map, as an illustration in a published atlas and as a carved, inlaid or painted representation on a decorative piece of furniture. In each case, the image might be said to have been simultaneously the same and different in terms of the skills that produced it, the ambient context which leant it meaning and the way in which it was used. Simon Werrett's recent book on the history of fireworks, to name another suggestive source, traces the movement of a developing body of knowledge and goods from the contexts of gunnery and court pageantry, through chemical laboratories to gas light manufacturing. It would be a profitable exercise to consider the changes undergone by the embodied representation of knowledge in this evolving historical context as it moved from gunnery manuals to pageant displays to chemistry texts books and demonstrations, to advertisements for and demonstrations of gas lighting.[21]

In some situations, it might be more appropriate to speak of circulating objects less in terms of embodying knowledge and skill and more in terms of embodying challenges or invitations to the new environments they enter. This point is perhaps best introduced by returning to the words of Simon Kuznets, whose discussion of 'useful knowledge' remains instructive. As he wrote,

> The key feature of an innovation is that it is *new* – and thus a peculiar combination of new *knowledge* sufficiently useful and promising to warrant the attempt to apply it; and of *ignorance* of the full range of possibilities and improvements that can be learned only in extended application.[22]

Kuznets' insight bears some similarity to that developed in a more philosophical vein by the sociologist Karin Knorr-Cettina and philosopher Hans-Jorg Rheinberger, in their discussions of 'epistemic objects' and 'epistemic things'. For both authors, what characterizes these objects is their incompleteness; that is, the simultaneity of their material presence and the absence of their fully being known in the context of their ongoing development or of the inquiry being made about them. Knorr-Cettina writes:

> Since epistemic objects are always in the process of being materially defined, they continually acquire new properties and change the ones they have. But this means that objects of knowledge can never be fully attained, that they are, if you wish, never quite themselves.

To help make sense of this poetic point, she offers a number of concrete examples, ranging from detectors used in high-energy physics experiments to computer programs, which take on different forms, characters, qualities and abilities through their various modifications, deployments and uses.[23]

If an examination of embodied knowledge leads us to recognize the historically dynamic and undetermined nature of embodied knowledge, then, it also signals the importance of (contexts of) appropriation and use. We can give additional historical substance to this by recalling Maxine Berg's argument that we cannot understand the origins of the so-called industrial revolution, without reference to Great Britain's trade with China.[24] Her point is that the extensive export of Chinese luxury goods to Europe was crucial, but should not be seen as having simply spurred import substitution schemes. Rather than presenting commodities such as ceramics and textiles as transparent embodiments of knowledge and skill that could be absorbed and put to work, she describes their presence in Europe as invitations to the creative application and further development of domestically available (embodied) knowledge and skill. The industrial revolution, on this count, was not about aping Chinese methods, tools and commodities. It was about finding productive solutions to the challenge of manufacturing new and more desirable or, at least, attainable goods – solutions which built on and further spurred locally present mechanical and social knowledge and skills.

Berg's historical examination makes clear that the circulation of knowledge is far from a geographically straightforward proposition. Rather, developmental trajectories of material production can draw on different geographically extensive networks through which knowledge and its embodiments are produced and move. Knowledge embodied in imported commodities at the point of production can be extracted elsewhere through the local analysis of goods; that is, domestic knowledge and skill can be applied to reveal knowledge coming from elsewhere. Alternatively, knowledge about production processes can be gathered abroad, translated into the languages and modes of domestic representation and understanding, and then circulate in the form of illustrations, publications and reports. Berg argues that British manufacturers opted for a third approach. Rather than seeking to adopt the foreign production processes which left their traces in Asian luxury goods as embodied knowledge or which were described in publications such as Malachy Postlethwayt's *Universal Dictionary of Trade and Commerce*, they harnessed locally available knowledge, skill and resources to produce alternative goods and to redirect consumer demand towards these novel products and fashions.[25] This tells us that the ignorance to which Kuznetz refers (see above) in fact bears two primary facets. He and many others focus on producers' ignorance regarding the possible futures implicated in their appropriation of knowledge and skills to new endeavours, which necessarily imbues their work with an element of entrepreneurial risk. In the first instance, we can use this as a starting point from which to trace out the further history of European responses to Asian luxury goods, claimed by Berg to have unfolded as the industrial revolution. But we can also recognize ignorance as a culturally constructed phenomenon which colours the perception of the past and informs the context in which future-directed activities unfold. In this case, prejudices regarding 'Oriental' culture helped draw attention away from (interest in) available knowledge about Asian practices and desire for Asian goods, towards an emphasis on and demand for local inventiveness and increasingly novel domestic goods.[26]

Both the concept of epistemic objects/things and Berg's analysis of the global roots of British industrialization can thus be said to point to the temporal character of epistemology. They do so, however, with different emphases. For Berg, industrialization arose over time through the innovative application of locally present knowledge and know-how to objects imported from elsewhere. In the process, some measure of the knowledge which was originally embodied in the objects was lost, obscured or transformed. Knorr Cettina and Rheinberger adopt a more philosophical perspective and speak about epistemology in general as involving a never-ending process of becoming. Talk about embodied knowledge is thereby best recast in terms of an object or procedure's ongoing, context-bound development. It is not knowledge, then, that essentially defines what a thing or process is. Rather, knowledge unfolds as the situated 'biography' of that object or process evolves.[27]

We will return to the implications of this important revelation in the essay's next two sections. To conclude this section, we turn to the question of the routes traced out by what we will continue conventionally to call the circulation of (embodied) knowledge. Who populated these paths and where did they lead? If this section begins with a concern for the links between current analyses of these questions and the spectre of the linear model, what alternative geographies might be proffered to tie the circulation of knowledge to innovation in early-modern Europe?

In a recent volume entitled *The Mindful Hand: Inquiry and Invention from the late Renaissance to early Industrialization*, a number of colleagues and I developed the historical argument that, at least for the extended period under investigation in this special issue, the practical division between mental and manual work – between the mind and the hand, if you will – was often illusory, more the product of cultural and institutional claims than of mundane activity. As the volume's various essays demonstrate, this was just as much the case for the careers of individual artisans and philosophers, as it was for larger fields of endeavour such as mathematics and chemistry.[28] With this in mind, it should come as no surprise that the migrations and peregrinations of artisans and guild members provided an important vehicle for the productive circulation of knowledge.[29]

In fact, the range of trajectories along which knowledge was translated was far from limited to the *Wanderjahre* of craftsmen and passage through academies. Productive knowledge paths could just as likely pass through and gain approval from the market, for example, as scientific societies. Books and pamphlets which highlighted (at least what was advertised as) useful knowledge, were, after all, purchasable commodities, available to anyone with change in their pocket. So too might artisans, especially itinerants such as Italian glassblowers and instrument makers, ply their wares at the fairs they visited across Europe through entertaining public demonstrations of their products' revelatory capabilities.[30] Merchants also served as important knowledge brokers and producers, sometimes quite directly engaged in various forms of inquiry and experimentation as part of their communication with producers about the wares they wished to order.

In fact, the same person or business partnership might well have been involved in both production and sales (as well as the appropriation of knowledge generated elsewhere). For the eighteenth century, Boulton and Watt, along with Josiah Wedgwood, certainly spring to mind as premier examples. So too did Benjamin Huntsman, known mostly for developments in the production of crucible steel, and his business grow rich from an interactive involvement in production and international trade.[31] Among his firm's trading partners and productive collaborators were Margaret Elizabeth Aumerle and her husband William Blakey, who operated a fashionable toy shop on the rue St. Honore in Paris, and at various times manufactured and sold pinion wire, medical trusses and steam engines, all of which were rooted in Blakey's own experimentation and design. One could go another step here and note that the design of Blakey's steel trusses, for example, were further modified through correspondence between Blakey and his customers who related their experiential knowledge so that he might produce a better fitting truss.[32] While historians have had much to say these past years about the relations between commerce and the productive circulation of knowledge in the age of global trading companies, these examples emphasize the value of paying closer attention to the role of individual merchants as well.[33]

FROM EMBODIED KNOWLEDGE TO LEARNING, KNOWING AND DOING

We saw in the previous section that discussions of knowledge which take a diachronic perspective (such as those by Kuznets, Knorr-Cettina and Rheinberger) lead to a consideration of how knowledge is apprehended. Knowledge and (not) knowing, that is to say, are analytical siblings; in order for knowledge to have a practical impact – to be useful and reliable, it has to be cognized or learned somewhere by some means. But where and how does this take place? The traditional answer is that knowing occurs in the individual mind, but a number of other answers have been posed with profitable implications for our understanding of the historical process of innovation. Explorations of the concept of tacit knowledge, for example, have proven an important avenue for furthering our understanding of how laboratory and factory workers, artisans and engineers come to know what they do and do what they know. Learning in this case involves some sort of apprenticeship or repeated practice, the content of which has traditionally been opposed to mastering rules of reason. If we return to the words of Diderot, for example, we find him building on this distinction to justify his encyclopaedic project: he claimed that the mute, but pregnant abilities of artisans needed the organizing voice of a reasoned dictionary in order to discipline and enhance their productivity. In the twentieth century, the Marxist sociologist Edgar Zilsel enshrined the distinction between tacit craft knowledge and scholarly reason in his classic description of the origins of modern science. In both cases, mundane familiarity with the material world and the willingness to experiment characterized craftwork; what artisans apparently lacked was the ability to articulate and thereby harness the rules of their art in a productively organized way. By disciplining the processes of material manipulation and experimentation, what historian of technology Edwin Layton would later call 'cut and try empiricism', rationally trained individuals – socially engaged *philosophes* for Diderot, scholars and humanists for Zilsel – enriched natural inquiry by grounding it in the direct, rationally informed examination of material phenomena and processes while they contributed to material progress by lending discipline and knowledgeable principles to artisanal practices.[34]

Of particular interest here is that the concept of tacit knowledge has been used to explore and explain the nature of scientific as well as artisanal or technically oriented work.[35] Building on an insight of fellow sociologist Jerry Ravetz, for example, Harry Collins argues that '[a]ll types of knowledge, however pure, consist, in part, of tacit rules which may be impossible to formulate in principle'.[36] Based on this claim, Collins uses an examination of a set of experimental physicists engaged in the construction of lasers to suggest that contextually specific tacit knowledge is, in practice, what holds a scientific group together. He and others have further argued for the socially adhesive epistemological role of tacit knowledge in areas such as the development of nuclear weapons, biological procedures, evidence-based medicine, veterinary surgery and the quality measurement of sapphire crystals.[37]

Collins cites Thomas Kuhn's influential argument that the 'normal science' practiced by a scientific community is held together by a paradigm as his starting point, which makes his focus on tacit knowledge even more intriguing.[38] Here it is of interest to note three things: (1) tacit knowledge can thus be seen as a way of referring to contextually specific rules for what Kuhn calls 'puzzle solving', which cannot be articulated, but which circulate through personal contact between senior and junior members of a (scientific) community; (2) tacit knowledge operates effectively in contexts of 'normal' science and, by extension, to comparable contexts of mundanely productive – as opposed to innovative or revolutionary – work in which a community of practitioners engages (a point to which we will return); (3) this view does not offer a determination of precisely where tacit knowledge 'resides' at the individual level.

In his analysis of engineering design, Eugene Ferguson responds to this third point by distinguishing between bodily skill and tacit knowledge, situating the latter in the mind as a kind of trained intuition. Similarly, Walter Vincenti accepts this distinction and goes on to argue that: 'tacit knowledge and prescriptive knowledge are closely related in practice in that they have to do with procedures'. Though not amenable to articulation, in other words, it is tacit knowledge that directs skill; it is the mind that learns and disciplines the body.[39]

Others refuse to base their views on an initial acceptance of Cartesian dualism and locate learning throughout the body. Phenomenologists ranging from Maurice Merleau Ponty to Don Ihde argue that we are always engaged with the world through the directive agency of tools, whether our bodily senses or the material instruments we make and yield.[40] But while phenomenologists conceive of embodied cognition as an ahistorical truth about how individuals cognitively relate to the world, we have already seen that learning invariably takes place over time in historically specific environments, which one might expect to have an impact on the learning process as well. Hence, for example, historical examination reveals that chemists situated the use of their senses and interpreted sense-based findings differently before and after the chemical revolution at the end of the eighteenth century, thanks to the coupled introduction of a constellation of new instruments and a new disciplinary protocol regarding what constituted chemical evidence.[41]

Among the first to bring together the view, in the 1930s, of embodied learning with a recognition of the specifying role played by sociocultural context was the sociologist and anthropologist Marcel Mauss. Beginning with a definition of *techniques du corps* as the traditional means by which people know how to make use of their bodies, Mauss insisted that these *techniques* involve an indissoluble union of the biological, the psychological and the social. Learning, he argued, predominantly entails the repeated imitation of evidently successful acts performed by figures of trust and authority (Mauss' conception of education). Not only does this unite the psychological and the physical, it situates their bodily union in what might be called the classroom of ambient culture.

The body, according to Mauss, learns within a historically specific sociocultural environment, with equally specific abilities and cultural continuity as a result. While most of his discussion is larded with examples drawn from observations of the bodily gestures found in various 'primitive' cultures, he offers his own experience of having to replace thousands of French shovels with English shovels during World War I so that English soldiers could take over the task of digging trenches, as corroborating evidence.[42]

Like Kuhn and others after him, however, Mauss carefully distinguishes between this kind of mundane 'normal' activity and innovative change, which apparently cannot be accounted for solely by reference to imitative learning within a community. Since at least the 1970s, however, economists and economic historians have discussed mechanisms whereby innovation can indeed result from shared learning opportunities. Robert Allan, for example, introduced the concept of 'collective invention' to express his claim that innovation can occur through processes akin to what economist Eric von Hippel calls 'informal know-how sharing'. Through channels ranging from conversations between employees working at different firms to the publication of articles in engineering journals, information about changes in plant construction or production processes which is not patented or patentable but which can provide a crucial increment in what Von Hippel calls the 'distributed innovation process', firms take part in networks of communal learning.

Allan examines 'communal invention', however, as an economic rather than cognitive phenomenon. For his part, Von Hippel explicitly describes relevant 'know-how' as 'held in the minds of a firm's engineers who develop its products and develop and operate its processes'. Intriguing as these insights are, then, they are not really helpful in opening the black box of cognition as a group dynamic.[43] By turning instead to recent discussions of the concept 'socially distributed cognition', we see how this gap can be bridged without having to return to a view of cognition as an individual mental process. The concept of 'socially distributed cognition' was first introduced by Edwin Hutchins in his book *Cognition in the Wild* (1995). Based on studies which examine navigation on board a ship and flying an airliner as jointly accomplished cognitive processes, Hutchins argues that cognition is social because it is distributed among people and objects who play different but collaborative roles in the problem-solving process. Because this form of cognition involves a socially distributed process in which knowledge is apprehended through its exercise in joint projects, we might call it 'learning by doing together'.[44]

A small number of historians have used Hutchins' method to inform their own work. Evelyn Tribble has discussed the collaboration between early-modern Protestant church architecture and parishioners in affording the memorization of sermons, as well as that between the Globe Theatre's layout, props, actors, costumes and so forth in the memorization and performance of a play's parts.[45] With Hutchins' work as an inspiration, Pamela Smith glosses the considerable interaction she has traced among early-modern artisans, their natural materials and processes in their workshops with the term 'artisanal epistemology'. One of the things she wants to signal with this term is that artisans' engagement with each other and the material world interactively led to artistic production

and understanding of nature; as such, it proved a source of discovery and innovation . . . so much so, according to Smith, that it came to inform the scientific
revolution's development of experimentalism as a favoured method.[46]

Of most interest in this discussion is Chandra Mukerji's recent book
Impossible Engineering: Technology and Territoriality on the Canal du Midi. While one
might expect such a study to be about the application of knowledge to a major
infrastructure project, Mukerji claims that building the Canal du Midi was
'less a product of knowledge than productive of it'.[47] At core, in other words,
it was an extended learning experience, the reward for which was enhanced
power over the physical and human landscape. To demonstrate this, she
examines the canal's construction as having taken place in a highly complex
context, one which involved the orchestrated collaboration among a variety
of communities – each with its own culture – and elements of nature. Along
the way she displays the innovative potential of socially distributed cognition,
both within individual communities and in cases involving intercommunity
collaboration.

Mukerji begins by arguing that one of the driving motivations behind the
canal's construction during the reign of Louis XIV was the French sover-
eign's equation of France with the 'new Rome'. She then sets out to recover,
among other things, how originally Roman engineering knowledge, embodied in phenomena such as local water supply systems, had been adaptively
kept alive through the centuries in the Pyrenees. Though ultimately rooted
in Roman designs and practices, these hydraulic lifelines evolved over time as
village inhabitants interactively learned to manage the ambient changes they
experienced in both the physical and social environment, the latter brought
about by contact with other cultures. Centuries of environmentally engaged,
collaborative learning built up a dynamic reservoir of tacit engineering knowledge which was part of daily local life and which could be called upon along
with migrant female workers from the Pyrenees who were hired by Pierre Paul
Riquet, the project's entrepreneur, to solve otherwise intractable construction
challenges.

Rather than casting this story simply as one of knowledge application, however, Mukerji is keen to present the overall construction of the Canal du Midi
as an ongoing process of joint learning. To do so she emphasizes the interdependent roles played by a large and heterogeneous cast of human actors ranging from royal advisors and mathematically trained engineers to unschooled
male and female workers who nonetheless possessed practical wisdom and
ability. The interaction among this motley assemblage, Mukerji insists, is what
led to the project's many innovations. But they could not have accomplished
this alone. To round out this productively interactive equation, Mukerji further
insists on the collaboratively constructive roles played by a range of non-human
actors including tools and cartographic documents, elements of nature and
hybrid building materials composed from a combination of natural substances
and human ingenuity.

Referring to such networks as the active locus of socially distributed cognition in which both humans and non-humans are engaged resonates with
the work of authors such as Bruno Latour, Michel Callon and John Law who

developed the interpretative approaches of actor-network theory (ANT) and heterogeneous engineering. According to ANT, when individual actors – both human and non-human – come together and work in concert, a hybrid network is formed which can also be seen as possessing constructive agency. In order for such unlike elements to collaborate constructively, both material and conceptual relations have to be forged by what John Law dubbed 'heterogeneous engineering'. In the words of historian John Krige, this involves:

> . . . not just technological innovation with refractory natural materials, but also the mobilization of obdurate human and material resources, the building of alliances, the deflection or silencing of opposition, and the development of persuasive rhetorics.

Heterogeneous engineering and ANT have been used to explain phenomena ranging from the successes of European cartography, Tycho Brahe's astronomy, Pasteur's microbiology and the discovery of the field particles that communicate weak interaction to the successful restocking of St. Brieuc Bay to produce more scallops and Portuguese maritime expansion during the fifteenth–sixteenth centuries.[48]

Ironically, the hybridity of actor-networks claimed by this approach can perhaps best be recognized by noting that, when considered on their own, the agency of the individual actors – both human and non-human – of which they are composed, is limited in nature. While certainly needed for the successful pursuit and management of engineering projects, for example, maps – which can themselves be seen as the products of socially distributed cognition – are not foolproof tools of engineering power and control because they cannot always 'keep up' with changes to the environment wrought either by engineering or nature. Neither can such material embodiments of hard-won knowledge and skill capture and hold on to the distributed cognitive processes ('learning by doing together') that go into their construction in a demonstrable way.[49] Much of the collaborative work needed to make them is, rather, rendered invisible by their abstract visual appearance and subsequent interpretation. At one and the same time, these things present themselves as too rigidly concrete to exert control over changing environmental conditions and too abstract to display all the sources of their meaningful existence. The same can be said of the Canal du Midi, returning to Mukerji's study.[50] On one hand she describes the canal as the embodiment of distributed cognition. On the other hand, she admits that it was neither capable of fully containing the dynamic forces of nature and society, nor of stably representing the distributed work carried out by the network which brought it into being. Storms destructively battered harbour walls which simultaneously depended on water pressure to keep them intact and political jealousies impeded productivity, for example, while broad-based, collaboratively designed and pursued innovations were narrowly credited retrospectively to elite engineers and courtly managers. The challenge to the historian, then, is to recover the hybrid, material–conceptual character of such projects, to tease out the dynamically interdependent roles played by all parties – human and non-human – in projects which embodied and contributed to productive innovation.

IS FOCUSING ON KNOWLEDGE ENOUGH?

There is yet one more reason to turn to Mukerji's book, which stems from the way in which she distinguishes her analysis from ANT. As she cogently argues,

> ANT might be a good way to explain knowledge-making . . . but network models in the ANT tradition are not particularly useful for explaining political regimes that derive power from using natural knowledge to shape the advantages and disadvantages of built environments.[51]

Here Mukerji places her finger on a crucial challenge to those interested in examining the productive circulation of knowledge through time. While we need to attend to the historical roles played by knowledge in economic development, it is equally important that we recall that the knowledge-power equation is not constituted by a unidirectional vector moving from knowledge to power. The power wielded by political and economic regimes, social movements and cultural values, which both feeds off and informs the productive (and sometimes destructive) circulation of knowledge, needs also to be taken into account.

For some historians, such as David Landes and Joel Mokyr, this recognition has the positive virtue of identifying the essential difference between 'the West and the rest'; that is, what they see as the historical character of European – especially British – society, which directed the growth of knowledge and know-how in a way that brought about 'the great divergence' between Europe and the rest of the world by the nineteenth century. Mokyr explains his position by rooting the so-called Industrial Revolution in a prior 'Industrial Enlightenment', which he describes as having linked a trend towards the realization of institutional adaptability, secure property rights and the rule of law with the ideals of economic freedom, competition, equal access and dedication to the generation and popularization of useful knowledge.[52] Needless to say his and Landes' perspectives are controversial; the latter because of its pairing of Euro-chauvinism and historical inaccuracies, the former because of its sharply stated and challenging thesis.[53]

This is not the place to rehearse the extensive debate surrounding the question of 'the great divergence', but given the way in which it implicates the perceived historical relationship between knowledge, power and economic growth, a few comments are in order. I begin with reference to John Brewer's excellent study, *The Sinews of Power*, in which he incontrovertibly links the rise of British economics and power in the eighteenth century to orchestrated government and institutional intervention in the form of taxation, military (naval) spending, deficit financing and the growth of a large public administration.[54]

William Ashworth adds further detail to this interpretation of British history through a close study of the interrelation between the country's customs and excise system and the growth of useful knowledge. Of special interest here is his discussion of the role played by government policies in stimulating both official and commercial interest in chemical investigation, standardization techniques and instruments of precision. Because assessing duties and excise taxes on consumer goods ranging from soap to alcoholic beverages depended on the trustworthy determination of material contents and alcohol percentage, both government inspectors and producers had an interest in developing expertise in chemical analysis and precision measurement. As inspectors employed newly developed techniques to analyse products for evidence of adulteration, for example, manufacturers responded by developing product substitutes and innovative manufacturing processes. The productive circulation of knowledge and know-how, in these cases, resulted from an ongoing spiral of governmental assertion of control and the public's creative attempts to evade it. Like Brewer, Ashworth introduces his readers to a sophisticated understanding of eighteenth-century Britain which replaces the stereotype vision of a society smoothly moving towards a kind of Smithian paradise.[55]

If the formative presence of governmental power and intervention cannot be separated from the related histories of knowledge production and economic growth in Great Britain during the long eighteenth century, it is easy to recall similar interconnections in other times and places. The history of government support in early-modern Europe for the introduction and improvement of various industries – whether through granting monopolies, patents and prizes, international espionage, tax regimes or attempts to manage the international movement of artisans and ethnic or religious communities – is well known. What we need to keep in the forefront of our investigations is the manifold ways in which the productive power of knowledge, politics and economic interests and activities simultaneously fed off and gained direction, shape and strength from each other. By uncovering the power relations and imbalances among the actors who collaborated and competed within such identifiable networks of power and production, we can go a long way towards charting the complex role played by the circulation of knowledge in Europe's economic growth.

The historian Kapil Raj discusses one of the most telling cases of the productive interaction between knowledge, commerce and politics in his suggestive essay 'Eighteenth-Century Pacific Voyages of Discovery, "Big Science", and the Shaping of European Scientific and Technological Culture'.[56] Analytically comparing global maritime ventures of the eighteenth century with the twentieth-century concept of 'big science' in which the scale of human, financial and material investment in research is such that it can only be borne by the (sometimes uneasy and sometimes covert) collaboration between governments, scientists and commercial interests, allows Raj to show how these voyages simultaneously served different purposes. Neither solely vehicles for reaping harvests of natural knowledge, for furthering technological capabilities, for filling the coffers of national trading companies and merchant networks, nor for political domination of the globe, the cargoes and crews attached to these voyages found themselves buffeted between and communally serving all these goals.

Mention of maritime expeditions that traversed the globe allows us to return to the scene with which this article opens: the teeming harbours of European ports which variously grew rich or declined in keeping with the presence of international trade. These bustling centres provided lodging for sailors and goods from around the world. So too were they the entry point for raw materials, manufactured goods and knowledge gathered from the four corners of the earth. Given the global intercourse that characterized so much material and knowledge exchange during the early-modern period, a good place to end this section is with the question of the extent to which it is possible or desirable to distinguish between 'the West and the Rest' as the starting point for tracing the role of URK in the history of economic growth.

CONCLUSION

In this chapter I have sought to shed light on how we might consider the role of (useful and reliable) knowledge in the historical development of early-modern Europe by critically analysing the often-used phrase 'circulation of knowledge'. Because bringing together discussions of knowledge production, translation, apprehension and use involves reference to so many different types of literature and approaches, it is not easy to summarize what has been said. Nevertheless, a few points are worth underlining.

I would begin by arguing that we need to guard our inquiries against the still-present spectre of the 'linear model', represented in the literature by a continued tendency on the part of some authors to distinguish between knowledge production and the institutional settings in which this occurs or gains validation, on one hand, and its application on the other. Similarly, we need to be careful that historical attention to early-modern scientific societies, 'natural philosophers' (still sometimes considered simply as the predecessors of modern scientists, based on the view that one can draw an unproblematic line of development between natural philosophy and science) and their publications, does not come at the expense of recognizing the productive and intermediary roles played by a variety of hybrid actors, including artisans, merchants and manufacturers, and their practices (i.e. those which cannot so easily be pigeonholed as belonging either to the worlds of mental or of manual activity). Knowledge was just as likely to circulate productively as part of market-related activities as in the context of gentlemanly intercourse.

Tracing the 'circulation of knowledge', others and I have stressed, cannot be accomplished without an analysis of the circulating physical objects and entities taken to embody knowledge. But while this is an increasingly accepted point, we must be careful not to treat embodiment as simply providing a neutral vehicle for the transport of knowledge. Rather, we need to examine how various manners of material embodiment and the trajectories they traced out shaped both the form and content of the knowledge they conveyed. Further, while recovering the objects and entities responsible for the translation of knowledge across space, time and fields of meaning is crucial, it is only half the job. For knowledge to have any impact, it needs to be apprehended or appropriately used. To complete the cycle, then, we need also to interrogate knowing and learning as historical processes.

Examining the part played by knowing and learning in the productive circulation of knowledge need not mean forcing a marriage between cognitive psychology or cognitive neuroscience with history.[57] As discussed in this essay, especially with reference to the work of cognitive scientist Edwin Hutchins and historical sociologist Chandra Mukerji, recent approaches have reoriented the study of cognition away from the internal workings of individual minds and brains and towards the socially distributed character of learning.

In philosophical terms, considering the process of knowing is a matter of epistemological orientation. Though not usually discussed by historians, reflecting on the epistemological commitments which undergird our interpretations can prove enlightening. The dominant perspective in this regard remains one which privileges 'knowledge' as defining or determining the nature of that which embodies it.[58] What are the consequences of positing instead the historically open-ended nature of knowledge – that is, of taking up the view that 'knowledge' is not that which essentially defines an object, process or phenomenon, but that which emerges – ever incomplete – over time and across space from the dynamically changing ways in which an object, process or phenomenon is interactively situated in its environment?[59]

As we examine the historical role of useful and reliable knowledge, we also need to beware of de-politicizing our interpretations by isolating them from the multifaceted landscapes of which they are an integral part. At the other extreme, we need to take care that our efforts to weave our discussions of knowledge into a more complex historical fabric does not shade off into an idealized celebration of 'the European miracle'. Ignoring the formative impact of government fiscal and taxation policies, military spending and market policing in eighteenth-century England, for example, in favour of the ideals of free trade and representative government invoked by authors such as John Locke and Adam Smith, not only falsifies the complexities of the past, it robs us of important insight into the historical dynamics responsible for productivity and economic growth – insight which can be of enormous value for thinking about the challenges facing us today. This is not a question of claiming that government – often protectionist – intervention is necessary to stimulate and manage economic growth. Rather it speaks to a realization that political power, economic and commercial power, and the productive (or destructive) power of knowledge historically implicate and feed off each other. To see how this operated in the past, we must attend to the dynamic interactions among political regimes (especially as embodied in systems and institutions of taxation, encouragement and governance), and the sites (sometimes mobile, as in the case of maritime vessels) and networks in which processes of innovation and industrialization can be identified to have physically taken place.[60]

Finally, geography matters. Not only is it notoriously difficult to define what we ought to understand historically by the term 'Europe' and the phrase 'the West and the Rest', Europe during the early-modern period was suffused with global interaction. This is not just a question of the presence of foreign goods and information, though, as authors such as Maxine Berg argue, the Industrial Revolution was nurtured by the drive to supplant exotic imports with innovatively designed and produced domestic goods. More fundamentally, it is a reflection of the formative roles played by global travel and (inter-mediated) contacts around the globe – all of which implicated struggles for management and control which furthered the construction of global networks of asserted power and profit.

Notes

1. Daniel Defoe, *A Tour Through the Whole Island of Great Britain*, vol. 2 (London, 1748), 146–7.

2. Denis Diderot, 'Encyclopédie', *Encyclopédie ou dictionnaire raisonné des sciences, des arts et des métiers*, eds, Diderot and Jean le Rond d'Alembert (Paris, 1751), 635–49, quotation on 635. For an introductory discussion of how the phrase 'circulation of knowledge' has been taken up by historians of science, see James Secord, 'Knowledge in transit', *Isis*, 2004, 95: 654–72. For an examination of the phrase in a non-Eurocentric context, see Lissa Roberts, 'Situating Science in Global History: Local Exchanges and Networks of Circulation', *Itinerario*, 2009, 33: 9–30.

3. As we will see in the second part of this chapter, others would include objects such as presses and previously published works in this list. Still others would insist on including readers as well, based on the view that meaning is finally determined, not by an author, but through the appropriatively interpretative act of reading.

4. Robert Darnton, *The Business of Enlightenment* (Cambridge, 1986); Jacques Proust, *Diderot et 'L'Encyclopédie'* (Paris, 1967).

5. Proust, *op. cit.* (4), especially 192–5. On the epistemological challenges of obtaining and presenting technical knowledge in the *Encyclopédie* see Joanna Stalnaker, *The Unfinished Enlightenment: Description in the Age of the Encyclopedia* (Ithaca, 2010), 99–123. For an overview of Diderot's contribution to technical education, see John R. Pannabecker, 'Diderot, the Mechanical Arts, and the *Encyclopédie*: In Search of the Heritage of Technology Education', *Journal of Technology Education* 6 (1994). Electronic journal accessed 25 August 2011. http://scholar.lib.vt.edu/cjournals/JTE/jte-v6n1/pannabecker.jte-v6n1.html.

6. Diderot, *op.cit.* (2), xl, xxxv.

7. Diderot, *Lettre sur les sourds et muets à l'usage de ceux qui entendent et qui parlent* (Paris, 1751), 161.

8. Ibid., 161–2.

9. Benoît Godin, 'The Linear Model of Innovation: The Historical Construction of an Analytical Framework', *Science, Technology and Human Values*, 2006, 31: 639–67; Barry Barnes, 'The Science-Technology Relationship: A Model and a Query', *Social Studies of Science*, 1982, 12: 166–72.

10. Recourse to the linear model, unfortunately, can still be found in policy-making circles and the popular press. For an interesting discussion of how knowledge is seen to be related to policy decisions, see Susan Cozzens and Michele Snoek, 'Knowledge to Policy', prepared for 'Workshop on the Science of Science Measurement', Washington DC, December 2010. www.nsf.gov/sbe/sosp/social/cozzens.pdf, accessed 25 August 2011.

11. Robert Allan, *The British Industrial Revolution in Global Perspective* (Cambridge, 2009); Joel Mokyr, *The Gifts of Athena: Historical Origins of the Knowledge Economy* (Princeton, 2002). While these authors draw on Margaret Jacob, *Scientific Culture and the Making of the Industrial West* (Oxford, 1997), such a claim is, in fact, ultimately rooted in the argument put forward by W. W. Rostow, *The Stages of Economic Growth: A Non-Communist Manifesto* (Cambridge, 1960), though he refers back to Francis Bacon rather than Isaac Newton.

12. On the distinction between production or – more traditionally put – discovery and justification, see Jutta Schickore and Friedrich Steinle, eds, *Revisiting Discovery and Justification: Historical and Philosophical Perspectives on the Context Distinction* (Dordrecht, 2006).

13. Ian Inkster, 'Potentially Global: 'Useful and Reliable Knowledge' and Material Progress in Europe, 1474–1914', *The International History Review*, 2006, 28: 237–86, 242.

14. 'To pass a threshold of reliability, continuity, and influence, such sites needed expert markets: an audience that harboured but tested the new and was characterized by an accepted minimal degree of trust and civility, itself a basis for both celebration and authentication'. Ibid., 246.

15. Ibid., 249. Note Inkster's ambivalence; he also speaks of how these two elements were sometimes to be found in a single person. We might take such tensions in his essay as indicative of a field in transition and the evolution of Inkster's own views. For a later, more critical perspective, see, for example, Ian Inkster, 'The west had science and the rest had not? The queries of the mindful hand', Lissa Roberts and Ian Inkster, eds, *The Mindful Hand in Global Perspective* (*History of Technology* 29) (2009): 205–11.

16. Secord, *op. cit.* (1).

17. Darnton, *Business of Enlightenment*; idem., *The Forbidden Bestsellers of Pre-Revolutionary France* (New York, 1996); Roger Chartier, *Inscrire et effacer: culture écrite et literature, XIe–XVIIIe siècle* (Paris,

2005); Adrian Johns, *The Nature of the Book: Print and Knowledge in the Making* (Chicago, 1998); Miles Ogborn and Charles Withers, eds, *Geographies of the Book* (London, 2010).

18. It would be wrong to assume that this is simply a story of linear 'progress' away from mistaken ideas and faulty practices towards either more precise measurement or more correct understanding. It is a much more intriguing and complicated story than that. Lissa Roberts, 'A Word and the World: The Significance of Naming the Calorimeter', *Isis*; idem, 'Calorimeter', Robert Bud and Elizabeth Warner, eds, *Instruments of science: An Historical Encyclopedia* (New York, 1997), 77–80. Contrast this view with Gaston Bachelard's view of scientific instruments as 'reified theorems'. Gaston Bachelard, *La nouvelle esprit scientifique* (Paris, 1934); Graeme Gooday, 'Instrument as Embodied Theory', ed., Arne Hessenbruch, *Readers' Guide to the History of Science* (London, 2000), 376–8.

19. Lissa Roberts and Simon Schaffer, *The Mindful Hand: Inquiry and Invention from the Late Renaissance to Early Industrialization* (Amsterdam, 2007); Pamela Smith, *The Body of the Artisan* (Chicago, 2006).

20. Kapil Raj, 'Circulation and the Emergence of Modern Mapping: Great Britain and Early Colonial India, 1764–1820', Claude Markovits, Jacques Pouchepadass and Sanjay Subrahmanyam, eds, *Society and Circulation: Mobile People and Itinerant Cultures in South Asia, 1750–1950* (Delhi, 2003), 23–54, reprinted in Kapil Raj, *Relocating Modern Science: Circulation and the Construction of Scientific Knowledge in South Asia and Europe* (London, 2010), chapter 2.

21. For an introduction to intermediality, see 'Intermediality', David Herman, Mandred Jahn and Marie-Laure Ryan, eds, *Routledge Encyclopedia of Narrative Theory* (Abingdon, 2005), 252–6. Benjamin Schmidt, 'Knowledge Products: Exotic Geography circa 1700'. Paper presented at the conference 'Transformations of Knowledge in the Dutch Expansion' (Collaborative Research Centre Series: 'Pluralisation and Authority in the Early Modern Period'), Historisches Seminar der Ludwig-Maximilians-Universität, Munich, October 2010. Simon Werrett, *Fireworks: Pyrotechnic Arts and Sciences in European History* (Chicago, 2010).

22. Simon Kuznets, *Economic Development, the Family and Income Distribution: Selected Essays* (Cambridge, 2002), 10.

23. Karin Knorr-Cettina, 'Objectual Practice', Massimo Mazzotti, *Knowledge as Social Order: Rethinking the Sociology of Barry Barnes* (Aldershot, 2008), 83–97, quotation onpage 89. Hans-Jorg Rheinberger, *Toward a History of Epistemic Things* (Palo Alto, 1997); idem., 'A Reply to David Bloor: "Toward a Sociology of Epistemic Things"', *Perspectives on Science*, 2005, 13: 406–10. For the sake of presentation, I have collapsed their discussions into one that articulates their shared basic points.

24. Maxine Berg, 'In Pursuit of Luxury: Global History and British Consumer Goods in the Eighteenth Century', *Past and Present*, 2004, 182: 85–142.

25. See especially Ibid., 114–18.

26. On not knowing and the politics of ignorance, see Robert Proctor and Londa Schiebinger, eds, *Agnotology: The Making and Unmaking of Ignorance* (Palo Alto, 2008).

27. Compare this insight with Arjun Appadurai, ed., *The Social Life of Things: Commodities in Cultural Perspective* (Cambridge, 1986).

28. Roberts, et al., *op. cit.* (19).

29. Liliane Perez and Catherine Verna, 'Dissemination of Technical Knowledge in the Middle Ages and the Early Modern Era: New Approaches and Methodological Issues', *Technology and Culture*, 2006, 47: 536–65 discusses numerous examples.

30. Lissa Roberts, 'Going Dutch: Situating Science in the Dutch Enlightenment', William Clark, Jan Golinski and Simon Schaffer, eds, *The Sciences in Enlightened Europe* (Chicago, 1999), 350–88. For instrument makers with their own shops, see Jim Bennett, 'Shopping for Instruments in Paris and London', Pamela Smith and Paula Findlen, *Merchants and Marvels* (New York, 2002), 370–97.

31. Liliane Perez, 'Steel and Toy Trade Between England and France: The Huntsmans' Correspondence with the Blakeys, 1765–1769', *Historical Metallurgy*, 2008, 42: 127–47; Chris Evans, 'Crucible Steel as an Enlightened Material', *Historical Metallurgy*, 2008, 42: 79–88.

32. Lissa Roberts, 'Full Steam Ahead: Entrepreneurial Engineers as Go-Betweens During the Late Eighteenth Century', Simon Schaffer, Lissa Roberts, Kapil Raj and James Delbourgo, eds, *The Brokered World: Go-Betweens and Global Intelligence, 1770–1820* (Sagamore Beach, 2009), 193–238.

33. Harold Cook, *Matters of Exchange* (New Haven, 2007); Siegfried Huigen, Jan. L. de Jong and Elmer Kolfin, eds, *The Dutch Trading Companies as Knowledge Networks* (Leiden, 2010); C. A. Davids,

'Dutch and Spanish Global Networks of Lnowledge in the Early Modern Period: Structures, Connections, Changes', ed., Lissa Roberts, *Centres and Cycles of Accumulation in and Around the Netherlands* (Berlin, 2011), 29–52. Sarah Easterby-Smith, 'Cultivating Commerce: Botany, the Plant Trade and Connoiseurship in London and Paris, 1760–c.1793', PhD dissertation, University of Warwick, 2010 discusses nursery owners' contribution to the growth of botanical knowledge in the context of their entrepreneurial intermediation between urban markets and broader networks through which plants and seeds were made available.

34. Edgar Zilsel, 'The Sociological Roots of Science', *The American Journal of Sociology*, 1942, 47: 544–62. For an alternative view, see Roberts, et al., *op. cit.* (19). Edward Layton, 'Mirror-Image Twins: The Communities of Science and Technology in Nineteenth-Century America', *Technology and Culture*, 1971, 12: 562–80, 562.

35. On tacit knowledge see Michael Polyani, *Personal Knowledge: Towards a Post-Critical Philosophy* (Chicago, 1958); Harry Collins, *Tacit and Explicit Knowledge* (Chicago, 2010). Eugene Ferguson, *Engineering and the Mind's Eye* (Cambridge, 1994), 59, 196. Onpage 196 he cites Harry Collins for this distinction. See Harry Collins, 'Expert Systems and the Science of Knowledge', Wiebe Bijker, Trevor Pinch and Thomas Hughes, eds, *The Social Construction of Technological Systems* (Cambridge, 1989), 331.

36. Harry Collins, 'The TEA Set: Tacit Knowledge and Scientific Networks', *Science Studies*, 1974, 4: 165–86, quotation on 167; Jerry Ravetz, *Scientific Knowledge and its Social Problems* (Oxford, 1971), 103.

37. Donald Mackenzie and Graham Spinardi 'Tacit Knowledge, Weapons Design and the Invention of Nuclear Weapons', *American Journal of Sociology*, 1995, 101: 44–99; Alberto Cambrosio and Peter Keating, 'Going Monoclonal: Art, Science and Magic in the Day-to-Day use of Hybridoma Technology', *Social Problems*, 1988, 35: 244–60; Tim Thornton, 'Tacit Knowledge as the Unifying Factor in Evidence Based Medicine and Clinical Judgement', *Philosophy, Ethics, and Humanities in Medicine*, 2006, 1: E2; Harry Collins, *Artificial Experts: Social Knowledge and Intelligent Machines* (Cambridge, 1990); idem., 'Tacit Knowledge, Trust and the Q of Sapphire', *Social Studies of Science*, 2001, 31: 71–85.

38. Thomas Kuhn, *Structure of Scientific Revolutions* (Chicago, 1962). Kuhn, in turn, compares his 'paradigm' to Michael Polanyi's discussion of tacit knowledge. See 44, note 1.

39. Walter Vincenti, *What Engineers Know and How They Know It* (Baltimore, 1990), 198.

40. Maurice Merleau Ponty, *Phénomélogie de la perception* (Paris, 1945); Don Ihde, *Technics and Praxis* (Dordrecht, 1978).

41. Lissa Roberts, 'Death of the Sensuous Chemist', *Studies in History and Philosophy of Science*, 1995, 26: 503–29.

42. Marcel Mauss, 'Les techniques du corps', *Journal de Psychologie*, XXXII (1936): 271–93.

43. Robert Allan, 'Collective Invention', *Journal of Economic Behavior and Organization*, 1983, 4: 1–24; Eric von Hippel, *The Sources of Innovation* (Oxford, 1988), quotation on 76.

44. Edwin Hutchins, *Cognition in the Wild* (Cambridge, 1995); idem., 'How a Cockpit Remembers Its Speeds', *Cognitive Science*, 1995, 19: 265–88. The phrase 'learning by doing together' is mine, not Hutchins.

45. Evelyn Tribble, 'Distributing Cognition in the Globe'. *Shakespeare Quarterly*, 2005, 56: 135–55; idem, '"The Chain of Memory": Distributed Cognition in Early Modern England', *Scan: Journal of Media Arts Culture*. http://scan.net.au/scan/journal/display.php?journal_id=53, accessed 18 September 2011.

46. Pamela Smith, *The Body of the Artisan* (Chicago, 2006). It might be interesting to bring her line of inquiry together with work done by historians such as Stephen Epstein who have argued for the guild structure as having been conducive of innovation over time. Stephen Epstein and Maarten Prak, eds, *Guilds, Innovation and the European Economy, 1400–1800* (Cambridge, 2008).

47. Chandra Mukerji, *Impossible Engineering: Technology and Territoriality on the Canal du Midi* (Princeton, 2009), seepage 219 for quotation.

48. Bruno Latour, *Reassembling the Social: An Introduction to Actor-Network Theory* (Oxford, 2005); Michel Callon, 'Some Elements of a Sociology of Translation: Domestication of the Scallops and the Fishermen of St. Brieuc Bay', ed., John Law, *Power, Action and Belief: A New Sociology of Knowledge* (London, 1986), 196–233; John Law, 'Technology and Heterogeneous Engineering: The Case of Portuguese Expansion', W. E. Bijker, T. P. Hughes and T. J. Pinch, eds, *The Social Construction of Technological Systems: New Directions in the Sociology and History of Technology* (Cambridge, 1987), 111–34;

John Krige, 'The 1984 Nobel Physics Prize for Heterogeneous Engineering', *Minerva*, 2001, 39: 425–43, quotation on 426.

49. Compare this with Hutchin's discussion of the distance between abstract mathematical computation as developed by Turing and the cognitive work of mathematicians. 'What Turing modeled was the computational properties of a sociocultural system'. Hutchins, *Cognition in the Wild* (*op. cit.* 44), 362. Latour highlights this characteristic of detachability from the complex local processes of production in a more positive light in his discussion of 'immutable mobiles'. Bruno Latour, *Science in Action: How to Follow Scientists and Engineers Through Society* (Cambridge, 1988).

50. Indeed, Mukerji writes that 'the canal became more substantial as the situation became more unstable'. Mukerji, *op. cit.* (47), 93. See alsopage 221.

51. Chandra Mukerji, 'History and Technology Forum: Author Response', *History and Technology*, 2011, 27: 213–22, quotation on 215–16.

52. David Landes, *The Wealth and Poverty of Nations* (New York, 1998), especially chapter 14 'Why Europe? Why Then?' and chapter 15 'Britain and the Others'; Joel Mokyr, *op. cit.* (11). I do not mean here to imply that there are no differences between Landes, who argues that what distinguished Europe from the rest of the world comes down to a question of 'culture', and Mokyr's more historically rooted and nuanced analysis.

53. For severe criticism of Landes, see WIlliam McNeil's review in the *New York Review of Books* (23 April 1998): 37–9 and the review by Andre Gunder Frank, available at http://rrojasdatabank.info/agfrank/landes.html, accessed 20 September 2011.

54. John Brewer, *The Sinews of Power: War, Money and the English State, 1688–1783* (Cambridge, 1990). For a model analysis of how the looming presence of the Admiralty affected the production, translation and management of knowledge in the field of ship building, see Simon Schaffer, 'The Charter'd Thames: Naval Architecture and Experimental Spaces in Georgian Britain', Lissa Roberts et al., *op. cit.*, (19), 279–305.

55. William Ashworth, *Customs and Excise: Trade, Production and Consumption in England 1640–1845* (Oxford, 2003); idem., 'The Ghost of Rostow: Science, Culture and the British Industrial Revolution', *History of Science*, 2008, 46: 249–74.

56. Kapil Raj, 'Eighteenth-Century Pacific Voyages of Discover, "Big Science", and the Shaping of European Scientific and Technological Culture', *History and Technology*, 2000, 17: 79–98.

57. For examples of how cognitive psychology has been used to interpret the history of experimentation and invention, see David Gooding, *Experiment and the Making of Meaning* (Dordrecht, 1990); idem, 'Mapping Experiment as a Learning Process: How the First Electromagnetic Motor was Invented', *Science, Technology and Human Values*, 1990, 15: 165–201; W. B. Carlson and M. E. Gorman, 'Understanding Invention as a Cognitive Process: The Case of Thomas Edison and Early Motion Pictures, 1888–1891', *Social Studies of Science*, 1990, 20: 387–430; idem, 'A Cognitive Framework to Understand Technological Creativity: Bell, Edison, and the Telephone', R. J. Weber and D. N. Perkins, eds, *Inventive Minds: Creativity in Technology* (Oxford, 1992).

58. What comes first to mind here is Gaston Bachelard's previously cited definition of scientific instruments as 'reified theories', but consider also the way in which texts often continue to be read as (transparent) vehicles for their content.

59. One cannot help but notice here the resonance between this stance and discussions of how closure and black-boxing are achieved in cases of scientific controversy and product design. For pioneering work, see Harry Collins, 'The Seven Sexes: A Study in the Sociology of a Phenomenon, or the Replication of Experiments in Physics', *Sociology*, 1975, 9: 205–24; Trevor Pinch and Wiebe Bijker, 'The Social Construction of Facts and Artefacts: Or How the Sociology of Science and the Sociology of Technology Might Benefit Each Other', *Social Studies of Science*, 1984, 14: 399–441.

60. See Ian Inkster's discussion of 'sites of endeavour' in his 'Thoughtful Doing and Early Modern Oeconomy', Roberts et al., *op. cit.* (19), 443–52.

Gatekeeping. Who Defined 'Useful Knowledge' in Early Modern Times?

KAREL DAVIDS

(Afdeling Geschiedenis VU University, Amsterdam)

INTRODUCTION

'Useful knowledge' has been defined in many different ways. According to Ian Inkster, 'useful and reliable' knowledge 'embraced the knowledge that was brought to bear at points of significant technological advancement'.[1] Joel Mokyr defined 'useful knowledge' as 'knowledge of natural phenomena and regularities that had the potential to affect technology'.[2]

Both these definitions are *ex post*: they determine with hindsight which knowledge was 'useful', namely knowledge with an actual (Inkster) or a potential (Mokyr) technological impact. But 'useful knowledge' is not only a construct of present-day historians. Marcus Popplow has shown that concepts of 'new', 'useful' and 'ingenious' to describe technical knowledge came into use in Germany, Italy and France as early as the sixteenth century, especially among authors of 'machine-books'.[3] Jesuits were interested in the 'utility' of knowledge, too, but in a slightly different sense. Rule number eight of the Revisers-General – the censors who reviewed all publications by Jesuits since c. 1600 – stipulated 'that Jesuit books should be useful and edifying'. 'Magical instruments' invented or described by Jesuits like Athanasius Kircher and Kaspar Schott were intended for practical purposes as well as for entertainment. The ultimate measure for judging the utility of such knowledge was whether it could serve the religious goals of the Society of Jesus.[4]

In the English-speaking world, 'useful knowledge' seems to have first emerged as a distinct concept in *An Essay Towards Promoting All Necessary and Useful Knowledge, Both Divine and Human,* published in 1697 by Reverend Thomas Bray, founder of the Society for the Promotion of Christian Knowledge, whose activities extended from England and Wales to the British colonies in North America. Bray's idea of 'useful knowledge' included knowledge useful to clergymen, physicians and lawyers as well as knowledge on history, travel, classical literature, agriculture and 'all such noble arts and sciences', as will render 'young gentle-men' 'serviceable to their families and countries'.[5] Benjamin

Franklin laid stress on the sciences and practical arts instead.[6] In his tract *A Proposal for Promoting Useful Knowledge among the British Plantations in America* (1743), which sparked the foundation of a host of societies of 'useful knowledge' in the American colonies, Franklin proposed to form a new society which would concern itself with:

- All new-discovered Plants, Herbs, Trees, Roots, &c. their Virtues, Uses, &c.
- Methods of Propagating them, and making such as are useful but particular to some Plantations [colonies] more general.
- Improvements of vegetable Juices, as Ciders, Wines, &c.
- New Methods of Curing or Preventing Diseases.
- All new-discovered Fossils in different Countries, as Mines, Minerals, Quarries, &c.
- New and useful Improvements in any Branch of Mathematicks.
- New Discoveries in Chemistry, such as Improvements in Distillation, Brewing, Assaying of Ores, &c.
- New Mechanical Inventions for saving Labour; as Mills, Carriages, &c. and for Raising and Conveying of Water, Draining of Meadows, &c.
- All new Arts, Trades, Manufactures, &c. that may be proposed or thought of.
- Surveys, Maps and Charts of particular Parts of the Sea-coasts, or Inland Countries; Course and Junction of Rivers and great Roads, Situation of Lakes and Mountains, Nature of the Soil and Productions, &c.
- New Methods of Improving the Breed of useful Animals; Introducing other Sorts from foreign Countries.
- New Improvements in Planting, Gardening, Clearing Land, &c.
- And all philosophical Experiments that let Light into the Nature of Things, tend to increase the Power of Man over Matter, and multiply the Conveniencies or Pleasures of Life.[7]

In the Dutch Republic, the first book to employ 'useful knowledge' explicitly as a guiding concept was the *Nieuw en volkomen woordenboek van Konsten en Wetenschappen bevattende alle takken der nuttige kennis*, a ten-volume encyclopaedia compiled by the translator and hack-writer Egbert Buys which appeared in Amsterdam between 1769 and 1777. Among the subjects discussed by Buys were both items that figured on Franklin's list, such as machines, instruments, tools or designs, and topics fitting with the idea of 'useful knowledge' as conceived by Thomas Bray, such as history, geography, topography, linguistics and natural history. Buys' encyclopaedia soon also found its way to Japan, where *rangaku*-scholars perused it as an important source for the state of 'Western' knowledge.[8]

'Useful knowledge' thus has known its *ex ante* definitions, too. Contemporaries, like twenty-first-century scholars, put forward their own ideas about the 'usefulness' of knowledge. But these definitions of 'useful knowledge' varied in many ways. Meanings of concepts like 'useful', 'utility' and 'usefulness' could differ by period and social context. Thus, as Koen Vermeir has insisted, the notion of 'useful' itself can and should be historicized.[9] This is exactly what I intend to do in this chapter.

Who defined 'useful knowledge'? On the basis of what criteria and in what ways? Which variations in definition occured and why? These are the key questions that will be addressed in this chapter. The focus of this contribution will be on changes in the late seventeenth and eighteenth centuries and on variations in the region of the North Atlantic, including Britain, British America and the western part of the European continent. The emphasis in this paper is thus on the analysis of changes in articulated views on knowledge,[10] not on the development of knowledge itself, whether in crafts, scholarly circles or other settings.

The analysis and comparisons in time and space will proceed in several steps. The first section traces changes in the meanings and relative importance of the 'usefulness' of knowledge in the late seventeenth and eighteenth centuries. Section two introduces the notions of 'gatekeeping' and 'gatekeepers' as tools for understanding definitions of 'useful knowledge'. Section three discusses how a broad conception of 'usefulness' lost support when groups that, as gatekeepers, could have taken a more inclusive view of the purposes of seeking knowledge vanished from the scene. The fourth section analyzes which groups in different regions of the North Atlantic world pushed through a narrow definition of 'usefulness' and by what factors the rise of these groups as gatekeepers of knowledge can be explained. The conclusion summarizes the argument of this chapter and discusses the meaning of its findings for the debate on the nature and importance of 'useful knowledge'.

CHANGING CONCEPTS OF USEFULNESS

At the end of the eighteenth century, educated elites in the North Atlantic world meant by 'useful', 'utility' or 'usefulness' of knowledge something different to 150 years before. The gist of the change was not a complete transformation of content but a progressive slimming-down of meaning. 'Useful', 'utility' or 'usefulness' of knowledge changed from a broad, multistranded concept into a narrow, onesided notion. By 1800, 'useful knowledge' had a much more specific meaning than in 1650. Some interpretations of 'usefulness' had in the meantime been discarded or discredited, others had received more emphasis than before. 'Usefulness' in a limited sense became a desired quality of knowledge.

The change in meaning can be illustrated with the help of Figure 5.1. For those who search for knowledge, the quest can be justified with a variety of reasons, which may be expressly stated or tacitly assumed. The gamut of possible reasons reaches all the way from seeking knowledge for its own sake to gathering knowledge as a means to a particular, practical end. Knowledge may be sought to satisfy curiosity or to master nature, but also for all sorts of purposes in between, such as: to seek enlightenment, to obtain salvation in the hereafter, to create entertainment, to enhance comfort or to increase power. And these purposes are, in principle, not mutually exclusive; combinations of reasons are conceivable as well.

In the middle of the seventeenth century, all of these reasons still peacefully existed next to one another. The pursuit of knowledge could be vindicated with

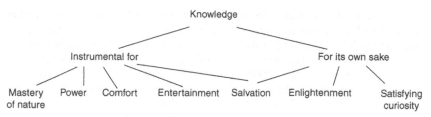

Figure 5.1 Purposes of searching for knowledge

instrumental arguments, but also with arguments that appealed to other sorts
of values, or with arguments that rested, tacitly or explicitly, on a mixture of
various considerations. Brian Wormald pointed out that the Baconian vision of
knowledge, for example, consisted in fact of two programmes: 'know thyself'
and 'know the universe of nature'. Bacon contended that man should strive
both to improve extant knowledge of his own mind and body and to achieve
new knowledge about the world of nature (of which man himself, too, formed
a part).[11] His vision thus combined elements ('enlightenment', 'satisfying curiosity', 'mastery of nature') at different ends of the spectrum. Bacon's thinking
was in this respect not unlike the approach followed by the Society of Jesus.
Jesuits, too, held a broad view of the purposes of seeking knowledge, which
accommodated knowledge for practical uses as well as knowledge for entertainment or knowledge as a means to attain salvation. The main difference with
the Baconian programme was that for Jesuits, at the end of the day, the quest
for knowledge remained subordinate to missionary goals.[12] In the Republic of
Letters before 1750, it was commonly accepted that scholars produced knowledge for each other rather than for society at large. Knowledge was normally
not supposed to serve any use outside the community of scholars themselves.
Scholarship and political convictions were assumed to be located in separate
spheres.[13]

During the eighteenth century, the meaning of 'usefulness' in the North
Atlantic world began to change in various ways. In France, the purpose of the
pursuit of knowledge was after 1750 redefined as 'the service of humanity'
rather than the 'service of truth'.[14] In Britain, the ideal of the scientist har-
nessing knowledge for the benefit of mankind by helping to 'improve' agriculture, industry and even society itself became increasingly dominant.[15] In the
British American colonies, as Meyer Reinhold has observed, a 'new utilitar-
ian mood', which had a 'anti-theological and anti-classical' tendency, became
manifest since the 1720s. Franklin's working definition of 'useful knowledge'
in his *Proposal* of 1743 exemplified this general trend. 'Useful' knowledge, as
James Delbourgo put it, more and more 'came to be understood in material
rather than spiritual terms', perhaps even to a higher degree than in contemporary France or Britain. Lending libraries, colleges and societies for promotion
of 'useful knowledge' which sprung up after 1750 in Philadelphia, New York,
Boston and other towns in North America laid stress on the instrumental value
of knowledge for the 'conduct of life' or the 'improvement of the country'.

'Pure scholarship' in general and the study of metaphysics or 'dead languages' in particular were branded as 'useless' knowledge.[16]

How could such variations in definitions of 'usefulness' occur? More specifically: how can the progressive narrowing of the meaning of 'usefulness' in the eighteenth century be explained? Before addressing this question, let me first discuss a concept that may serve as a helpful analytical tool, namely the notion of 'gatekeepers'.

GATEKEEPERS

'Gatekeepers of knowledge' and 'gatekeeping of information' are notions that are used by economic geographers and communication scientists as instruments to study flows of technical information in present-day organizations or economic regions. I would like to suggest that these notions also may be valuable tools to analyze the definition of 'useful knowledge' in early modern times.

In its original form, introduced by Thomas Allen, the concept of 'gatekeepers' of knowledge referred to key people in R&D organizations who identify external sources of technical information, then interpret and absorb this information and translate it to a local or site-specific context. 'Gatekeepers' mostly are 'technically competent', 'people-oriented' 'first-line supervisors', who frequently participate in meetings and networks both inside and outside their organizations. In general terms, 'gatekeepers' constitute a small community of individuals, are at the core of an information network, are overexposed to external sources of information and mostly have informal linkages with external actors. Scholars have subsequently extended the concept from individuals acting as 'gatekeepers' in organizations to firms operating as 'gatekeepers of knowledge' in industrial districts.[17] Joyce Chaplin used the notion of 'gatekeepers in the republic of letters'.[18]

Starting from this basic nation, I propose to use the concept of 'gatekeepers' in this essay in a slightly adapted form. 'Gatekeeping', I would suggest, does not necessarily only concern a small community, and external linkages of 'gatekeepers' do not necessarily always possess an informal nature. Gatekeeping is practised by *people*, that is, 'human gatekeepers', in particular *settings*, which can be both of an informal and a formal, or institutional, nature. Gatekeepers may hold for instance a position at a university, a learned society, a state agency or a publisher's house. Unlike Allen and other social scientists, I suggest to imagine gatekeeping as a *two-way process*. And gates can open in two directions. Gatekeeping does not only allow knowledge from outside to flow inwards but also knowledge from inside to flow outwards. It allows knowledge of a global, generic nature to be turned into local, site-specific knowledge and vice versa.[19] The function of gatekeepers can be characterized as managing two-way flows of knowledge between local/site-specific and global/generic spheres. Managing flows of knowledge means: selecting, translating and focusing. Some knowledge is promoted or at least allowed to pass, other knowledge is neglected or rejected. The instruments for positive or negative sanctions can vary over time. They can range from premiums, patents or publications in highly ranked journals to disqualification, defilement or outright destruction of texts or artefacts.

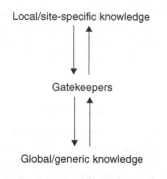

Producers and transmitters of knowledge

Local/site-specific knowledge

Gatekeepers

Global/generic knowledge

Producers and transmitters of knowledge

Figure 5.2 Gatekeepers and knowledge

Gatekeepers thus can profoundly affect the ways in which 'useful knowledge' is conceived.

Analytically, the role of gatekeepers should be distinguished from that of producers or transmitters of knowledge, who are active at a local or a global end of the process (although these roles may of course be combined in one and the same person). It should not be confused either with the role of 'go-betweens' – people who made 'sustained encounter and interaction across different cultures possible throughout history' and helped to create the 'modern world' in the 'domain of knowledge and sciences'.[20] Figure 5.2 gives a visual representation of the relations and functions discussed so far.

The different functions and relations can be illustrated with the case of an eighteenth-century Swiss/Dutch professor, Jean Nicholas Sébastien Allamand. Jean Allamand was born in Lausanne, Switzerland, in 1713. After being trained as a protestant minister in his native country, Allamand moved to Holland, where he entered the service of Willem Jacob 's Gravesande, professor of mathematics, astronomy and philosophy at the University of Leiden and the foremost Newtonian on the Continent, as tutor of his two sons. During his stay in the Gravesande household till 1739 and his study of law in Leiden thereafter, Allamand developed a keen interest in science himself, which led to his assistance in the experiments of Van Musschenbroek and Cunaeus with the Leiden jar and the publication of his first paper, on electricity, in 1747. These early achievements appear to have jump-started Allamand's career in academia and the Republic of Letters at large. Having first received an appointment at the university of Franeker in 1748, Allamand was soon invited to accept the prestigious chair of mathematics and philosophy in Leiden, thanks to the intervention of his friend and patron, count Willem Bentinck, one of the most powerful noblemen in Holland and member of the governing board of Leiden university. In addition to this professorship, Allamand in 1751 obtained the post of curator of the university's cabinet of minerals, naturalia and instruments; he also built a private collection of models and instruments, which was even larger than the university's. From the 1760s onwards, he began to teach courses on natural history and experimental physics as well. He continued to combine all these functions until his death in 1787. Allamand was member of several learned societies, including the Royal Society and the *Hollandsche Maatschappij der Wetenschappen* in Haarlem and the *Bataafsch Genootschap der Proefondervindelyke Wijsbegeerte* in Rotterdam.[21]

As a student, professor and curator at Leiden university, Allamand played an important role as (co-)producer and transmitter of 'useful knowledge' in the Mokyrian and Inksterian sense, turning local/specific knowledge into global/generic knowledge, and the other way around. Not only did he make a seminal contribution to the 'knowledge of natural phenomena and regularities that had the potential to affect technology', by assisting in the development of the Leiden jar (a crucial device for Franklin's experiments with electricity about 1750),[22] he also helped to give wider circulation to Franklin's idea that pouring oil on water could, under certain conditions, be usefully employed to still the waves and thus to enhance the safety of ships and crews.[23] In 1773, Allamand, jointly with Willem Bentinck and his son John, captain in the Royal Navy, witnessed one of Franklin's experiments with pouring oil on water in Green Park, London.[24] After returning to the Netherlands, Allamand repeated these trials with the stilling effects of oil in the canals of Leiden, in the presence of a number of friends: a retired naval captain, a natural philosopher and a merchant and cloth manufacturer, Frans van Lelyveld.[25] Lelyveld later published a 200-page pamphlet with reports on similar observations from many parts of the world, plus translations of selections from the writings on the topic by 'the very famous English philosopher Benj. Franklin'. This pamphlet also appeared in a French translation a year later.[26] It was Allamand, too, who took care of editing the collected works on mathematics and experimental philosophy by his late friend Gravesande and forwarding copies to contacts in England, France and Geneva.[27] This Leiden professor moreover revealed himself as one of the foremost champions of steam technology in the Dutch Republic and a true propagandist of 'useful knowledge' in the Inksterian sense – 'knowledge that was brought to bear at points of significant technological advancement'. Aside from buying a model of the Savery engine for the university's collection of physical instruments, he added models of a Newcomen engine and one of the type invented by William Blakey. In 1772, he gave a lecture for the *Bataafsch Genootschap* about 'the great benefit' which might accrue to the Netherlands from substituting 'fire machines' for wind-powered drainage mills. And last but not least, Allamand was also the 'eminent teacher' of Rinze Lieuwe Brouwer, who in 1780 built a small-size engine of the Newcomen type for raising water on Jan Hope's estate Groenendaal in Heemstede.[28]

Allamand has been characterized as 'pre-eminently a builder of networks'.[29] Thanks to his positions as professor and curator of university's collections, his membership of learned societies, his connections with's Gravesande and Bentinck, and very probably, his excellent command of French, Allamand got to know many of the leading lights and rising stars in the Republic of Letters in the Dutch Republic, France, Switzerland, Germany, Scandinavia, Britain and the British colonies in America. Visiting scholars from abroad were eager to call on Allamand and take a look at his large collection of models and instruments.[30] Allamand used his extensive network to operate as a kind of 'literary agent' between publishers in Leiden and Amsterdam, Elie Luzac and Marc-Michel Rey, and potential authors in the Republic of Letters, both foreign and Dutch. He made contacts, brought in manuscripts, reviewed and translated. Most of the publications in which he was involved appeared in French.[31] Thus, Allamand effectively acted as a gatekeeper of flows of knowledge between local and global spheres of circulation.

DECLINING SUPPORT FOR A BROAD DEFINITION

Let us now turn to the question of why the meaning of 'usefulness' in the course of the eighteenth century was increasingly narrowed. This is a story in two parts. On the one hand, the social basis for a more inclusive view of 'useful knowledge' became steadily weaker. On the other hand, forces in support of a narrow definition of 'usefulness' gained ever more strength.

First, the negative part of the story. Keeping the role of gatekeepers in mind, I would suggest that a key factor in this process was the gradual removal, or withdrawal, of those groups that, as gatekeepers, could have taken a more 'catholic' view of the purposes of seeking knowledge than the vision that ultimately prevailed. The social backing for a more inclusive view of 'usefulness', in short, became steadily weaker. Three groups in particular deserve a closer look in this respect: women, regular clergy and the constituency of the *virtuoso*. Each of these groups can be seen as supporter of a broader view of the uses of knowledge, which spanned a large part of the spectrum sketched in Figure 5.1 above. Each of them, however, ceased to exert a meaningful influence on the definition of 'usefulness' of knowledge before the eighteenth century came to a close. Each of them eventually vanished from the scene as a relevant actor in the gatekeeping of knowledge, although not entirely in the same way.

'Gender politics', Londa Schiebinger has written, led in the eighteenth century, for example, 'to a distinctive body of ignorance in the case of abortion practices'. 'Europeans chose to remain ignorant' of abortive properties of a certain plant common in the West Indies, the peacock flower (*Poinciana*).[32] Although specimens of the peacock flower were carried to Europe and the plant actually was grown in botanical gardens in Paris, Amsterdam, Leiden, Uppsala and Chelsea Physic Garden near London, 'the knowledge of its use as an abortifacient did not take root there'. This is all the more remarkable as the anti-fertility effects of the Poinciana were known among slaves in the West Indian colonies and among male and female European observers who at the turn of the eighteenth century travelled to the Caribbean themselves, such as Hans Sloane and Maria Sibylle Merian.[33] According to Schiebinger's account, this particular item of knowledge' was *ignored* in Europe rather than actively suppressed. The reason why it was not acknowledged as 'useful' knowledge in Europe appears to have lain in the dominant image of women as being destined to 'reproduce' and thus to aid population growth, which tallied neatly with emergent mercantilist views about the interests of the state. And as these ideas about gender roles were primarily defined by men, 'much useful knowledge' about birth control 'was lost'.[34]

Thus, if women could have acted as gatekeepers on the same terms as men, it might well have happened that knowledge that ran the risk of being discarded would have been recognized as 'useful' after all. How did the marginalization of women as gatekeepers of 'useful knowledge' actually come about? Even before the middle of the eighteenth century, women generally had not been regarded as equal partners of men in the pursuit of knowledge. Women were allowed to undertake scientific activities such as observing stars, studying plants or writing books, but they were as a rule not admitted as members of state-sponsored learned societies like the Royal Society or the *Académie des Sciences* nor were they considered to be eligible for an appointment at a university or to an official position at other scholarly institutions. Eminently learned women such as Margaret Cavendish, Anna Maria van Schurman, Emilie du Châtelet or Maria Winckelmann were permitted to participate in scholarly discourse and contribute to the growth of knowledge, but only in informal, indirect ways. They were barred from achieving positions of formal power.[35] Some of these *femmes savantes* nevertheless spoke up for the rights of women to partake as full members in the world of scholarship in a very public way. Anna Maria van Schurman, reputedly the most learned Dutch woman of her time, did so in a skilfully crafted treatise published in 1641, the *Dissertatio de ingenio muliebris ad doctrinam & melioris litteras aptitudine*. Schurman argued in this tract that women, like men, fully possessed the aptitude to study all the arts and sciences that could be 'of use to getting to know and love God better'.[36] Maria Winckelmann in 1710 submitted a request to the *Akademie der Wissenschaften* in Berlin to succeed her late husband Gottfried Kirch as assistant astronomer. In the end, this request was declined 'because of concern about the effect on [the Academy's] reputation of hiring a woman'.[37]

One of the exceptions to this general pattern of unfriendliness to females had to do with social hierarchy. Noble females and women with a craft background often enjoyed more opportunities to get some scholarly education or a training in scientific practice than women in other social ranks. Cavendish, Van Schurman and Châtelet, for instance, were all of noble birth.[38] Maria Winckelmann exemplified the strength of craft traditions in Germany, Londa Schiebinger has argued. In the late seventeenth and early eighteenth centuries, female astronomers were not an unusual presence in Germany because women still could enter crafts as apprentices or through marriage and because astronomy itself possessed craft-like aspects.[39] Another exception of a different nature could be found in Italy. Academies of science in Bologna, Padua and Rome in the seventeenth and eighteenth centuries sometimes *did* admit women as members. Universities more than once awarded doctorates to women and the university of Bologna in 1733 appointed a woman (Laura Bassi) as professor of physics.[40]

The prevailing tendency in the later eighteenth century was to restrict the scope for 'agency' by women in the pursuit of knowledge still further. True, the 1750s, 1760s and 1770s were the heyday of the *salonnières* in Paris. Founding and running a salon with a glittering cast of eminent *philosophes* gave bourgeois and noble women an opportunity to keep themselves informed about new developments in science and to participate in intellectual discussions. But this was something different from making an active contribution to the growth of knowledge or acting out the role of gatekeeper. *Salonnières* offered facilities for meetings and took pains to maintain the rules of polite conversation but they did not seek to create new knowledge or even to select, interpret or translate information. Their conception of usefulness was not broader than that of the male *philosophes* whom they received in their salons. 'Their definition of utility was the same as that of the philosophes', Dena Goodman remarked: 'they contributed to the good of humanity by joining the Enlightenment Republic of Letters, and furthering its work'.[41] Moreover, salons were as central meeting places for exchange of knowledge in the 1780s supplanted by a new type of organization, called *musées*, which were dominated by men, although a few of these, such as the *Musée de Monsieur*, allowed more than a token participation by women.[42] A learned society founded by and for (well-born) women in Middelburg in the Dutch Republic in 1785, the *Natuurkundig Genootschap der Dames*, actually discussed the same sorts of topics in the physical sciences as many learned societies with an all-male membership.[43] In Britain, the rise of botany as a popular subject of study since the 1760s did not signify a change in the subordinate status of women in the pursuit of knowledge either. Although 'women of the middle classes, gentry and aristocracy joined the new workforce of polite botany as plant collectors, illustrators and students of taxonomy', Anne Shteir observed, they remained 'excluded from formal participation in the public institutions of botany and science. They could not be members of the Royal Society or the Linnean Society, could not attend meetings, read paper or (. . .) see their findings published in the journals of those societies'.[44]

Another group that might have sustained a more inclusive view of the uses of knowledge was the regular clergy. Jesuits, as noted above, always nourished a much broader conception of the utility of knowledge than merely knowledge expedient to increase power, improve comfort or enhance the mastery of nature. Edification and striving for salvation were eminently worthwhile aims, too. The leading light of the Society of Jesus in the mid-seventeenth century, Athanasius Kircher, showed an 'exuberant curiosity' for all sorts of facts and objects and aspired to achieve a truly encyclopaedic grasp of all branches of learning.[45] In Kircher's view, almost every piece of knowledge was worth being collected, described and preserved. It was this all-embracing scope of his scholarship that conduced to Kircher's formidable reputation among many educated people in his lifetime, laymen and fellow-clergymen alike.

Unlike women, regular clergy were for a long time certainly *not* considered to be unqualified as participants in scholarly or scientific organizations. Despite mistrust and suspicion among Protestant scholars, Jesuits received recognition as members of the Republic of Letters.[46] Jesuits were eagerly sought after as specialists for scientific expeditions overseas sponsored by the French state and the *Académie* in the time of Richelieu and Louis XIV. Actually, the Jesuit astronomers who sailed to Asia in 1685 on a scientific mission on behalf of the *Académie des Sciences*, 'by a particular privilege' *did* receive membership of the Paris Academy.[47] Both Jesuits and members of other religious orders and corporations, such as Dominicans, Franciscans, Oratorians or Maurists got appointments to prestigious and powerful positions in institutes of higher education. The Colegio Imperial de San Isidro in Madrid, for instance, which since 1625 also incorporated the Royal Mathematical Academy, was staffed by Jesuit teachers.[48] Many teaching posts at the training colleges for naval officers established in France in the time of Colbert were occupied by members of the Society of Jesus, too.[49] Monks of the *Congrégation de Saint-Maur* played a prominent role in military academies established by the government in 1776 to improve the quality of future army officers. In five of the 12 newly created academies, Maurists made up the majority of the teaching staff.[50]

The decline of Kircher's reputation, manifest by the 1720s,[51] reflects the onset of a larger shift in the status of the regular clergy in the realm of knowledge which gathered pace in the course of the eighteenth century. The devaluation of Kircher did not only spell a rejection of all pretensions to universal knowledge but also a demotion of the regular clergy as qualified judges of knowledge as such. During the second half of the eighteenth century, regular clergy were increasingly relegated to a kind of ancillary status in the process of collecting, transmitting and evaluating knowledge, or they were even removed from the scholarly scene entirely. The new regulation of the *Académie des Sciences* made in 1699 stipulated that henceforth only the lowest category of membership, *honoraire*, would be open to members of religious orders. From 1716 onwards, members of religious orders could no longer even be admitted as *honoraires*; they were only eligible in a new class of membership that, in contrast with *honoraires*, lacked any voting rights in the Academy's assembly at all: the *associés libres*. As a result of these rules, members of religious orders were also deprived of the chance of ever reaching the highest, most powerful rank in the *Académie*, namely *pensionnaire*.[52] The Paris Academy 'seemed increasingly unwilling' to grant Jesuit missionaries in China 'the parity they desired'. In the eyes of French *académiciens*, the China Jesuits fell back to a status of, at best, mere collectors of data instead of respected scholars in their own right.[53] Although Jesuits of the Portuguese-sponsored mission in China for a while were more successful in nurturing their scholarly connections in Europe (and even managed to get astronomical observations published in the *Philosophical Transactions* of the Royal Society),[54] they were no more able to ward off the onslaught on the part of 'enlightened' rulers after 1760 than their colleagues in other countries in Europe. By the mid-1770s, the Society of Jesus, and the huge network of learned institutions that went with it, was almost completely destroyed. A similar fate befell many other religious orders and corporations in the 1780s and 1790s. Thousands of monasteries in the lands of the Habsburg monarchy, in France and in other states in Central and Western Europe were dissolved and the contents of their age-old repositories of learning, the monastic libraries, were dispersed or destroyed.[55] As gatekeepers of knowledge, regular clergy had effectively been removed from the scene.

Finally, the social basis for a broader view of usefulness was also weakened by the withdrawal of people who had cultivated the ideal of the *virtuoso*. The *virtuoso* ideal of knowledge entailed that (almost) all knowledge was worth collecting and transmitting. *Virtuosi* were, in John Gascoigne's words, people 'who had the time and leisure to advance knowledge either by collecting rarities or by promoting experiments'.[56] 'Virtuous collectors of information', who professed to seek knowledge primarily for its own sake, first emerged as a type in Renaissance Italy and then proliferated all over Western Europe during the early modern period, both among laymen and clergy. They were known as *liefhebbers* in the Netherlands, *Liebhaber* in Germany and *amateurs* in France.[57] It were *virtuosi*, who first arranged cabinets of natural and man-made curiosities and who created the earliest museums, and it were *virtuosi*, too, who started to make long travels abroad to visit interesting historical sites, study the natural environment, collect 'wondrous objects' and converse with famous scholars. Athanasius Kircher was in a sense a specimen of the kind, too.

The *virtuoso* style of pursuing and evaluating knowledge continued to exert a powerful attraction on the leisured, landed, educated classes in Europe until the middle of the eighteenth century.[58] Unlike women or regular clergy, supporters of the *virtuoso* ideal were not sidelined or brushed aside as competent judges of knowledge, but rather gradually superseded by another, new-fashioned type of scholar: the disciplinary specialist. The comprehensive ideal of knowledge represented by the *virtuoso* tradition slowly gave way to a more circumscribed vision which laid stress on specialization and the formation of clearly defined scientific disciplines. This transition did not only occur through the substitution of one generation of scholars by another but also, as Gascoigne showed in his case study of Joseph Banks, by a change of profile of individual scholars during their lifetime. Between the 1770s and the 1820s, Banks underwent a transformation from a *virtuoso* into a botanist.[59] The shift from a cult of 'omniscience' to a 'world of increasingly specialized and jealously guarded expertise' thus could be performed within the mind of an individual as well.[60] As a result of these changes at a macro- and micro-level the social support for a broader concept of usefulness dwindled. Gatekeeping came to rest with people who nurtured a more narrow, one-sided view.

TURNING TO A NARROW DEFINITION

The decline of social support for a more inclusive view of 'useful knowledge' is only half the story, however. If the shift to a narrow notion of 'usefulness' would have solely depended on the removal, or withdrawal, of supporters for the broader vision, one would expect that the trimmed-down version of 'utility' would have found acceptance sooner in societies where women, regular clergy or adherents of the *virtuoso* ideal ceased to matter as gatekeepers of knowledge at an early date than in societies where they continued for be relevant for a much longer time. This may explain a difference in timing in the utility discourse between, say, Britain and Italy, but it certainly does not hold true in every case.

An exception can be found in the Dutch Republic. Contrary to expectations, the United Provinces did *not* lead the way in the emergence of the narrow view of 'usefulness'. Although regular clergy were eliminated as a relevant factor during the Dutch Revolt in the late sixteenth century, women were assigned a secondary status in the pursuit of knowledge (despite the achievements of

Anna Maria van Schurman and Maria Sibylle Merian) and the *virtuoso* ideal never attracted quite as large a following as in Italy or Britain, and the shift to a more restricted view of usefulness did not take place in the Netherlands until the middle of the eighteenth century. 'Practical utility' was not a common argument used to justify scientific pursuits until after 1750.[61] It was no accident that the first Dutch book to employ 'useful knowledge' as a guiding concept, Egbert Buys' encyclopaedia, did not appear until 1769. The claim by Jacob and Sturkenboom that 'the theme of usefulness (was) already prominent' in 'the earliest scientific lectures given for the public by D. G. Fahrenheit in 1718' is not borne out by the source in question.[62] In the 234-page manuscript with notes of Fahrenheit's lectures taken by Jacob Ploos van Amstel the words 'utility' or 'usefulness' (*nut, nuttigheid*) only appeared three times. And they occurred in a particular setting: Fahrenheit called knowledge of specific gravity useful to determine whether metals were pure or forged.[63]

While gatekeeping of knowledge thus became more and more an affair of males, laymen and disciplinary specialists rather than females, regular clergy and generalists, the timing of the turn to a narrow practical view of usefulness also depended on other contextual variables, including the social profile of the gatekeepers themselves. In the Dutch Republic, the quintessential gatekeepers of knowledge were professors attached to an institution of higher learning such as a university or a *illustre school*. Willebord Snellius, Adriaan Metius and Joseph Scaliger in the late sixteenth and seventeenth centuries or Herman Boerhaave, Willem Jacob's Gravesande, Jean Allamand, Johan Lulofs and Jan Hendrik van Swinden in the eighteenth century were typical examples of this kind. Although professors at Dutch universities from the very start of these institutions in the late sixteenth century were intermittently engaged in evaluating, creating or transmitting knowledge that *ex post* may be called 'useful' according to Mokyr's or Inkster's definition, it was not until about mid-eighteenth century that they became involved in the creation, selection and communication of 'useful' knowledge on a more regular and general basis, and with a stronger emphasis on the practical, instrumental aspect of usefulness.[64]

This change was partly a response to a growing demand for expert advice on technical matters from public or semi-public bodies such as provincial governments, city governments, Admiralties and the Dutch East-India Company, partly an outcome of a paradigmatic shift in academia itself towards ways of thinking with a more empirical, practical bent than the Aristotelian or Cartesian mindsets which long dominated the world of higher learning. Professors at Dutch universities, foremost 's Gravesande, belonged to the early adopters of experimental philosophy on the Continent and later also came under the influence of an emergent field of study focused on technical artefacts and practices, called *Technologie*, which flourished in state bureaucracies and newly founded institutions of higher learning in Germany, such as the university of Göttingen. The connections between Dutch and German universities in the eighteenth century were after all quite close: of the 16 professors in Utrecht in 1760, for example, nine came from Germany.[65]

In other societies in the North Atlantic world, however, the turn to a narrow definition of 'useful' knowledge was performed by different sorts of gatekeepers, in different contexts and in different ways than in the Dutch Republic. In these societies, gatekeepers of knowledge in the eighteenth century were primarily based at academies, societies, state agencies or publishing houses rather than at universities or similar institutions of higher learning. Most gatekeepers of knowledge were not university professors – although many of them had been trained at a college or a university, but editors of journals, publishers, *académiciens*, members of learned societies or government officials. The rise of these groups as gatekeepers of knowledge was made possible by a combination of changes in the structure of patronage, the nature of communication of scientific information, the extent of consumer demand and the opportunities for careers in scholarly pursuits. From the late seventeenth century onwards, scientific academies sponsored by secular rulers or elites became a more important channel for patronage for scholars than support via personal relationships or sponsorship by ecclesiastical rulers or institutions. Communication networks based on 'weak ties', such as correspondence, printed texts and personal encounters through travelling, became increasingly significant for exchange of scientific information next to 'strong ties' in 'closed circles', such as learned societies.[66] The expansion of market economies and the increased spending power of consumers led to a growth of demand among educated publics for news about scientific or technical subjects.[67] And both the expansion of markets and the growth of state support for science and technology, through the creation of universities, engineering schools or technical departments, increased the opportunities for people to pursue a professional career in seeking and 'selling' knowledge.

The shift to a narrow view of 'useful' knowledge was not a smooth process. In each case, the turn towards a more instrumental, practical concept of 'usefulness' went not only together with all sorts of verbal disputes but with a more or less drastic change in a balance of power between institutions as well. In France, the change appears to have taken place in two stages: first, the King and his ministers arranged that the gatekeeping function was increasingly concentrated at the *Académie Royale des Sciences*, and that the Academy would provide expertise on practical matters such as assessments of new inventions,[68] and next, the commanding role of the Academy was weakened by the rise of several other actors and institutions which laid claim to a leading part as gatekeepers of knowledge themselves. The gatekeeping function partly devolved from the Academy to the *Maison du Roi*, which was directly controlled by the King,[69] partly to learned societies outside Paris, which tried to influence the development of 'useful' knowledge through prize competitions,[70] and partly to the emerging movement of *philosophes* who, independently from the state and learned societies, attempted to set their stamp on public discourse via meetings in Parisian salons and the medium of print, especially through the great publishing project of the *Encyclopédie*.[71] Whatever their differences, all these gatekeepers came to share a preference for an instrumental 'logique utilitaire', as Daniel Roche has called it.

In Britain, the Royal Society and its journal *Philosophical Transactions*, as John Gascoigne insists, may long have been 'the nation's unchallenged repository of scientific knowledge', reaching its apogee during the presidency of

Joseph Banks (1778–1820),[72] but it did never quite succeed in becoming the pre-eminent authority in defining what knowledge could be regarded as 'useful'. Larry Stewart had pointed out that tensions between the Society's *virtuosi* and artisans arose as early as the Restoration and that Isaac Newton 'could no more control the market in philosophy than he could the laws of gravity'.[73] Joseph Banks himself was, as a *virtuoso*, now and then made an object of mockery in public opinion.[74] Outside the Royal Society, the market for information on scientific and technical information in the eighteenth century developed to that extent that many natural philosophers could earn a living as entrepreneurs in 'useful' knowledge by giving lectures, conducting experiments and writing books. Some of them even operated as a sort of gatekeeper themselves. John Theophilus Desaguliers, for example, enjoyed a reputation 'as one to be trusted both before the rarified audience at the Royal Society and as an advertized brand that conveyed quality to the London public'.[75] Newly founded 'elite associations' such as the Royal Society of Arts, based in London, and the Manchester Literary and Philosophical Society, began to practice gatekeeper functions, too. State agencies in Britain acted as intermediaries in the evaluation, transmission and promotion of 'useful' knowledge as well, though did not behave as proactively as in France.[76] Support from patrons in government anyway remained highly important, even for a high-profile gatekeeper of knowledge like Joseph Banks.[77]

Finally, back to Benjamin Franklin and the definition of 'useful knowledge' in the American colonies. Like in Britain, 'private enterprise took full responsibility for organizing the pursuit of knowledge'. In contrast with the metropolis, however, 'the gentleman scientist [*virtuoso*] was a relative rarity' and 'private resources were less substantial'.[78] There were no established institutions at the top of the hierarchy of the knowledge infrastructure such as the Royal Society and support from state agencies for science and technology was not forthcoming either. While the Americans were creating their own network of 'weak ties' of correspondence networks, for a long time they looked to London as the centre of the universe of knowledge. Benjamin Franklin himself was a prime example of this colonial mentality, as Joyce Chaplin has demonstrated. Having 'friends and patrons' among natural philosophers in London was 'an absolute necessity for doing work in the sciences', Franklin realized in the 1740s. 'The gatekeepers in the republic of letters' who had 'to pay attention to him' were located in the metropolis.[79] The meteoric rise in Franklin's international reputation as a natural philosopher was due to the recognition of his achievements (foremost his experiments with electricity) by the Royal Society in the 1750s. He received the Copley Medal in 1753 (the first colonial to receive this honour) and was elected as Fellow three years later.[80] Thanks to his elevated status in the Atlantic network of science, Franklin could next turn into a gatekeeper himself and lend his considerable prestige to the shift to a more instrumental, practical definition of 'useful knowledge' in the American colonies. In 1768 he was 'crowned as supreme among American philosophers' by being elected president of the newly formed American Philosophical Society for Promotion of Useful Knowledge in Philadelphia.[81]

CONCLUSION

Historians normally define 'useful knowledge' retrospectively. They conceive 'useful' knowledge *ex post* as knowledge with an actual or a potential technological impact. But contemporaries have not always looked at 'usefulness' purely from this practical, instrumental perspective. 'Utility' of knowledge has for a long time in fact carried a variety of meanings. During the eighteenth century, this range of meanings progressively become more restricted. The emergence of 'useful' knowledge as present-day historians conceive it, is also a story of loss: a whole set of meanings has been discarded or forgotten. 'Usefulness' today means much less than it used to do a few centuries ago.

Why did the view of 'useful knowledge' become more and more narrow in the late seventeenth and eighteenth centuries? This essay has looked at two sides of the background of this process. One part of the context was the gradual removal, or withdrawal, of those groups that, as gatekeepers, could have taken a broader view of the purposes of seeking knowledge than the vision that ultimately prevailed: women, regular clergy and people who had nourished the ideal of the *virtuoso*. On the other hand, a comparison between different societies on both sides of the Atlantic shows that the turn to a narrow definition was engineered by gatekeepers of knowledge mostly based at academies, societies, state agencies or publishing houses, whose rise to power can be explained by a combination of changes in the structure of patronage, the nature of communication of scientific information, the extent of consumer demand and the opportunities for careers in scholarly pursuits. Thus, the shift to a practical, instrumental definition of 'useful' knowledge was a general phenomenon in North Atlantic societies, with characteristics that transcended 'national' borders, but it was not always and everywhere performed in exactly the same context, and in exactly the same way.

The findings in this chapter on the definition of 'useful knowledge' in early times are also relevant for the debate on the nature and importance of 'useful knowledge' in general. The shift to a narrow concept of usefulness was not a necessary condition for technological development or economic growth, as the case of the Dutch Republic attests. The Dutch Republic, after all, was a technologically advanced society which witnessed substantial economic growth long before a restricted, instrumental view of 'utility' came into vogue.[82] The turn to a narrow definition of 'usefulness' may have been facilitated by the expansion of markets and technological change but it did not *cause* these developments. The example of the Dutch Republic also demonstrates that commercialization and technological advancement were not sufficient conditions to give rise to a restricted, instrumental concept of 'usefulness' either. Thus, the discourse on 'useful knowledge' appears to have been only intermittently connected to the actual development of technology. Situations in which the *concept* of 'useful knowledge' interacted with technology in *practice* were exceptions rather the rule. One of these exceptions can be found in Britain in the eighteenth century. Eighteenth-century Britain is a rare case where a particular, narrow vision of 'useful knowledge' actually *did* interact with what happened with technology on the ground.

Notes

1. I. Inkster, 'Potentially global: "Useful and reliable knowledge" and material progress in Europe, 1474–1914', *The International History Review*, 2006, 28: 237–86, esp. 238.

2. J. Mokyr, *The Enlightened Economy. An Economic History of Britain 1700–1850* (New Haven: Yale University Press, 2009), 35.

3. M. Popplow, *Neu, nützlich und erfindungsreich. Die Idealisierung von Technik in der Frühen Neuzeit* (Münster: Waxmann, 1998).

4. D. Stolzenberg, 'Utility, edification, and superstition: Jesuit censorship and Athanasius Kircher's Oedipus Aegyptiacus', in *The Jesuits II: Cultures, Sciences, and the Arts 1540–1773*, ed. J. O'Malley (Toronto: University of Toronto Press, 2006), 336–54, 343, K. Vermeir, 'Athanasius Kircher's magical instruments: an essay on "science", "religion" and applied metaphysics', *Studies in History and Philosophy of Science*, 2007, 28: 363–400, 382–84.

5. M. Reinhold, (1975), 'The quest for "useful knowledge" in eighteenth-century America', *Proceedings of the American Philosophical Society*, 119, 108–32, esp. 111–12.

6. Reinhold, 'The quest for "useful knowledge"', 114–22.

7. B. Franklin, *A Proposal for Promoting Useful Knowledge among the British Plantations in America* (Philadelphia: By the author, 1743).

8. E. Buys,, *Nieuwe en volkomen woordenboek van konsten en wetenschappen, bevattende alle de taken van nuttige kennis*, 10 vols. (Amsterdam, 1769–78); Jacques Proust Baalde, 'De quelques dictionnaires hollandais ayant servi de relais à l'encyclopédisme européen vers le Japon' *Dix-huitième siècle*, 2006, 38: 17–38.

9. Vermeir, 'Athanasius Kircher's magical instruments', 363, 394–95.

10. See Inkster, 'Potentially global', 259.

11. B. H. G Wormald, *Francis Bacon. History, Politics and science, 1561–1626* (Cambridge: Cambridge University Press, 1993), 32–45.

12. Vermeir, 'Athanasius Kircher's magical instruments', 382–85.

13. A. Goldgar, *Impolite Learning. Conduct and Community in the Republic of Letters (1680–1750)* (New Haven: Yale University Press, 1995), 6.

14. D. Goodman, *The Republic of Letters. A Cultural History of the French Enlightenment* (Ithaca/London: Cornell University Press, 1994), 28, 33.

15. J. Gascoigne, *Joseph Banks and the English Enlightenment. Useful Knowledge and Polite Culture* (Cambridge: Cambridge University Press, 1994), 3–4, 57–63, 67–9, 185–6.

16. Reinhold, 'The quest for "useful knowledge"', 113–14, 117, 119, 122–5; J. Delbourgo, 'Common sense, useful knowledge, and matters of fact in the late Enlightenment', *The William and Mary Quarterly*, 2004, Third Series: 61, 643–84, esp. 650.

17. Y. J. Allen, *Managing the Flow of Technology: Technology Transfer and the Dissemination of Technological Information within the R&D Organization* (Cambridge MA: MIT Press, 1977), 141–51, 166–80, A. Morrison, 'Gatekeepers of knowledge within industrial districts: Who they are, how they interact', *Regional Studies*, 2008, 42(6): 817–35, Nathalie Lazaric, Christian Longhi and Catherine Thomas, 'Gatekeepers of knowledge versus platforms of knowledge: From potential to realized absorptive capacity', *Regional Studies*, 2008, 42(6): 837–52

18. J. E. Chaplin, *The First Scientific American. Benjamin Franklin and the Pursuit of Genius* (New York: Basic Books, 2006), 93.

19. About this relation see for example, Mario Biagioli, 'From print to patents. Living on instruments in early modern Europe', *History of Science*, 2006, 44: 139–86, esp. 152; J. Secord, 'Knowledge in transit', *Isis*, 2004, 95: 654–72, esp.655.

20. S. Schaffer, L. Roberts, K. Raj and J. Delbourgo,'Introduction', in *The Brokered World. Go-betweens and Global Intelligence 1770–1820*, eds S. Schaffer, L. Roberts, K. Raj and J. Delbourgo (Sagamore Beach: Science History Publications, 2009), IX–XXXVIII, esp. XI.

21. R. Van Vliet, 'Makelaar in intellect. Johannes Nicolas Sebastiaan Allamand (1713–1787) als intermediair tussen schrijvers en uitgevers', *Tijdschrift voor Sociale en Economische Geschiedenis*, 2004, 1: 103–22, 102–7, J. Mertens, 'The honour of Dutch seamen: Benjamin Franklin's theory of oil on troubled waters and its epistemological aftermath', *Physics Today*, 2006, 59(1): 4.

22. Chaplin, *The First Scientific American*, 109, 114.

23. B. Franklin, W. Brownrigg, and Mr Farrish, 'Of the stilling of waves by means of oil', *Philosophical Transactions of the Royal Society*, 1774, 64: 445–60.

24. Mertens, 'Honour of Dutch seamen', 4–5; H. Hardenberg, 'Benjamin Franklin en Nederland', *Bijdragen voor de Geschiedenis der Nederlanden*, 1950–1, 5: 213–30, esp. 215–17, 219–20.

25. Mertens, 'Honour of Dutch seamen', 6–9.

26. Ibid., 7.

27. Van Vliet, 'Makelaar in intellect', 108–13.

28. P. De Clercq, 'In de schaduw van's Gravesande. Het Leids Physisch Kabinet in de tweede helft van de 18ᵈᵉ eeuw', *Tijdschrift voor de Geschiedenis der Geneeskunde, Natuurwetenschappen, Wiskunde en Techniek*, 1987, 10: 149–89, esp. 165–7; J. G. Büsch, *Bemerkungen auf einer Reise durch einen Teil der Vereinigten Niederlande und Englands* (Hamburg: Carl Ernst Bohn, 1786), 70–1; R. L. Brouwer, *Wederlegging der aanmerkingen van den heer P. Steenstra over de vuur-machines* (Amsterdam: Doll, 1774), 5.

29. Van Vliet, 'Makelaar in intellect', 113.

30. See for example, G. W. Kernkamp (ed.) 'Bengt Ferrner's dagboek van zijne reis door Nederland in 1759', *Bijdragen en Mededelingen van het Historisch Genootschap*, 1910, 31: 314–509, esp. 465, 479.

31. Van Vliet, 'Makelaar in intellect', 113–19; R. Van Vliet, *Elie Luzac (1721–1796). Boekverkoper van de Verlichting* (Nijmegen: Vantilt, 2005), 68, 78, 124, 228.

32. L. Schiebinger, *Plants and Empire. Colonial Bioprospecting in the Atlantic World* (Cambridge MA: Harvard University Press, 2004), 226, 230.

33. Schiebinger, *Plants and empire*, 107–10, 128–42, 150–3.

34. Ibid., 232–39

35. L. Schiebinger, *The Mind has No Sex? Women in the Origins of Modern Science* (Cambridge MA: Harvard University Press, 1989); M. De Baar and B. Rang, 'Anna Maria van Schurman, A historical survey of her reception since the seventeenth century', in *Choosing the Better Part. Anna Maria van Schurman (1607–1678)*, eds M. de Baar, M. et al. (Dordrecht: Kluwer Academic Publishers, 1996), 1–23, esp. 1.

36. C. Van Eck, 'The first Dutch feminist tract? Anna Maria van Schurman's discussion of women's aptitude for the study of arts and sciences', in *Choosing the Better Part*, eds De Baar et al. (1996), 43–53, esp. 44–5.

37. L. Schiebinger, 'Maria Winckelmann at the Berlin Academy: A turning point for women in science', *Isis*, 1987, 78: 187–200, esp. 186–7.

38. L. Schiebinger, *The Mind has No Sex*, 36–67, De Baar and Rang, 'Anna Maria van Schurman', 1.

39. Schiebinger, 'Maria Winckelmann', 175, 177–9.

40. Schiebinger, *The Mind has No Sex*, 14–16, 26.

41. Goodman, *Republic of Letters*, 54, 90–135.

42. Ibid., 259–75; M. R. Lynn, 'Enlightenment in the public sphere: The Musée de Monsieur and scientific culture in late-eighteenth-century Paris', *Eighteenth-Century Studies*, 1999, 32: 463–76, esp. 469–70.

43. M. C. Jacob, and D. Sturkenboom, 'A women's scientific society in the West: The late eighteenth-century assimilation of science', *Isis*, 2003, 94, 217–52, esp. 217–18, 225–40.

44. A. B. Shteir, *Cultivating Women, Cultivating Science. Flora's Daughters and Botany in England 1760 to 1860* (Baltimore: The Johns Hopkims University Press, 1996), 37.

45. P. Findlen, 'Scientific spectacle in Baroque Rome: Athanasius Kircher and the Roman College Museum', in *Jesuit Science and the Republic of Letters*, ed. M. Feingold (Cambridge MA: MIT Press, 2003), 225–84, esp. 229; P. Findlen, 'Introduction: "The last man who knew everything". or did he?: Athanasius Kircher S. J. (1602–80) and his world', in *Athanasius Kircher. The Last Man Who Knew Everything*, ed. P. Findlen (New York/London: Routledge, 2004), 1–48, esp. 7, 9.

46. M. Feingold, 'Jesuits: Savants', in *Jesuit Science*, ed. M. Feingold 2003, 1–45, esp. 23–4; M. Baldwin, 'Pious ambition', in idem, 2004, 285–329, esp. 320, N. Malcolm, 'Private and public knowledge: Kircher, esotericism and the Republic of Letters', in idem, 2004, 297–308, esp. 299–300; Goldgar, *Impolite Learning*, 197.

47. N. Safier, *Measuring the New World. Enlightenment Science and South America* (Chicago: University of Chicago Press, 2008), 214; Baldwin, 'Pious ambition', 320; F. C. Hsia, 'Jesuits, Jupiter's satellites and the Académie Royale des Sciences', in *The Jesuits. Cultures, Sciences, and the Arts, 1540–1773*, eds John W. O'Malley et al. (Toronto: Toronto University Press, 1999), 241–57, esp. 244, 249–50.

48. M. M. Portuondo, *Secret Science. Spanish Cosmography and the New World* (Chicago: University of Chicago Press, 2009), 86.

49. A. Anthiaume, *Évolution et enseignement de la science nautique en France et principalement chez les Normans*, 2 vols. (Paris: Dumont, 1920), vol. II.

50. R. Chartier, D. Julia and M.-M. Compère, *L'éducation en France du XVIe au XVIIIe siècle* (Paris: Société d'édition d'enseignement supérieur, 1976), 217–20; F.-B. Artz, 'L'éducation technique en France au XVIIIe siècle (1700–89)', *Revue d'Histoire Moderne*, 1938, 13: 361–47, passim; J. McManners, *Church and Society in Eighteenth-century France*, 2 vols. (Oxford: Oxford University Press, 1998), I, 600.

51. Findlen, 'Introduction', 7, 9.

52. F. C. Hsia, *Sojourners in a Foreign Land. Jesuits and their Scientific Missions in Late Imperial China* (Chicago: University of Chicago Press, 2009), 117–19.

53. Ibid., 120–1, 125.

54. Ibid., 126.

55. F. Buchmayr, 'Secularization and monastic libraries in Austria', in *Lost Libraries. The Destruction of Great Book Collections since Antiquity*, ed. James Raven (London: Palgrave Macmillan, 2004), 145–62, D. Varry, 'Revolutionary seizures and their consequences for French library history', in idem, 2004, 181–96.

56. Gascoigne, *Joseph Banks and the English Enlightenment*, 59–60.

57. H. J. Cook, *Matters of Exchange. Commerce, Medicine, and Science in the Dutch Golden Age* (New Haven: Yale University Press, 2007), 72.

58. Gascoigne, *Joseph Banks and the English Enlightenment*, 60–6; I. F. McNeely and L. Wolverton *Reinventing Knowledge from Alexandria to theInternet* (New York: W.W. Norton, 2008), 142–53.

59. Gascoigne, *Joseph Banks and the English Enlightenment*, chapter 3.

60. See Findlen, 'Introduction', 7.

61. K. Davids, *The Rise and Decline of Dutch Technological Leadership. Technology, Economy and Clture in the Netherlands, 1350–1800*, 2 vols. (Leiden: Brill, 2008), 521–3.

62. Jacob and Sturkenboom, 'A women's scientific society', 219, note 6.

63. University Library Leiden Ms. BPL 772 Natuurkundige lessen van Daniel Gabriel Fahrenheit f. 88 [170], 92v [176], 95v [182].

64. K. Davids, 'Universiteiten, illustre scholen en de verspreiding van technische kennis in Nederland, eind 16ᵉ – begin 19ᵉ eeuw', *Batavia Academia*, 1990, VIII: 1–34, esp. 11–22.

65. Ibid., 30–1.

66. Baldwin, 'Pious ambition', 319–20; D. S. Lux and H. J. Cook, 'Closed circles or open networks? Communicating at a distance during the Scientific Revolution', *History of Science*, 1998, 36: 179–211, esp. 181–2, 201–3.

67. J. R. Wigelsworth, *Selling Science in the Age of Newton. Advertising and the Commoditization of Knowledge* (Aldershot: Ashgate, 2010); L. Hilaire-Pérez and M. Thebaud-Sorger, 'Les techniques dans l'espace publique. Publicité des inventions et literature d'usage au XVIIIe siècle (France, Angleterre)', *Revue de Synthèse*, 2006, 127: 393–428.

68. R. Briggs, 'The Académie Royale des Sciences and the pursuit of utility', *Past and Present*, 1991, nr. 131: 38–88, esp. 39, 65–6, 85–7.

69. L. Hilaire-Pérez, *L' invention technique au siècle des Lumières* (Paris: Albin Michel, 2000).

70. D. Roche, *Le siècle des Lumières en province : académies et académiciens provinciaux 1680–1789*, 2 vols. (Paris: Mouton, 1978), I, 283.

71. Goodman, *Republic of Letters*, 23–54, 183–232.

72. Gascoigne, *Joseph Banks and the English Enlightenment*, 258.

73. L. Stewart, 'Philosophers in the counting houses: commerce, coffee-houses and experiment in early modern London', in *Urban Achievement in Early Modern Europe. Golden Ages in Antwerp, Amsterdam and London*, eds, Patrick K. O'Brien et al. (Cambridge: Cambridge University Press, 2001), 326–45, 334–44.

74. Gascoigne, *Joseph Banks and the English Enlightenment*, 61–4.

75. L. Stewart, *The Rise of Public Science. Rhetoric, Technology, and Natural Philosophy in Newtonian Britain, 1660–1750* (Cambridge: Cambridge University Press, 1992), 213–54; Wigelsworth, Selling science, 147.

76. Inkster, 'Potentially global', 265–6, 267, 269; P. Minard, 'Le bureau d'essai de Birmingham, ou la fabrique de la réputation au XVIIIe siècle', *Annales Histoire Sciences Sociales*, 2010, 65: 1117–46.

77. J. Gascoigne, *Science in the Service of Empire. Joseph Banks, the British State and the Uses of Science in the Age of Revolution* (Cambridge: Cambridge University Press, 1998).

78. J. C. Greene, 'Science, learning, and utility: Patterns of organization in the early American Republic', in *The Pursuit of Knowledge in the Early American Republic. American Scientific and Learned Societies from Colonial Times to the Civil War*, eds A. Oleson and S. C. Brown (Baltimore: The Johns Hopkins University Press, 1976), 1–21, 1

79. Chaplin, *The First Scientific American*, 93.

80. Ibid., 133–4, 155.

81. Ibid., 203.

82. As is shown in my survey of the technological development of the Netherlands between 1350 and 1800 in Davids, *Rise and Decline*.

Introduction. Patent Agency: Problems and Perspectives

IAN INKSTER

Nottingham Trent University, UK.

The papers selected below were presented at the Workshop on Patent Agency, of the British Academy Patents in History Network, held at Sant Marti, Spain in October 2008.

This was intended to develop preliminary thoughts and existing works that touch upon the subject of agency and patenting in history. This introduction further reflects on some major themes of the subject and the period.

It seemed clear enough that we could usefully begin with some notions of what we meant by agency, the possible range of its applications and how any such future work might relate to concerns within the wider historical enterprise of history of technology, industrial and economic history and work on the institutions of intellectual property more generally. We may assume that agency is that of human beings working within the informal or formal constraints of prevailing institutions, and that all patent systems take on institutional forms that may or may not be characteristic or 'of a type'.

Secondly, it also seemed reasonable to begin with what historical material we have, in particular with agency material that overlaps with or is tangential to existing scholarly work on patents in history. To that extent, at the very least, this workshop may be seen as a direct outcome of earlier meetings (2002–8) under the auspices of the British Academy, and the focus provided by the volume of essays of this group, published in an earlier special issue of *History of Technology*.

Thirdly, it is surely useful to begin to hazard how such perspectives and such *ad hoc* historical materials might be formulated into a research-based project into the future, a major purpose of the present small collection of papers. What systematic material might be researched that could be used as data-type across divergent national systems? Of such material, may we now hazard the important historical questions? What other seemingly ancillary institutional or other investigations would need to be undertaken?

The agency focus fits well with the major concerns of such analysts as Douglass North.[1] A perhaps obvious application of patent history is also to the Gerschenkronian early-developer/late-developer dichotomy.[2] That is, it might be possible to interpret the undoubted array of patent systems among industrial, industrializing and colonized nations as a feature of the more general Gerschenkronian process of 'institutional substitution'. So, as I will suggest further in this chapter, British patenting agency was more integrated into the industrial and urban system and less formalized and institutionalized than, say, that of Germany prior to 1914. The principal agents were likely to be more creatures of the market place than in Germany, where they were perhaps extensions of state encroachment into the late-industrializing, heavy-industry based economy.[3] Patent systems were pursued as a nascent science policy, not only in aid of intellectual property protection but also as information systems and mechanisms of technology transfer-in. This was so in an era when little in the way of alternative effective, institutionalized (regulated) information and transfer systems existed. We might hazard the differences between systems within the developing international regime. In an early-start nation such as Britain much emphasis was on a cumulative relationship between the patent system and its agencies or organization on one hand and individual patentees on the other, much of that relationship forged in information dispersal and search, and tested in a bewildering variety of courts of law where rising experts determined the commercial valuation of useful and reliable knowledge. That is, patent systems were part of a process whereby information markets were described and regulated and wherein new products were defined. In more peripheral Spain, the slimmer line of manufacturing needed a more formal backing. In a case of very late-development, such as that of Meiji Japan, policies regarding patents were more overtly strategies for information and technique transfer, but worked alongside a gamut of human capital and cultural policies designed to force industrialization at as fast a rate as was compatible with good social and public order.[4]

The British case shows the intricacy of the advantage of the earlier start, more widely conceived than merely economic or even strictly technological. An argument about public order in the 1870s had emerged from an early radicalism of community in the 1830s. Note the brilliant elisions of E. P. Thompson in reflecting on the intellectual and libertarian traditions of the radical skilled artisan clubs and associations into the 1830s:

> This was perhaps the most distinguished popular culture England has known. It contained the massive diversity of skills, of the workers in metal, wood, textiles and ceramics, without whose inherited 'mysteries' and superb ingenuity with primitive tools the inventions of the Industrial Revolution could scarcely have gone further than the drawing board. From this culture of the craftsman and the self-taught there came scores of inventors, organizers, journalists, and political theorists of impressive quality.[5]

Now, while Thompson is set to argue for periodical renewals of an underground political culture from the 1830s, he is also providing for a different notion and a contrary process. In this culture of the radical astisan was spawned machinofacture,[6] and in this emerged an era of precision, detail and exactitude associated with the resulting Golden Age of artisan–engineer innovation and civic consciousness.[7] Such a notion of the civic engages well with the notions of precision and system. It might be postulated that in great centres such as

London or Birmingham, an older artisan radicalism among the aristocrats of the working class evolved at least partially into a new emphasis on precision, standardization, exactness – all qualities at the centre of the civil society of negotiation taking place in patent offices, agencies and court rooms through-out urban Britain. Through this evolution in innovation artisans became small manufacturers *en masse et en passant*, and Britain retained greatness in manufacturing industry for a longer period than could be explained by such factors as investment in physical or human capital. Later industrial Britain was living on a radicalism and artizanship borrowed from an earlier age.

There can be little doubt that in our conception here, patent agency owed little obligation to elites, whether political or cultural. It also explains why Martin J. Weiner was always wrong on *English Culture and the Decline of the Industrial Spririt*.[8] Whatever Weiner ever did say about the non-industrial or even anti-industrial reflexes of the British cultural elite, none of it could touch the coteries and sites of innovative endeavour. Manufacturing innovation had a life and a place of its own, pervasive and resolute and unplanned. As the poets and ministries slept so too the industrial spirit was up and about early in the morning in Southampton Buildings, in Warwick Court and Chancery Lane, or in Manchester around St Ann's Square, or in Birmingham on Martineau Street, Temple Street or Colmore Road or in the offices of Triangle Chambers. We would thus come to conclusions closer to that of one great outsider, Karl Mannheim, who recognized the detachment of the elite from all such realities, and in turn the disengagement of Britain from its intellectuals.[9]

Within this sort of broad perspective, a principal task of a study of patent agency would be to *incorporate discussions of agency and organization into historical analysis, and to begin to develop some comparative or integrative perspective on the major agents of:* national patent offices; all patentees, partnerships and private enterprises engaged in using the systems; all patent agents/attorneys who organized relationships and information flows within systems; all law courts and other regulatory organizations that settled disputes and awarded values to inventions or their products; all experts drafted in by patentees or courts, including scientists and engineers; all those neighbouring knowledge components and incentives that influenced the individual patentee.

Following the reform in the system during 1851–2, Britain illustrates well the manner in which patent agency worked alongside a veritable mess of legalities. Increased attention to technical novelty combined with rules that more easily permitted foreign lodgement of patents through a British intermediary, meant that there was a huge increase in the role of patent agents in London from mid-century. Many such patent agents specialized either by industry or by foreign location – thus the English and Foreign Patent Office in Finsbury seems to have concentrated upon textile machinery, while Richard Brooman of the Fleet Street Patent Office specialized in motive power innovations. During the 1850s several agencies opened multiple centres, such as the offices in London, Manchester, Liverpool and Halifax of Hughes, Fletcher and Co, who apart from their basic work of registering for provisional protection at a fee of £10, managed the whole post-1851 gamut of specification drawings, revisions, settlements of oppositions, solicitation of prolongations and so on.[10]

Undoubtedly, this more specialized patent agency encouraged the upsurge of professional engineer patentees and long chains of incremental patents based on breakthrough advances. These included Bessemer (iron and steel), Collier (textile finishing), Goodyear (india rubber), Platt (textile machinery), Lister (textile preparation), Nasmyth (forging) or Whitworth (firearms), each of whom as early as the first proper year of the new system (1852–3) was active in precisely those areas that they were to dominate for years to come. Of course, such patenting still involved artisans through strategic partnerships – so George Collier of Halifax (above) was in partnership with many machinists and tradesmen, while the famous engineer Joseph Roberts of Manchester enlisted the special expertise of local power loom workers and overlookers.[11]

Below the Court of Queen's Bench, the provincial legal system at times had to deal with increasingly complex cases after 1851. On of the most testing was that involving Ewald Riepe's invention for improvements in the manufacture of steel, originally obtained as a patent in Britain in 1850. The invention was based on halting the decarbonization process at the point where sufficient carbon remained to constitute high-quality steel within a standard puddling furnace.[12] Heard before Judge James P. Wilde (1816–99) at the Liverpool Assizes in April 1860, the case enlisted the expertise of Lyon Playfair FRS, MP, Professor of Chemistry at Edinburgh, Edward Frankland PhD, FRS, Frederick Calvert, the Manchester-based chemist and manufacturer, the great technical advocate Frederick Bramwell, the analytical chemist Dugald Campbell and several other notables. The plaintiff's case rested on observations by the named experts of the process as being used by James Spence and Frederick Worthington at their Derwent Works at Workington, Cumberland. In turn, the two defendants claimed that the patentee had not adequately described his invention and that it was 'not of any use or advantage to the public'. On the side of the empirics, William Clay, managing partner of the Mersey Steel and Iron Works, gave convincing evidence that the Riepe specification could be directly applied to good effect without any other specialized knowledge but using the tacit knowledge of experienced puddlers. Clay had for some time manufactured such puddle steel under license of the patent and concluded that the 'language of the specification is sufficient to instruct an ordinary workman as to the process to be adopted, and it has done so'. Furthermore, the process was used by several other firms under license, including that of Messrs Naylor, Vickers and Co. of Sheffield who also acted as agents for Riepe in Britain. His evidence was confirmed by a number of practical men experienced at the Derwent Works including engineers, puddlers and steel heaters. The experts seemingly concurred with the practical men, judging the processes as basically the same with the exception of the manner in which oxygen was effectively excluded and with the proviso of a distinction between a process and its results.

But, in answer, the defence questioned the adequacy of terms such as 'cherry-red' and claimed that any workman would be at a loss as how to apply the specification in practice: indeed, the original patent was calculated to mislead and those parts of it that were of utility were well-established in Britain and elsewhere prior to 1850. However, the core of the defence was the expert evidence of Playfair who began with a barrage of authorities and continued with the claim that 'if Riepe's description were followed steel could not be made; certainly not if the temperature there mentioned were adhered to'. Furthermore, the process as used by Spence and Worthington differed as to air exclusion and temperature and thereby produced a better result. He then admitted his own 'want of practical experience' in distinguishing between the colour and the welding heat of shear steel. Calvert confirmed Playfair and was followed by a civil engineer who testified to the impracticality of the Riepe formulation, while an ironmaster of Smethwick near Birmingham and a steelmaker of Tipton both testified to producing steel at a commercial level in the puddling furnace prior to the 1850 patent, but at a considerably higher temperature. The result of this case was the failure of the patentee to defend the patent, and this arose because in a situation where the expert evidence appeared at a stalemate, evidence of prior working was fatal to the plaintiff. In cases where simple evidence of prior working or non-working did not apply, then the move towards expert evaluation within systems of intellectual property was likely to be associated with a new complexity of agency and a new formalization of knowledge.[13] In particular more investigation is required into the way in which law courts became sites for the vigorous activities of technological compradors, those who acted as persuasive middlemen translating and mediating the obstructions that existed between formal knowledge and real practice.

We would argue that patent systems provide good measure – better than most – of what has happened in the material history of the world since around 1830 and the varieties of agency associated with technological change in the leading national systems. In the period dealt with in the chapters of this collection, we might suggest that patent systems were at once systems of intellectual property right, mechanisms of technology transfer and blockage and information systems, and at different times in different places succeeded or failed on each of these levels. More particularly – the years 1830–1914 were the ones in which patent systems helped in the forging of an interconnected club of machinofacture through a combination of their informational and transfer functions.

It is not too much to suggest that in the great industries in the great cities, and in dockyards and arsenals and engineering emporiums, there was something of a ferment of useful and reliable knowledge, and that while this was certainly passing into the hands of the capital goods industries, our wider array of agencies still signified in technological progress. The skilled tradesmen in particular benefited from proximity to one another within industrial and workshop districts. In the words of the great economist Alfred Marshall of Cambridge (a theorist who actually entered factories), in such places quality of production 'is rightly appreciated, inventions and improvements in machinery, in processes and the general organization of the business have their merits promptly discussed: if one man starts a new idea, it is taken up by others and combined with suggestions of their own; and thus it becomes the source of further new ideas'.[14] Not so far removed from Hagerstrand's notion of 'neighbourhood effects'[15] this formulation explains both the importance of specific urban locations and the survival of artisanal tacit knowledge systems in the process of incremental technological change well into the twentieth century. Thus our variety of patent agency.

This may read like an attempt at colonization! But such a range of possible connections and relations seems natural to any study of the activities of the gamut of institutions whose common functions are intellectual property protection on the one hand and knowledge capture, utilization and dispersal on the other. By the time we enter the twentieth century, of course, the whole problem of agency expands still further. Patents protection joins with many other institutional systems such as designs, copyright and trademarks, but at the same time patents become merely one of a range of formal devices to capture and profit from new technologies or products, most of which now centered on corporate activity rather than individual initiatives or small inventive partnerships.

So, if we focus on the United States in the years 1936–55, total patents issued per annum ranged from 20,000 to around 44,000, the proportion of these to corporations were estimated at ranging around 50 per cent to 62 per cent, the proportion to foreign corporations from less than 2 per cent to 7 per cent. Thus at the peak of twentieth-century machinofacture, individual patenting still composed around 35–45 per cent of all patenting, with the US government taking up a residual of up to 2 per cent. But of the 20,000 corporations taken in this estimate, the largest 157 obtained around 30 per cent of all corporate patenting during the 1930s. For the entire 1939–55 period, General Electric obtained 10,757 patents, ATT 8,539, Radio Corp. 7,894.[16] The agents of technological advancement had changed.

The years 1914–70 saw patent systems serving a larger process of technological and industrial containment just as they matured as systems of intellectual property right. The only regions that escaped entrapment were white-settler ones such as Australia or Canada, and of course Japan.[17] The former evolved their own derivations of the systems at the centre of machinofacture, the latter played a canny game of institutional improvization and opportunism. But generally, the short twentieth century (1918–71) represents a vital failure of industrial prosperity to spread, and a partial explanation must be that patent systems were a regulative portion of an institutional system that nurtured machinofacture but did not transfer it to systems elsewhere. There were those who thought that patents were vital to the poor nations of the world, that exclusion from the system spelt doom, Thus 'China grants no patents to foreigners, which probably is a factor in that nation's limited industrial development'.[18] However, a more considered position was that of Patel and others, who saw that patenting was now part and parcel of a great divergence of the world. As patents moved out of the hands of a myriad of competing industrial agents and into those of large corporations so too did the twentieth century for most of its length fail to create prosperity in new nations.[19] Agency really mattered. So it was that the modernization of surprising East Asia awaited the moves of US President Richard Nixon in 1971 to take the dollar off gold and change the rules of the global exchange system, and the surely more profound turn from metals and chemicals towards micro and biological technologies at around the same time.[20]

It seems that we can not claim that at all times the agency of individuals, partnerships, collectivities and urban sites were either of fundamental importance or especially benign in the advancement of technological change. It is certainly possible that our period of the nineteenth-century and earlier twentieth-century particularly illustrates the ubiquity of patents as both intellectual protection and encapsulations of practical knowledge. But it most certainly cannot be argued that at that time the variety of agency as here depicted was necessarily a force for technological change into colonized, poor or marginalized areas of the world. Where the agency of the central places such as Britain or Germany or Italy actually travelled with technology, usually to white-settler outposts such as Australia, or Canada or South Africa, then peripheral patent systems could emerge as part and parcel of small sites of high technological capability. Systems transferred and were part of a process of technology capture.[21] But in most colonial or outsider systems the history of the nineteenth century was one of simple exclusion, the history of the twentieth century was one of expensive technological disaster. In the earlier period a myriad of agency failed to transform outsiders. In the later period, the twentieth century, patent agency was simply one of a great host of elements in the process of dynamic underdevelopment. That history could only change, not so much with an institutional revolution of agency, but through technological revolutions that ushered in microelectronics and information systems, biotechnologies, marine technologies and environmental technologies that had as their shared imperatives a movement of global knowledge rather than the location of capital and specialized agencies.

Notes

1. Douglass North, *Understanding the Process of Economic Change* (Princeton, NJ, 2005).

2. P. A. Gerschenkron, *Economic Backwardness in Historical Perspective. A Book of Essays* (Cambridge, MA, 1962).

3. Of course influence may have occurred through state contracting with large industrial concerns. Anna Guagnini has pointed out to me that in Germany in many cases, large industrial concerns played a decisive role in the development of patent law; what they tried to protect was their own interests, whether that coincided or not with political concerns.

4. K. Sugihara, 'The development of an informational infrastructure in Meiji Japan', in *Information Acumen. The Understanding of Knowledge in Modern Business*, ed., Lisa Bud-Frierman (London, 1994), 75–97: Ian Inkster, 'Politiques, Brevets et Savoirs établis: une approche institutionnelle de l'apogée des années 1850–1914' ["Policies, Patents and Reliable Knowledge – An Institutional Approach to the Climacteric 1850–1914'], *Economies et Sociétés* [Histoire Economique Quantitative], 2008, 38(1): 461–81; Inkster, 'Japan. Cultural Engineering and Late Development', in *Reconceptualizing the Industrial Revolution*, eds, Merritt Roe Smith, Leonard N. Rosenband and Jeff Horn (Cambridge MA, 2010), 291–308.

5. E. P. Thompson, *The Making of the English Working Class* (London, 1963), 831.

6. For the best exposition of machinofacture in engineering work see Joseph Whitworth, *Miscellaneous Papers on Mechanical Subjects* (London, 1858).

7. Ian Inkster, Judith Rowbotham Jeff Hill and Colin Griffin. eds, *The Golden Age 1850–1870 Essays in British Social and Economic History 1850–70* (London, 2000).

8. Martin J. Weiner, *English Culture and the Decline of the Industrial Spirit* (Cambridge, 1981).

9. Karl Mannheim, *Diagnosis of Our Time. Wartime Essays of a Sociologist* (London, 1943), quote page 42.

10. *The Inventors' Gazette*, 1857, 1(26): 17.

11. For example, for Roberts, Patent No. 1251 of 1855.

12. Thus no lengthy and costly recarbonization process or cementation was required as a process beyond the puddling furnace, and the invention rested on acting on the molten metal just at the point where bubbles or grains appeared on the surface by 75 per cent closure of the damper in order to reduce heat. At the point at which the mass became cherry-red (the welding heat of shear steel) and waxy the damper was shut. The patentee was claiming the sequencing of the heat regulation, exclusion of atmospheric air and addition of iron to the mass during the last part of the process, a series of claims difficult to specify precisely in words.

13. For the details of the Liverpool case see 'Scientific Adjudication', *Newton's London Journal of Arts*, 1860, 1 October: 232–44.

14. A. Marshall, *Principles of Economics* (London, 1920), quote on page 271.

15. T. Hagerstrand, *Innovation Diffusion as a Spatial Process* (Chicago, 1967).

16. For references and historical context see footnote 18 below and Ian Inkster, 'Intellectual Property, Information, and Divergences in Economic Development – Institutional Patterns and Outcomes circa 1421–2000' in *The Role of Intellectual Property Rights in Biotechnology Innovation*, eds, David Castle and Richard Gold (London, 2009), 413–36.

17. For several examples of which see Ian Inkster, *Japanese Industrialisation. Historical and Cultural Perspectives* (London and New York, 2001). It is noteworthy that when Japan's intellectual system finally did open up to foreign registrations during 1897–8, the rush of applications was not so much in patenting, as in trademarks, which doubled that of Japanese applications; see *Japan Times*, 25 February 1898, 3; *The Engineer* 13 may 1898, 464.

18. W. B. Bennett, *The American Patent System* (Baton Rouge, LA, 1943), 227.

19. See S. J. Patel, 'The Patent System and the Third World', *World Development*, 1974, 2: especially 9–11; C. Vaitsos, 'Patents Revisited: Their Function in Developing Countries' in *Science, Technology and Development*, ed., C. Cooper (London, 1973), 71–86; [P. J. Frederico], Distribution of Patents Issued to Corporations, 1939–55, *Subcommittee on Patents, Trade Marks and Copyright of US Senate*, eighty-fourth Congress, Washington, 1957.

20. For some time now there have been vigorous efforts at reform of the global patent system to recognize and protect indigenous knowledge in peripheral and poor nations. Debates in the World Intellectual Property Organization over protection of traditional knowledge, genetic resources and traditional cultural expressions (in global jargon known as TKGRTC) have not come to a firm resolution yet.

21. Between 1848 and 1918 some 87,000 patent applications were made in the Australian colonies, for which see Ian Inkster, 'Intellectual Dependency and the Sources of Invention. Britain and the Australian Technological System in the Nineteenth Century', *History of Technology*, 1990, 12: 40–64.

Patent Agents in the European Periphery: Spain (1826–1902)

DAVID PRETEL
University of Cambridge

and PATRICIO SÁIZ
Universidad Autónoma de Madrid

INTRODUCTION

Although some recent studies have provided fresh intellectual insights on the role of patent practitioners during the nineteenth century, they have largely overlooked the activity of these actors in international patenting and peripheral countries. The focus of much of this historical writing about patent advisers and intermediaries has been the 'core' industrial countries of Western Europe and North America, and not the so-called peripheral countries.[1] However, given that patent institutions became increasingly interdependent in the second half of the nineteenth century, it is also necessary to study the connections among various national systems and the broad role of patent practitioners as links in international patenting.

This study will fill a gap in the existing scholarship through an examination of the role and influence of patent agents in Spain from the introduction of the country's first modern intellectual property law in 1826 to the regulation of agents' practice in 1902. The study explores the range of activities carried out by those individuals employed by Spanish and foreign patentees to deal with both the patent application process and the commercialization of property rights. Our argument here is that a focus on patent agents and other forms of agency can provide us with a better understanding of processes of invention, innovation and technology transfer in the European periphery during the nineteenth century. The history of technology in the periphery requires attention not only to the incentives for innovation but also to the social procedure of transmission of knowledge, ideas and information as well as the actors involved in this activity. It is important to note that our focus cannot be solely on the transfer and communication of knowledge and information from advanced industrial nations to 'backward' ones; it must also include the processes of interaction, exchange and appropriation that occurred in both directions.

The essential insight of this chapter is that patent agents were significant actors in the functioning and historical evolution of the Spanish patent institution during the nineteenth century, especially its final decades. We begin the next section by briefly reviewing the main characteristics of the Spanish patent system, which was designed in a hybrid way that guaranteed property rights to original inventors while promoting technology transfer and industrialization. In the third section we will explore the origins of industrial property agency in Spain before 1878 – that is, before the new patent law and the institutional changes achieved during the last quarter of the century.[2] The fourth section will show that from the end of the 1870s, when professional patent specialists began to dominate national and international patenting in Spain, their activities became indispensable for successful patent and trademark application and management. The final section will explore the regulation of Spanish patent agents' activity at the turn of the twentieth century.

THE NINETEENTH-CENTURY SPANISH PATENT SYSTEM AS A HYBRID INSTITUTION

The establishment of patent systems throughout the Atlantic economies in the nineteenth century has been analysed mainly as the twofold result of the extension of intellectual property rights observance and the widening of international agreements signed with respect to intangible assets, such as those derived from invention activity. Patent systems have also been studied as the natural consequence of the industrial development, technological change and expansion of scientific knowledge that stemmed from capitalist expansion and, additionally, a consequence of the necessity of guaranteeing appropriation of intangibles in order to foment inventions and economic progress. Hence, many economists and economic historians, with few exceptions, have used and are using patent data as a partial technological proxy, aggregating each and every patent statistic from different countries and periods, and making international comparisons without regard to the fact that there were huge differences among national systems. There has likewise been a failure to take into account the hidden aspects of laws and their enforcement, which in turn reflect on institutions and agents.

We maintain that the nineteenth-century Spanish industrial property institution can only be explained through the study of its interactions with other national patent regimes and systems of innovation. In that sense, the patent system in Spain was explicitly designed to promote technological emulation, rather than to protect and foster domestic inventive activity. The modern patent laws of 1820 and, mainly, 1826 were aimed at stimulating technology transfer as a strategy for improving the country's relatively backward industrial position.[3] During the whole nineteenth century and even most of the twentieth century, Spanish patent legislation stimulated technological diffusion with a variety of policies including patents of introduction, utility models, a lack of technical exams and compulsory working clauses.[4] The diffusion and emulation of foreign technology was also facilitated by a weak, non-specialized judicial system.

During the nineteenth century a close interdependence existed between the different patent systems and the political economy of the different nations. Nineteenth-century patent institutions were the product of a particular historical period in which core industrial nations acted as technological leaders, yielding the greatest number of patents, while peripheral-dependent countries sought to emulate foreign technology and stimulated international patenting (patents of introduction included) in their own systems. It is likely that the degree of institutional diversity in patent systems during those years stemmed from the relative position of their home nations as innovative or emulative. Nineteenth-century patent systems were designed not only as economic institutions for protecting invention activity and fostering innovation processes but also, and above all, as a mercantilist political strategy by which to promote industrialization. This was the predominant viewpoint during a time when technology transfer and human capital movements mattered greatly and when copying or establishing new technologies from other countries was encouraged by all nations.

It was especially after the 1870s that national patent systems began a process of interconnection, harmonization and, to certain point, unification that influenced international agreements on patent law. In the last decades of the nineteenth century, Spanish politicians, political economists, industrialists and engineers widely agreed that patent protection was a good way to promote technological imitation and encourage national exploitation of patented technologies imported from abroad. Among them, industrialist and patent practitioners – many of them engineers – were some of the most enthusiastic advocates of the patent institution.

PATENT AGENTS IN SPAIN DURING THE FIRST INDUSTRIALIZATION PROCESS

From the establishment of the Spanish patent register in 1826 through 1850, only 890 patents were requested in Spain, half of them patents of introduction. The limited scope of the Spanish patent system in that period precluded the participation of actors other than inventors. The proportion of individuals acting as representatives, assistants or patent traders was decidedly low. Although there were several privileges of introduction and property rights assignments granted through intermediation, it was not yet possible to clearly identify a community of Spanish patent practitioners.

As the original patent files reveal, until the 1850s no one had specialized in patent issues, not even as a complementary professional activity. Only a few foreign diplomats and engineers living in Spain occasionally stepped outside their primary activity to dabble in patent-related business during the first 25 years of the country's patent system, usually assisting foreign inventors in registering their technologies.[5] Likewise, the duties of 'patent jobbers', who obtained patents on behalf of their clients, seem to have been recurrent during the first decades of the patent institution's existence, as they were in other countries.[6] It is nevertheless difficult to assess the importance of patent jobbers' activities during these formative years because of the lack of complementary sources that could allow us to define who the 'first' and 'true' inventor was.

As Graph 7.1 shows, the number of patent applications channelled through intermediation rapidly increased from the 1850s. Although this chart reflects

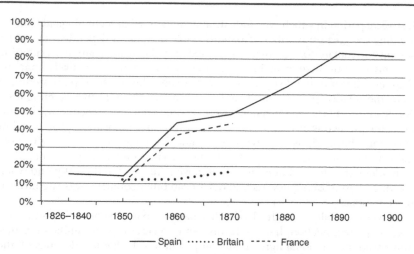

Graph 7.1 Percentage of Spanish Patent Applications Involving an Agent (1826–1900)

Source: Spain: OEPM, Historical Archive (1826–1900); France: Philippe Peyre, 'Les Armengaud, la Petite École et le Développement de l'Innovation', *Les Cahiers d'Histoire du CNAM*, 1994, 4: 93–113; and Britain: Ian Inkster, 'Machinofacture and Technical Change: The Patent Evidence', in *The Golden Age: Essays in English Social and Economic History*, eds Colin Griffin, Ian Inkster, Jeff Hill and Judith Rowbothamet al. (Aldershot, Ashgate, 2001).

only patent applications (not consultancy, assignments or litigation services), it accurately reflects the increasingly significant role of patent practitioners in the Spanish system during this period. The growth of patent intermediation from the 1850s was primarily rooted in the increasing technical complexity of inventions and the new regulations on industrial property law. The growth of patent intermediation from the 1850s was also facilitated by the favourable economic conditions stemming from the new liberal policies of the 1840s and 1850s – years during which significant legislation on land disentailment, railways, bank and financial systems were promulgated. Indeed, the increasing industrialization process trigged patenting. However, compared to leading industrial nations, the patent activity in Spain was still extremely limited, as were the economic incentives for foreign inventors to protect their property rights in that country.

The nature of the technical memoranda presented by patentees to the patent office before 1850 did not require specialized assistance. Before the 1850s, the level of formalization of the patent text was reduced and technical explanations were usually based on practical experience. From the early 1850s a series of more strict requirements became necessary to effectively secure patents. After 1849, for instance, independent notarized reports of patent work were required by the state, thereby increasing control over the actual implementation of patents. A public notary had to assess whether a given invention had

been put in practice and an engineer had to certify it. Formal patent specifications and precise technical drawings thus became essential for effectively
securing valuable and technically complex inventions in Spain.[7] The use of
standardized language, mathematical representations, chemical formulas and
professional technical drawings also became a tacit requirement.

Despite the increasing percentage of patentees who resorted to representatives after 1850, the application for patents did not yet necessarily require the
specialization of engineers and lawyers, and the individuals who assisted patentees were not yet full-time professionals dedicated to patent issues. Indeed, direct
patenting by Spanish inventors and firms remained commonplace through the
1850s and 1860s. In contrast to France, Britain and the United States, individuals working on patent issues in mid-nineteenth-century Spain were not yet
professionally engaged as patent agents and did not recognize themselves as
such. In the third quarter of the century, the vast majority of these individuals worked in an extremely diverse array of activities and comprised a very
heterogeneous community. Rather than serving as professional patent agents,
they were employed, primarily, as general attorneys, international merchants,
mechanical draftsmen, machinists, model builders, engineers and scientists,
and some of them were important patentees in their own right.

Rather than the consolidation of a new profession, before the mid-1870s we
could identify an increasing rent-seeking behaviour among pre-existing professionals and firms who smoothly entered the patent system. Above all, lawyers,
general trade firms and commissioning houses provided non-professional patent services for an increasing number of foreign capitalists seeking individuals
to mediate in patent rights applications in the Spanish system and facilitate
trade with patented technology. The lawyers Juan and Leopoldo Barrié y
Aguero and the commercial house C. A. Saavedra dominated the field during
the 1850s and 1860s, most notably in the extension of patent rights to foreigners in Spain. Although agency-related activities were part of their principal
business, none of these were specialized as patent lawyers, consultants or intermediaries. They were in fact subagents of large foreign agencies based in Paris
and London. The lawyers 'Barrie y Aguero' worked mainly as correspondents
in Spain for the French engineering firm Maison Armengaud Aîné, which specialized in patents.[8] Between 1853 and 1878, these lawyers, based in Madrid,
procured 'letters patents' in Spain for, among others, the German engineers
Carl Wilhelm Siemens and Alfred Krupp.[9] However, it was the commercial
firm C. A. Saavedra,[10] often subcontracted by the international industrial property agency of the French civil engineer Charles Thirion, that was most active
in the provision of patent services from the 1850s through the mid-1870s. With
offices in Madrid, Paris and London, the C. A. Saavedra business engaged in
diversified international activities, including the import and export of a variety
of products; translations and interpretations; consignments; representation of
foreign railway companies in Spain and so on.

Business partnerships around a patented invention also became commonplace from the 1850s. This strategy reduced the costs and risks encountered
by foreign inventors seeking to patent in Spain. The series of patent agreements undertaken between the Basque commercial and steel company Ybarra

Brothers and renowned foreign inventors during the late 1850s is an excellent example. Although the history of the Ybarra Company is well known,[11] the patent strategies this firm developed are worth investigating. José de Vilallonga, a Catalan metallurgist and manager of Ybarra Brothers, oversaw the signing of patent agreements between foreign inventors such as the French mining engineer Adriane Chenot and the British industrialist and engineer Henry Bessemer.[12] In 1856, for instance, Vilallonga signed a £5,000 licence agreement with Bessemer for the exclusive use of his converter in Spain to produce iron and steel from pig iron without fuel.[13] Interestingly, apart from signing a patent licence with Bessemer and Chenot, Vilallonga acted as an industrial property intermediary and business partner, making all the administrative arrangements required for the extension of Bessemer's and Chenot's patents in Spain.[14] In 1854, Vilallonga, Ybarra and Chenot established a firm in Bilbao for the improvement, management and application of Chenot steelmaking inventions in Spain.[15]

THE PROFESSIONALIZATION OF AGENCY AT THE BEGINNING OF THE FIRST GLOBALIzATION

The 1870s marked a transition in the organization of innovative activity in Spain. In the last quarter of the century, a community of specialized engineers, lawyers, consultants and business partners who assisted and interacted with inventors emerged in the country's largest cities. From that moment onwards, the participation of these techno-legal actors in the Spanish industrial property system dramatically increased and became highly significant. Patent practitioners came to occupy a central position in the increasingly larger and more complex Spanish innovation system. As Graph 7.1 shows, the percentage of patent applications in Spain involving an agent increased from 50 per cent in the 1870s to over 80 per cent at the century's end. Unfortunately, the data available for France and Britain (also represented in Graph 7.1) is limited to the period 1850–70, but recent scholarship, using contemporary accounts and reports, maintains that in the late nineteenth-century agents in both countries likewise monopolized industrial property application and management.[16]

A series of changes occurred in the second half of the nineteenth century that may help explain the division of innovative labour and increased professionalization of the patent business throughout the world, particularly in latecomers such as Spain. First, and foremost, the growth of patent activity managed by agents can be interpreted as a response to the increased incentives for assisting foreign inventors in extending their property rights to other countries. For instance, late nineteenth-century professional inventors, such as Thomas Alva Edison, Guglielmo Marconi, Alfred Nobel and William Thomson, as well as large companies, including Krupp, American Bell, Vickers Ltd., Siemens-Halske, General Electric and Schneider Cie., increasingly relied on Spanish engineers, lawyers and trade firms to secure their inventions in Spain. These changes were closely related to the international agreements on industrial property that transpired during the 1880s and facilitated international patenting through a reduction in uncertainty, costs and bureaucracy. Meanwhile, the 1878 Spanish industrial property law had incentivized patenting through a reduction in fees and the granting of two years of priority rights to inventions already patented abroad.[17] From the approval of the 1878 law, the system gained in dimension and complexity. The number of patent applications per year, the trade in property rights and the technical and economic value of the inventions protected increased significantly from that moment. From 1878 to 1902 there were approximately 31,000 applications for patents in Spain, versus around 5,000 during the much longer period of 1826 through to 1878.

Economic and political transformations that occurred from the 1870s in Spain were likewise a factor in increasing the propensity for patenting, especially from abroad. After a financial and political crisis that lasted from 1864–8 to 1874, the first phase of the '*Restauración*' (1875–1902), was a period of stability and industrial development, characterized by new and significant economic regulations including, among others, the Public Works Law (1875), the Railways Law (1877), the Patent and Industrial Property Laws (1878, 1902) and the new Commerce Law (1885). It was a period of economic convergence in which many institutional reforms were completed. That said, the patent data indicate that the industrial take-off of the last decades of the century had arisen out of technological dependency, insofar as Spain was heavily dependent on German, American, British and French patented technology, specifically in the metalworking, electrical, communication, chemical, railways and gas and lighting sectors.[18] Between 1878 and 1907 approximately 60 per cent of patent applications were by foreigners, a percentage of technological dependency that reached an average of almost 70 per cent if we include the patents of introduction on foreign technology for which Spanish residents applied.

The unprecedented amount of foreign patented technology that flooded Spain from the 1870s contributed to a mushrooming of new patent professionals in the country's two large urban centres: Madrid, where the patent office (*The Conservatory of Arts*) was established, and Barcelona, Spain's leading industrial city. The phenomenon was also reflected in the increasing number of advertisements for patent businesses in the specialized and general press and the growing number of technical journals devoted largely to industrial property issues. The steady stream of international enquiries for patents in Europe and America during the last decades of the century was noted in an 1885 article by the consulting industrial engineer Gabriel Gironi, director of *La Semana Industrial* (The Industrial Weekly).[19] Similarly, the engineer and patent agent Teodoro Merly, in a series of articles published in the daily *El Liberal* in March 1890, stressed how the 'enormous' transfer of technology to Spain during those years had fostered the rise of a number of occupations whose raison d'etre was to secure the rights of foreign inventors and firms.[20]

In the last decades of the century Spain's patent business underwent a process of professionalization. Specifically, this meant a transition from the generalist patent practitioner of the mid-nineteenth century to the specialized large patent agency that came to dominate at the turn of the century. The patent business was becoming a full-time professional niche for lawyers and engineers. Two agencies active in the 1870s – *El Centro Auxiliar de la Industria* (Industry Assistance Centre), created in 1871 in Barcelona by the aforementioned industrial engineer Teodoro Merly,[21] and the Vizcarrondo agency – can be considered the pioneers of the professional patent business in Spain. These agencies also epitomize the two distinctive types of patent firms that emerged during the last decades of the century: those formed by engineers and those set up by lawyers and business agents. The two types would merge during the first decades of the twentieth century.

The first Spanish professional agency to work intensively for foreign firms and inventors such as Thomas Alva Edison and the German steelmakers Krupp was the Anglo-Spanish General Agency and Commission House, established in 1865 by Julio Vizcarrondo (1829–89), a Puerto Rican lawyer based in Madrid. Although Vizcarrondo's general agency in Spain was founded in 1865, it did not come to specialize in industrial property management until ten years later. Vizcarrondo appears to have been the first professional agent (professional in that he had specialized knowledge of patent application, control and management) to engage in international patenting activities in Spain. He was also Spain's leading patent agent from the mid-1870s through the late 1880s, intermediating in about 20 per cent of Spain's total patent applications during this period. In yet another distinction, he was the first Spanish agent to become a member of foreign patent agent associations such as the French *Syndicat des Ingenieurs-Conseils en Matiére de Proprieté Industrielle* and *The British Chartered Institute of Patent Agents*.

Especially interesting was the tendency from the early 1860s of a number of distinguished engineers, machinists and chemists – many of whom owned patent rights themselves – to begin acting as patent professionals. Several of these engineers and scientists were trained in France and Britain and frequently doubled as technical assistants and draughtsmen. The new demands of the Spanish innovative system during those years provided opportunities for the relatively small number of professionals residing in Spain who had a technical and scientific background and shared a common technical language with inventors and industrialists.

Good examples of this tendency were the industrial engineer Magín Lladó and the chemist Federico Cajal, both editors of the weekly publication *El Porvenir de la Industria* (The Industrial Future), who in 1857 established a technical agency in Barcelona dedicated to mechanical and chemical consultancy, valuation of inventions and management of patents and trademarks.[22] A few years later, in 1865, José Alcover, also an industrial engineer and the director of the weekly review *La Gaceta Industrial* (The Industrial Gazette), established a consulting engineering firm in Madrid from which he advertised patented inventions and public exhibitions of foreign machinery, integrating engineering, commercial and patenting services.[23] This company operated until 1891, at which point it became an electrical consulting firm whose participation in the patent business was minimal owing to the emergence of larger specialized industrial property agencies during the last two decades of the century.

The expansion of agents' activities in Spain during the last third of the century was closely related to the increasing number of mechanical and chemical consultancies established in Barcelona and Madrid during those years. This relationship may explain why patent businesses began to be dominated in part by industrial engineers, a small elite community with close ties to the industrialization process. Moreover, in the second half of the century, Spain's industrial engineers were the preferred professionals selected by both inventors and the state to certify the practical implementation of patented inventions that had been required by law since 1849.

A look at late nineteenth-century business directories suggests how different the Spanish patent system had become by the last two decades of the nineteenth century. Over 30 Spanish individuals and firms were consistently listed and advertised in national and international patent directories in the late 1880s and 1890s.[24] However, although business and city directories give a sense of the increasing importance of the industrial property business in Spain, they do not reflect the fact that by 1900 a mere handful of agencies had come to monopolize the patent business via mergers between complementary firms. The overwhelming majority of Spanish agents and agencies during the last decades of the century were practising in Madrid or Barcelona for both economic and administrative reasons. As Table 7.1 shows, the services and economic sectors assisted by these agencies often differed, as did the qualifications and backgrounds of their employees.

At the turn of the century, the country's patent agency business was already consolidated and controlled by a very low number of increasingly large professional agencies specializing in different types of services. Among them, the two firms set up by lawyers – '*Vizcarrondo-Elzaburu*' and '*Clarke, Modet & Co.*',[25] both established in Madrid – worked almost exclusively for foreign corporations and inventors. These two firms did not offer technical assistance; instead, they functioned mainly as agents who communicated rights and knowledge as part of a transnational sociotechnical network of agents that dominated the field of communication of foreign industrial property rights to Spain. Engineering firms, for their part, occupied a separate niche of the market for patent professionals. Beyond their international clientele, the consultancies of Gerónimo Bolibar and Teodoro Merly, both in Barcelona, devoted a substantial part of their activity to assisting Spanish inventors and industrialists. Gerónimo Bolibar was the editor of the patent journal *Industria e Invenciones,* published weekly in Barcelona since 1884. Bolibar was a renowned professional who acted as Secretary of the International Engineering Conference celebrated in Barcelona in 1888.

These engineers tended to participate in various interrelated activities and offered their clients a wide range of services (testing, installations and exhibitions) that overlapped with those of electrical and mechanical consultancy and technology trade. In the 1890s the firm *El Fomento Industrial*, established by the registered business agent Agustín Ungría,[26] became an important player in the Spanish patent business. The company was a general commission house, not specialized in industrial property rights, that saw an opportunity to engage in the commercialization of patents and trademarks through its trade journal *El Fomento Industrial y Mercantil* (The Industrial and Mercantile Promotion).

According to patent documentation for the year 1900, a half-dozen industrial property firms controlled about 70 per cent of Spain's total patent applications along with the commercialization of patents; the leaders of this sector were *Vizcarrondo-Elzaburu, Clarke, Modet & Co.* and *The International Patent Office of*

Table 7.1 Services Provided by Main Industrial Property Agencies 1878–1900

	Year Foundation	City	Background agents (in origin)	Patents	Trademarks	Litigation	Technical Assistance	Colonial Patents	Technology Trading	Journal	Other literature
Alfonso Piquet	1860s	Madrid	Engineer	x			x	x	x		
Ezaburu-Vizcarrondo	1865	Madrid	Lawyers	x	x	x		x			x
'Agencia General de Patentes y Marcas, Clarke, Modet and Co.' (Alberto Clarke, Fernando Modet, José Gómez-Acebo)	1879	Madrid	Lawyers	x	x	x		x			x
'El Fomento Industrial y Mercantil' (Agustín Ungría)	1891	Barcelona Madrid Valencia	Business Agent	x	x				x	x	
'Oficina Internacional de Propiedad Industrial' (Gerónimo Bolibar)	1884	Barcelona	Industrial Engineer	x	x		x		x	x	x
'Centro Auxiliar de la Industria' (Teodoro Merly, Félix Sivilla, Ventura Serra)	1871	Barcelona Madrid Lisbon	Engineers	x			x	x	x		x
Carlos Bonet	1886	Barcelona Madrid	Engineer		x						
José Pella	1880s	Barcelona	Lawyer			x					x

Sources: Original Patent Files at the OEPM (1826–1900); *BOPI* (1886–1910); *International Directory of Patent Agents* (London: William Reeves, 1893, 1897, 1901); Advertisements and directories in *La Gaceta Industrial, Industria e Invenciones, La Semana Industrial, El Porvenir de la Industria, Revista de Obras Públicas* and *Anuario de la Electricidad.*

Gerónimo Bolíbar.[27] It seems that almost the totality of 'elite' foreign patents were channelled through these leading agencies. Meanwhile, four agencies monopolized trademarks application and management: Elzaburu, Ungría, *Clarke, Modet & Co.* and, above all, the industrial engineer Carlos Bonet. The latter, based in Barcelona, specialized almost exclusively in the application and management of trademarks and channelled approximately 44 per cent of trademark applications between 1885 and 1905.[28] As Graph 7.2 clearly shows, from the 1875 Restoration onwards, agents' intermediation grew exponentially – to such an extent that at the beginning of the twentieth century they managed virtually every trademark ever registered (93–94%).

Thus, it is clear that foreign inventors and entrepreneurs considered agents the best means of obtaining and controlling patent and trademark rights in Spain, given the reduction of transaction and information costs. Foreign patenting activity would have been constrained without the presence of these intermediaries. However, the indispensable participation of agents in international patenting and trademarking in Spain also reflects the various barriers to, and changing imperatives for, technology transfer to peripheral economies during the years of the Second Industrial Revolution and reveals, among other things, that foreign patenting in Spain was limited to inventors who could afford the high state and, especially, agent fees.

Once a patent had been issued, some patent professionals continued assisting foreign inventors in patent maintenance, the compulsory enactment of the invention and the sale and transfer of property rights. Indeed, assisting foreign patentees to assign and license their property rights and facilitate external investment may have been an important part of professional agents' activities, despite Spain's relatively small market for patented technology during the last decades of the century. Although the presence of professionals who assisted patentees in commercializing their inventions cannot be readily measured, by

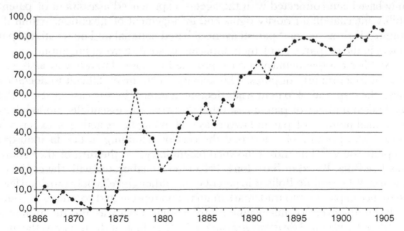

Graph 7.2 Spanish Trademark Applications Involving an Agent (1866–1905)
Sources: OEPM, Historical Archive, Trademarks 1866–1905.

the 1870s a commonality of technical and general press advertisements saw agents selling patents and inventions. In any case, agents' co-ownership and partnership with inventors and their activities as brokers who dealt commercially with patents were controversial, since these activities seemed to confer an excessive power to agents and entail a conflict of interest insofar as the agents' commercial and professional duties clashed.[29]

The study of dozens of assignment contracts of 'elite' patents from 1870 to 1900 makes two ideas clear.[30] First, all contracts of assignment and licence of foreign patents were established through professional industrial property agents. Second, from the 1880s, the same agents who provided assistance in patent procurement were drafting licences and providing counsel in property rights assignments. For instance, the patent firm *Clarke, Modet & Co.*, through its lawyers José Gómez Acebo and Alberto Clarke, assisted Guglielmo Marconi in the 1897 assignments of his Spanish patent on wireless technology to *The Wireless Telegraph and Signal Company Limited* of London. In 1896, following instructions from Edward's Carpmael's London-based patent firm, *Clarke, Modet & Co.* had mediated to obtain Marconi's Spanish patent. In 1897 the same Spanish agency intermediated with the state to officially prove that the invention was in practice following the legal requirements of the 1878 law.[31]

Spanish patent professionals may also have been active in the last two decades of the century in assisting Spanish industrialists and inventors in the process of information searching. Some industrial engineers, like Teodoro Merly and Gerónimo Bolibar, provided clients with summaries and copies of letters patent, specifications, technical memorandums and drawings of patents already granted confirming ownership, titles and assignments. This service was most likely a principal source of technical information contained in patents, along with patent journals and related literature, since the complete specifications were not published by the official organs of the patent office, namely the *Gaceta de Madrid* and, from 1886, the *Boletín de la Propiedad Industrial (BOPI)*. This service may have been connected with the agents' experienced assessment of patentability, international priority rights and infringement of inventions within the country. For this reason Spanish agents advised national and international patentees in the preparation of their applications so as to avoid litigation.

Another complementary service provided by some lawyers was assistance in industrial property disputes. This activity is extremely difficult to document given the dispersal of patent trials documentation.[32] In any case, it seems that the limited number of patent cases that occurred was essentially monopolized by a small number of patent lawyers as well as engineers acting as expert witnesses, who presumably increased the cost of obtaining justice in industrial property issues.[33] The most renowned patent lawyer at the turn of the century was José Pella. Based in Barcelona, Pella often collaborated with the engineering firm of Gerónimo Bolibar in patent trials, although Pella only provided legal assistance in patent and trademark matters and represented patentees in courts of law in the event of infringement proceedings. Pella was also the author of *Patents of Invention and the Rights of Inventors* (1892), which at the time was the most relevant doctrinal treatise on industrial property law in the Spanish language and a paradigmatic example of pro-patent discourse.[34]

THE INSTITUTIONALIZATION OF AGENTS ACTIVITY

Although industrial property professionals had placed themselves at the centre of the Spanish innovation system from the 1870s, neither the patent law of 1878 nor the minor regulations passed in the last two decades of the century regulated the participation of third parties in the acquisition and management of patent rights of invention. Apart from the acknowledgement that representatives could apply for patent rights under the inventors' names, no other references can be found in the 1878 law. This law reflected a lack of awareness among legislators that actors other than inventors and state officers could participate in the patent system. It was with the major reform of the patent law of 1902 that Spanish patent agents' activities became regulated by the state through the establishment of a mandatory register of industrial property agents as well as formal requirements for their practice.

The 1903 by-law regulating the 1902 Industrial Property Law established both a mandatory register of patent agents and formal requirements for their practice.[35] This regulation established that no one could intermediate in more than three files of patent and trademark applications without being registered in the *Negociado Especial de Patentes* (the Spanish Patent Office of the time) as an industrial property agent. The law, however, did not introduce clear barriers to entry into the profession. It simply specified that only Spanish citizens with a legal or engineering degree or an accredited equivalent competence could be registered as Industrial Property Agents. Registered agents also had to be members of the official *Colegios de Agentes de Negocios* (Associations of Business Agents) and have a minimum of five years of experience working as agents without any judiciary reclamation for malpractice.

As the patent lawyer Francisco Elzaburu pointed out in correspondence to the *Society of Patent Agents* of London, the new law passed by the Spanish Parliament represented 'great progress' for Spanish agents.[36] From that moment, the contours of the agents' occupation became both more controlled and more normalized. However, the new regulation left room for abuse. The main issue, according to professional and technical journals edited by agents, was that it remained unclear precisely what kind of expertise and qualifications were required in order to practise as a patent agent. The profession of 'industrial property agent', in short, was still fairly vague. Conversely, in the United Kingdom, France and the United States, no exam or specific training was required. Due to Spain's lack of official registration or exams, Spanish agents' reputation as experts in international patenting was obtained through personal and professional connections with colleagues in foreign cities and their participation as foreign members in international mutual associations.

The 1902 industrial property law opened up the patent business to the three types of professionals who had brought the most individuals into the industrial property field: engineers, business agents and lawyers. From the late 1870s, members of these three occupations had seen a professional opportunity in the patent business. Moreover, they represented the three realms that patent agents mediated: science, the market and the law. The 1903 patent regulation did not privilege any one of them. Engineers managed to preserve the exclusivity of drafting and signing technical memorandums, technical drawings and models that was already regulated by the budget law of 1893–7, even though it had not been acknowledged by the Spanish Patent Office.[37] Business agents and lawyers celebrated the new regulations insofar as they limited industrial property agencies to professionals with experience and sufficient economic resources for a mandatory deposit, thereby ensuring a minimum level of competence in the profession.[38] The register did not begin to function and was not published in the official organ of the Patent Office (the *BOPI*) until 1905.[39] In the first Register of Industrial Property Agents, in November 1905,[40] only 28 individuals were registered – 21 in Madrid, 6 in Barcelona and 1 in Bilbao, most of them working for Spain's six largest professional agencies, which had monopolized the country's industrial property business since the last years of the nineteenth century.[41] Interestingly, the regulation of agents' activities through the introduction of a mandatory register of agents seems to have stimulated large agencies to absorb smaller ones and increasingly integrate individuals with technical and legal backgrounds.

It was as late as 1907 that Spanish industrial property agents founded their first mutual organization, the *Asociación Española de Agentes de la Propiedad Industrial y Comercial* (The Association of Industrial and Business Agents), through the initiative of Francisco Elzaburu, the organization's first president. In May 1909 this organization acquired official character insofar as it was recognized by the state. It was a very late professional association considering that Britain, France and the United States had already established professional associations by the 1880s, while countries like Germany, Switzerland and Italy had done so by 1900. In December 1916 the *Consejo de la Propiedad Industrial y Comercial* (Council of Industrial and Business Property) was created as a state consultative cabinet for the reform of industrial property laws and related issues. In 1917, two of Spain's leading patent professionals, Francisco Elzaburu and Agustín Ungría, were among the cabinet's first members alongside representatives who were industrial engineers, members of the Academy of Sciences and industrialists; the cabinet was presided over by the former Minister of Public Works, Rafael Gasset. In any case, before the establishment of agents' associations and the state council, industrial property practitioners had never conformed an underrepresented collective. From the 1880s some agents – including Julio Vizcarrondo, Gerónimo Bolibar and Alberto Clarke – carried lobbying activities through their journals, privileged political connections and active membership in foreign associations such as the *London Chartered Institute of Patent Agents* and the *International Association for the Protection of Industrial Property*.

CONCLUSION

During the last two decades of the nineteenth century there emerged in Spain a community of specialized engineers, lawyers, consultants and business partners who assisted patentees. Although people acting as representatives and assistants of patentees could be found in Spain between 1826 and 1878, there was no inventive community in that country until the last two decades of the nineteenth century. Moreover, the activities of Spanish agents throughout most of the nineteenth-century were less specific than in other countries. Spain's lack of a qualifying exam, lax enforcement of property rights and reduced levels of indigenous patenting collectively explain its meagre agency activity and relatively late extension of a community of patent professionals.

This paper has demonstrated how, during the last decades of the nineteenth-century, foreign inventors and firms increasingly relied on the services offered by industrial property agents, who guided and assisted patentees in registering, publicising and commercializing their inventions in Spain. The increasing activity of patent agents in Spain in the second half of the century also reveals the increasing openness of the Spanish patent system – a finding consistent with previous studies on Spain's dependency on foreign technology during this period. The globalization of technological knowledge, the international agreements on industrial property law and the increasing amount of corporate 'elite' patenting in the Spanish system seem to explain the rise in the participation of these intermediaries and the professionalization of their activity.

The leading Spanish agents of the late nineteenth century had substantial expertise and considerable training in legal and technical issues. Spanish agents, specifically engineers and lawyers, were active in the last decades of the nineteenth century in assisting inventors and firms in translating their ideas into techno-legal documents and these documents into functional technologies. The activities of the leading Spanish patent practitioners during the late nineteenth century overlapped with other occupations, including the evaluation of inventions, legal assistance, commercialization of technology, technical journalism and engineering consultancy.

Given this dependent and peripheral nature, the history of the Spanish patent system during the nineteenth century should be seen not just as an example of the history of invention but above all as a significant historical case of the history of technology transfer and diffusion. During this period, the overwhelming majority of foreign inventors patenting in continental and colonial Spain used intermediaries. For large foreign industrial corporations and wealthy independent inventors, international networks of intermediary agents were the best way to reduce transaction costs – mainly information costs – and avoid spending time visiting Spain. The resort to agents became imperative for industrial property control and management in Spain, even as it also functioned as a barrier limiting international patenting and trademark activities to those foreign inventors and firms that could afford the high costs of intermediation.

Notes

1. Good examples of recent historiography on the subject focused on French, American and British cases are Gabriel Gálvez-Behar, 'Des Médiateurs au Coeur du Système d'Innovation: Les Agents de Brevets en France (1870–1914)' in *Les archives de l'invention: ecrits, objets et images de l'activité inventive* dirs. Marie-Sophie Corcy, Christiane Douyère-Demeulenaere and Liliane Hilaire-Pérez (Toulouse: Médiriennes, 2006): 437–47; Philippe Peyre, 'Les Armengaud, la Petite École et le Développement de l'Innovation', *Les Cahiers d'Histoire du CNAM* 1994, 4: 93–113; Anna Guagnini, 'Patent Agents, Legal Advisers and Guglielmo Marconi's Breakthrough in Wireless Telegraphy', *History of Technology* 2002, 24: 171–201; Naomi R. Lamoreaux and Kenneth L. Sokoloff, 'Intermediaries in the US Market for Technology, 1870–1920', in Stanley L. Engerman, Philip T. Hoffman, Jean-Laurent Rosenthal and Kenneth L. Sokoloff (eds), *Finance, Intermediaries, and*

Economic Development (Cambridge: Cambridge University Press, 2003): 209–46; Harry I. Dutton, *The Patent System and Inventive Activity: During the Industrial Revolution 1750–1852* (Manchester: Manchester University Press, 1984): Chapter 5; or Ross Thomson, *Structures of Change in the Mechanical Age: Technological Innovation in the United States, 1790–1865* (Baltimore: The Johns Hopkins University Press, 2009): Chapter 7.

2. Patricio Sáiz, *Propiedad industrial y revolución liberal. Historia del sistema español de patentes (1759–1929)* (Madrid: OEPM, 1995): 121–50.

3. Patricio Sáiz, 'Patents, International Technology Transfer and Spanish Industrial Dependence (1759–1878)' in *Les chemins de la nouveauté. Innover, inventer au regard de l'histoire*, dirs. Liliane Hilaire-Pérez and Anne-François Garçon (Paris: CHTS, 2003): 223–45.

4. Patricio Sáiz, 'The Spanish Patent System, 1770–1907', *History of Technology* 2002, 24: 45–79, section 2.

5. For instance, in the 1830s the secretary of the Belgian embassy Ernest Dalwin (OEPM, *Privilegio* 208) and the ambassador of France in Madrid, Juan Lagoanere (*Privilegios* 109, 110 and 119) were occasional representatives of inventors from their respective countries. Examples of foreign engineers living in Madrid and occasionally representing foreign inventors during these formative years are the Parisian Enrique Mambert (*Privilegios* 64 and 65) and the British Charles Green (*Privilegios* 207, 690 and 1,892). Similarly, renowned professionals like the Spanish botanist and utopian socialist Ramón de la Sagra (*Privilegios* 684, 694 and 695) and the merchant Enrique O'Shea (*Privilegios* 147, 148, 165, 167 and 300) were also occasional intermediaries of foreign inventors in their application to obtain patents in Spain in the 1830s and 1840s.

6. This practice also seemed to be frequent in international patenting in Spain before the international agreements of the 1880s. A good example of patent jobber activity is that performed by the lawyer of Madrid Antonio María Blanco (OEPM, *Privilegios* 257, 275, 276, 277 and 440).

7. Royal Order of the 11 January 1849.

8. For an illustration of Barrie's activities see OEPM, *Privilegios* 3,070, 4,195 and 4,609.

9. For an example of Barrie y Agüero as representatives of Siemens see OEPM, *Privilegios* 4,902 and 2,669. For their representation of Alfred Krupp see *Privilegio* 5,373.

10. C. A. Saavedra (for a while renamed Saavedra and Riberolles) and the commercial agents associated with this firm, like Telesforo and Domingo Algarra, channelled hundreds of patents from 1853 to the early 1880s, their services disappearing with the emergence of professional sizeable patent agencies specialized in patenting.

11. Pablo Díaz, *Los Ybarra. Una Dinastía de Empresarios, 1801–2001* (Madrid: Marcial Pons Historia, 2002).

12. For Henry Bessemer's profuse use of patenting for protecting his inventions see Ian Inkster, *Science and Technology in History: An Approach to Industrial Development* (Basingstoke: Rutgers University Press, 1991), 161.

13. For the series of agreements the Ybarra Brothers signed with the company Bessemer & Longsdon and with the inventor André Chenot, see Pablo Díaz, *Los Ybarra*, 83–95.

14. On January 1857, the Henry Bessemer Company, Bessemer & Longsdon, was granted a Spanish patent of invention for 15 years and immediately transferred the rights to Ybarra Brothers. A few weeks before, in December 1856, Ybarra Brothers had been already granted a five-year Spanish patent of introduction for the Bessemer converter. Thus, Ybarra Brothers had already obtained the Spanish patent rights for the Bessemer invention and, yet, decided to sign a patent license agreement with Bessemer in order to receive technical assistance and probably to extend the duration of the monopoly insofar as patents of introduction could only last 5 years. Bessemer himself supervised the installation of his invention in the Ybarra's plant of Santa María de Guriezo in December 1858 (OEPM, *Privilegio* 1,510).

15. OEPM. *Privilegio* 1,212.

16. Inkster et al. See note 1.

17. Patent Law of the 30 July 1878. See Patricio Sáiz, 'The Spanish Patent System (1770–1907)', Table 1.

18. Id. Ibídem, Tables 2 and 7 and comments.

19. Gabriel Gironi, 'Los Privilegios de Invención', *La Semana Industrial* (22 January 1886).

20. Teodoro Merly, 'La Unión Internacional para la Protección de la Propiedad Industrial: análisis de la misma', *El Liberal* (20–31 March 1890).

21. Teodoro Merly was a well-known industrial engineer, who often wrote in technical and professional journals like the prestigious *Revista de Obra Públicas*. The experienced industrial engineers Ventura Serra, editor between 1881 and 1883 of the patent journal *Gaceta de la Industria y las Invenciones* and director of the International Patent Agency, and Felix Sivilla, director of the *Centro Auxiliar Mecánico*, both established in Barcelona, joined Merly in his technical office in the late 1870s working all of them as consultants of patentees in Spain and Portugal.

22. Some examples are OEPM, *Patentes* 10,466 and 10,467.

23. See OEPM, *Privilegios* 4,561; 4,542; 5,774 and 5,778. See also David Pretel, 'Invención, nacionalismo tecnológico y progreso: el discurso de la propiedad industrial en la España del siglo XIX', *Empiria*, 2009, 18: 59–83.

24. Directories and advertisements of Spanish and foreign patent agents can be found in several technical journals and official publications, including the *Boletín de la Propiedad Industrial* (*BOPI*), the *Almanaque de la Gaceta Industrial* and the *Anuario de Electricidad*. For Spanish patent agents in international directories see the *International Directory of Patent Agents* (London: William Reeves, 1893, 1897 and 1901).

25. The firm *Clarke, Modet & Co.* originated in 1892 in the merge of *Agencia General de Patentes y Marcas* and *Clarke and Co.*, both established in Madrid in 1879. The lawyers José Gómez Acebo and Francisco Modet joined the firm in the late 1880s. See, for example, OEPM, *Patentes* 8,239 (Edison); 18,733; 21,771 and 23,158 (Vikers) and 20,041 and 23,449 (Marconi).

26. A fine literary description of Agustín Ungría's business agency activities in the 1920s in the 'hundreds of official departments' and the origins of this firm in the late nineteenth century can be found in Arturo Barea, *The Forging of a Rebel* (London: Davis-Poynter, 1972): 390–3. Examples of patents registered by Ungría in 1900 are OEPM, *Patentes* 25,314; 25,319 and 25,349.

27. OEPM, patent applications and assignment contracts for the year 1900.

28. OEPM, trademark register from 1885 to 1905.

29. For contemporary accounts of patent agents activity to commercially exploit inventions see Gerónimo Bolibar, 'Misión de los Agentes de Negocios', *Industria e Invenciones* 14 August 1908, 7: 61–2; and Frederick Walker, 'Patent Agents and Patent Brokers', *Journal of the Society of Patent Agents*, March 1902, 3(27): 39–41.

30. Assignment contracts of, among others: Edward W. Serrell, Charles F. Brush, George Westinghouse, *International Bell Telephone Co.*, *Marconi Wireless Telegraph*, Eugène Turpin, Thomas Alva Edison, Thorsten Nordenfelt, Isaac Peral, Nicolaus A. Otto, *Portilla & White Co.*, *Siemens & Halske A.G* and *Compagnie d'Electricité Thomson Houston*.

31. OEPM, *Patente* 20,041. Marconi applied patents for his invention in Britain, Austria-Hungary, France, Germany, Spain, Italy, Russia, United States of America and India. See Anna Guagnini, 'Patent Agents', 199.

32. A good indirect source of patent litigation trials for this period are the copies kept with patent files in the OEPM, as well as the contemporary accounts written by patent agents regarding patent infringement and litigation in Spain.

33. For a contemporary account on the high cost and time-consuming nature of the Spanish patent trials see Gumersondo Vicuña 'Complemento de la Ley de Patentes', *La Semana Industrial*, January 1886, year V, Vol. V: 7; and 'Sindicato de Inventores', Industria e Invenciones 28 August 1886, 139: 93.

34. José Pella, *Las Patentes de Invención y los Derechos del Inventor: Tratado de Utilidad Práctica para Inventores e Industriales* (Barcelona: Administración de Industria e Invenciones, 1892).

35. Royal Decree of 12 June 1903 (*Colección Legislativa de España, Nueva Serie*, XV). Section V on industrial property agents and their register. A translation to English furnished by Francisco Elzaburu was also published in London by the *Journal of the Society of Patent Agents*, 1903, IV(47–8): 162–6.

36. Letter from Francisco Elzaburu to the Society of Patent Agents reproduced in the *Journal of the Society of Patent Agents*, July, 1902, III(31): 109–10.

37. Gerónimo Bolibar, 'Observaciones al Proyecto de Ley de Propiedad Industrial', *Industria e Invenciones*, 2 November 1901, 18: 158–64.

38. See, for instance, the series of articles by Agustín Ungría celebrating the new regulation and the compulsory requirement to be registered as business agent: Agustín Ungría, 'Los Agentes de Negocios y la Propiedad Industrial', *El Fomento Industrial y Mercantil*, 20 June 1902, 404 : 991–2 and 20 July 1902, 407: 1016.

39. The remarks of the Royal Order of 22 May 1905 on this issue are eloquent. The Royal Order urged the introduction of a Register of Industrial Property Agents, arguing that 'the actual situation must no longer continue because it only protects those who [work as industrial property agents] without fulfilling any sort of requirement', and 'in detriment of those who from the beginning fulfill the legal requirements, thereby offering a guaranty to those who may need their services'. *BOPI*, July 1905, 453: 837–8.

40. *BOPI*, November 1905, 461: 72.

41. During the few years following the first registration, the number of individuals registered remained low, with most working for only a few patent firms. In March 1906 there were 32 individuals registered (*BOPI*, 470: 423–4); in April 1907, 36 (*BOPI*, 496: 616) and in June 1908, 37 (*BOPI*, 523, 810–11).

Highly Fraught with Good to Man: Patent Organization, Agency, and Useful and Reliable Knowledge in British Machinofacture Circa 1780–1851 and beyond

IAN INKSTER

Nottingham Trent University, UK.

INTRODUCTION

In the introduction to this special collection it was suggested that patent agency might be a subject of comparative analysis across the industrializing nations. The work of Alexander Gerschenkron and Douglass North could perhaps act as initial perspectives. However, we might push this further to argue that the distinction made by Douglass North between institutions and their *organizations* might also be of compelling application to patent systems in this period, and provide room for the modification of any such Gerschenkron-type modeling. That is, while the patent systems – qua institutions – of the major nations were at least nominally similar and constructed under a set of common understandings, in reality they were *organized* in such a way as to produce different outcomes in terms of technological advance and knowledge accrual and information circulation. Relatively backward systems adopted institutional nuances that favoured their own learning alongside improved access to the global technological shelf. But within all industrializing nations, patent systems were surely manipulated by commanding interests, demonstrative of North's famous adage that 'institutions are the rules of the game, organizations are the players'.[1] However much governments erected institutions of policy, outcomes were the results of organizational nuances and game-playing, of the huge range of activities of a myriad agents. In the case of the patent systems of our period, it seems clear that their role as economic institutions may have been strongly conditioned by their role as social organizations – as places or foci of competing/cooperating agents – and by how far such latter roles conflicted with or conformed to what North has called the 'perceptions of the entrepreneurs of political and economic organizations'.

In the case of Britain we may identify the character of patent agency both prior to 1852 when the patent system as an institution was insubstantial, costly, badly monitored or regulated, and after the reform (as in Anna Guagnini's contribution here) when it became less costly to operate within, harboured a much greater number of individual patentees and demanded greater specific knowledge and technical expertise, more documentation and specification on the part of those patentees and their agents. We will show how it was that prior to 1851 formal patent agency was very rare, but informal agency was vital to the registration and ownership of many technical innovations. After 1851 formal agency became far more common but acted alongside still flourishing, informal sites and networks of agency. In the terms of Douglass North, prior to 1851 agency belonged mostly to the organizations of patenting, after 1851 it increasingly emerged within the core regulations and activities of the more formalized patent institutions. We also add that any institution that works nominally across varying spaces and sites will surely absorb specific characteristics from those sites. Here we show that in the important industrial city of Birmingham, the nominal agency of patenting was conditioned not by legislation or rules (North's institution) but by the immediacies and intricacies of that specific urbanity (North's organization).

PATENT AGENCY. THE UNREFORMED SYSTEM IN BRITAIN PRIOR TO 1851

Under the unreformed British patent system, special patent agency was in little demand relative to its speedy growth after the 1851 watershed. William Newton, who as an engineer began to practise as a patent agent in 1820 was an exception to the rule yet exemplary of how patenting as an institution was actually being organized.[2] Born in London in 1786 of middle-class background and with little formal education, Newton followed in the footsteps of his land surveying father, and under training with his uncle Edward Baker broadened his scientific interests, becoming a member of the City Philosophical Society.[3] Alongside Michael Faraday and others he indeed delivered lectures there on scientific topics, and then joined the Royal Society of Arts. A particular interest in mechanical drawing brought him even more firmly into inventor environs, especially as a draughtsman to offices where specifications were recorded. This alerted Newton to the need for an improved system of information diffusion, especially concerning specifications, as well as their very deficient character under the ancient regulations. He became convinced of the entrenched inadequacy of the British system and the need for real expertise, as with Moses Poole and his evidence before the 1829 patent enquiry. According to Newton and some others such as Poole, few were capable of precisely describing the essential workings and novelties of a patent, including inventors themselves. So Newton established his role in the profession of patent agent on a basis of increased perspicuity and conciseness. An example of this was Wright's pin machine of 1824, hugely important to industry and scrutinized and tested before the Privy Council. From 1820 Newton edited the *London Journal of Arts and Sciences*, and for 14 years reported all patented inventions from first-hand inspection of rolls in the enrolment office. Newton and his journal became very important in improving the application of British mechanical drawing to patenting. A busy traveller round the Northern and Midlands industrial areas, Newton became especially a friend and advisor to the lace inventor John Heathcoat and 'ultimately the professional adviser of the whole of the lace manufacturers', and eventually branched out into tours of Europe on patent business.[4] In 1837 Newton was elected Associate of the Institute of Civil Engineers, and continued developing wider scientific interests. A great advocate of patent reform (we might instance the 1829 enquiry, and the 1836 pamphlet for an amendment), he lobbied for a special patent court to replace the confused complexity surrounding the Courts of Queen's Bench, the Exchequer and Common Pleas, to be paid for through the sales of patent literature 'in the chief manufacturing towns'.[5] Newton inherited a seemingly complete disregard for money and died in modest circumstances in 1861. Here there is strong parallel with Alexander Parkes of Birmingham (below) but also similarity with many other agents of technological progress.

William Newton's history seems to point to several characteristics of agency prior to reform. First it relied upon an urban network of association and information diffusion, one which strengthened considerably during the early nineteenth century. Second, active agency embraced a great deal of business lying beyond the formal institution of the patent system, including its vital advertising, informational and legal aspects. Thirdly, however tenuously, a few individuals were beginning to earn something of a living as ancillary agents of significant inventive efforts. Our study of Birmingham below further illustrates such points and how the connectivities between actual sites continually disturbed the supposed workings of national patent systems.

Long before reform was being planned, many patentees were very active in industrial civic life – as with Henry Clay of Birmingham (below).[6] As to the importance of urban associations in forging agency, beyond the city mechanics' institutes lay local artisan clubs and lecture societies that boasted huge memberships, and these proliferated throughout the English and British provinces.[7] To which should be added the travelling lecturers, giving substantial courses on practical and theoretical mechanics, replete with models and replicas and demonstrations, and including such men as Henry Adcock, Charles Sylvester, John Stancliffe, William Lester and Robert Addams, all of whom were successful patentees. Several inventive engineers sparkled as intellectual entrepreneurs within the urban culture, exemplary among them being John F. Daniell of Kings College, London, managing director of the Continental Gas Co., author of a great array of scientific publications, three times medallist of the Royal Society and a frequent patentee.[8] In its Civil Engineering Department, Putney College ran lecture courses delivered by scientists such as Edward Frankland (1825–99) and David Thomas Ansted (1814–80), but also lectures and classes in civil engineering, architecture and machinery from such professional or multi-patentees as Samuel Clegg (1800s–1840s on rotative engines, gas meters, valves), or J. V. Binns (woodworking).[9] Similarly, the Surveying and Engineering College set up on Russell Square by the patentee engineering partnership and firm of Hyde, Smith and Lewis, ran four distinct branches in Railway Surveying, Land and Estate Surveying, Engineering Surveying and Architectural and Machine Drawing at 10 guineas for each branch. The lessons on surveying, architecture and engineering run by the same partnership at one guinea were delivered under the auspices of University College, London, during the lecture courses there of Professor Harman Lewis, subscription £9.[10] Generally, we might note that patentees were very active in metropolitan scientific associations, such as the City of London Literary and Scientific Institution, established in 1825, whose officers and lecturers were drawn from among the innovating engineers.[11] This applies seemingly to even small groups such as the Kentish-Town Literary Institute's lectures on Philosophy Applied to Everyday Life, delivered by the patentee electrical engineer C. J. Varley (1781–1873), an instrument maker who demonstrated much in the way of electrical experimentation in his public courses.[12]

As a class the agents of the early nineteenth century demonstrated similar characteristics. Newton and Sons already published their own regular indexes to patents from the early 1840s, and pamphlets on how to patent from their office for patents in Chancery Lane.[13] M. Joselin Cooke, of the Office for Patents of Invention and Registry of Designs, 20 Half Moon St, Piccadilly, was boasting the obtaining of British and foreign patents, offering prizes for the best patents and designs taken out from his office, including a gold medal plus £100 and silver medals plus £50.[14] Patentees who could manufacture any excuse for widespread publicity, did so with alacrity. Thus in 1808 G. L. Needham advertised a range of his 'new inventions and improvements on their way to the Society for the Encouragement of Arts, Manufactures and Commerce, London' in handbills and newspapers as he travelled south, and in Nottingham offered exhibitions from 10–1 pm and from 2–8 pm at the corner of Church-Lane and Low Pavement showing a range of carding machinery, drawing frames, spinning machines and models of his improved steam engine illustrative of the process of feeding steam into the smoke flue to increase efficiency. Added to such unrelentingly masculine appeal was one to both ladies and gentlemen at 1/- per head to see all this plus his glass ropes for ladies headdresses.[15] Others, such as Alexander Prince puffed and blew through advertising his Office of Patents of Invention, at 14 Lincoln's Inn Fields as if it were the national centre for inventive activity.[16] In turn, a patentee like Charles Holtzapffel A.I.C.E. (1806–47) used publications, such as his 6-volume *Turning and Mechanical Manipulation*, which was devoted to very detailed machinofacture descriptions of materials, cutting tools, grinding and polishing and so on, to mark his expertise and reliability as an inventor and manufacturer.[17] G. T. Day, patentee of what he termed his 'archimedian ventilator', delivered public lectures on the ventilation and warming of public buildings, mines etc., as advertisement to his patent ventilation manufacturing works in Pimlico.[18] Similarly, tin plate worker Dederick Smith of 17 Gerrard St, London lectured publicly on gas lighting and thereby advertised his manufacture of all sorts of tin work and his newly invented carriage lanterns, reflectors, phosphoric matches and so on.[19] Robert J. Longbottom, patentee and secretary, lecturer and exhibitor to the Royal Polytechnic Institute, advertised and utilized new instruments constructed by W. C. Collins based at the RPI. By the 1840s, a commonality of press adverts saw patentees selling inventions and engaged in impressive entrepreneurship; new companies based almost entirely on new patents included civil engineering, salvage and gas lighting.[20]

Agency and technological journalism went hand in hand, a good example being the *Practical Mechanic's Journal* of the 1840s, published by the agent and consultant engineer William Johnson from his offices in Buchanan Street, Glasgow, which contained complete lists of all British and abstracts of many foreign patents and patentees, notes of scientific and technical associations and essays and printed lecture courses on physical sciences, chemistry, mechanics and mathematics, as well as numerous letters, news and notes from the diaries and notebooks of practising artisans and engineers. Similarly, the *Artizan* in London, at 1/- per issue was filled with engine engravings, plans of utilities, government enquiries in civil engineering, steam boilers, colliery explosions, the manufacture of sugar and other staples, patents and registrations and was published by Mathew Soul at the *Artizan* office, 69 Cornhill, from which also emerged the *Mechanical Gazette* that provided a register of all machinery and plant for sale, new patents and articles on them and organized a Great Exhibition Mutual Insurance Fund for Exhibitors in 1851. Articles were written commonly by such patentees as Robert Armstrong (1830s water-pressure engines), W. B. Adams (1830s–1850s on wheel-carriages), the Swansea civil engineer W. P. Struve (1840s ventilating mines and railway systems) or Frederick Grace Calvert (1840s and 1850s textile dyeing; also looms patented in partnership with Samuel Clegg 1851, see above) whose papers concerned bleaching cotton and flax.[21] Such journals were joined by a flourish of periodicals devoted almost exclusively to the world of patent agency, including the *Patent Journal and Inventors Magazine* at 6d issued from the patent office of Barlow, Payne and Parker, Chancery Lane, *The Practical Mechanics Journal* at 1/-, *The Repertory of Patent Inventions* at 3/- (begun way back in 1794 and including copious law reports), and the *Chemist*, which reported on all chemical patenting. A patentee activist such as the civil engineer John Bourne was well placed to develop an agency role as a leading member of the Artizan Club linked to the *Artizan* and author of *A Treatise on the Steam Engine and its Applications*, published by the Club and in its third edit at 27/- by 1851.[22]

Major journals of patent agency were fully engaged in reforming the institution itself. Thus William Johnson of the *Practical Mechanics' Journal* during 1849–50, reported the Lords Commissioners of the Treasury Report on the patent system and reform and went on to argue that much fault was to be found with the system but found little in the way of expert suggestions for change. He argued that presently lawyers were in no position to evaluate the 'very minute scientific or mechanical detail' involved in most cases, and supported the notion that all petitioners should provide a formal description, which would reduce fraud. He was against the planned reduction of patent fees to around £50 from the approximate £300 then in force, as this might 'encumber manufacturers by the number of patents so much, that it would be scarcely possible for them to make the slightest modification in their machinery or system, without interfering with some patent right'. For Johnson a more proper solution to this was to increase the stringency of examination, criteria for novelty and so on. Against such editorializing, a letter of Alfred Savage, a machinist of Cheapside, London argued that the prevailing least-cost patent of around £130 was beyond the means of the majority of inventors, this meaning that much useful invention was not registered or recorded. For Savage the obvious answer was to introduce a copyright of scientific designs as for books, which would be much cheaper, for 'as we all pay our share of the expenses of police and civil government, we are morally entitled to have our property protected, whether the property is in the form of inventions, or of the wealth produced by the use of inventions'.[23]

Agency at times emerged from engineering partnership, as in the case of George Hood, who worked with the scientist, civil engineer and inventor Charles Sylvester to develop a commercial exploitation of Sylvester's findings. The most financially lucrative of Sylvester's discoveries was possibly that of the galvanic covering of zinc on copper or other metals, and this was not exploited directly by Sylvester, but by agents and partners. Although Charles Hobson of Sheffield was certainly acting as patentee-manufacturer of malleable zinc in that town during late 1808,[24] so too was there a formal partnership between Sylvester and George Hood of Derby, only dissolved in November 1809.[25] Estimating Sylvester's exact business role is extremely difficult. In the first case, Sylvester does not seem to have been especially involved, commercial production being left to Charles Hobson, who entered business at the top of Pond Lane, Sheffield, producing malleable zinc primarily for covering copper and lead. However, the fact that Sylvester was independently advertising the properties of malleable zinc as late as 1809 suggests that some form of financial association remained.[26] Until that time also, the firm 'Silvester and Hood, Manufactures of Zinc' traded actively, but from that year George Hood continued on his own account. Hood, who retained his business as a plumber, glazier and general patent agent throughout this period[27] was a fellow member of the Derby Philosophical Society and an early supporter of the Derby Mechanics' Institute at a later time.[28] Thus patenting partnership and intellectual association worked together in this sort of enterprise to encourage the emergence of more formal agency work.

Scientific work and entrepreneurship was intimately linked to agency development in these early years. Amid a large correspondence of Macvey Napier in the early years of the century concerning his editorship of the supplement to the fifth edition of the *Encyclopaedia Brittanica*, the engineer John Farey wrote in February 1814 that he was kept perpetually busy by patent cases, and particularly as more than anyone else he was now engaged in 'research into the history, practice and theory of mechanical inventions, for the assistance of inventors who wish to procure patents', and for five years or so he had been 'greatly engaged' in giving advice to patentees and inventors, and been paid 'liberally by his employers to do so'.[29]

Hardly surprisingly from this sort of background, the agency of academics was enrolled in order to exploit patents commercially. A good example of this was the promotion of the Irish Peat Company formed to exploit the technologies of the chemist Rees Reece in 1851 at a capital of £120,000 formed of 6,000 shares at £20 each. The key patent processed peat to yield commercially competitive volumes of sulphate of ammonia, acetate of lime, volatile oils and naptha and this was all publicly demonstrated (presumably at fee) by Dr John Frederick Hodges (1815–99), the Professor of Agriculture at Queen's College, Belfast and by Prof William Thomas Brande (1788–1866) in his lectures at the Royal Institution, London on 31 January 1851. The tar bi-product of the process was projected to go to Caffey and Sons of the Bromley works 'who have determined the paraffin contents'. The Prospectus of the company aimed at potential shareholders was sold alongside Brande's lecture at offices in the Old Jewry Chambers.[30] Similarly, the proposed Cambrian Copper Company planned smelting of copper ores, 'upon an improved principle for which a patent has been obtained', raising a capital of £100,000 from £100 shares. The boast was that this company was different from any other scheme being both thoroughly practical, and 'quite unlike any previous in being properly scientific'. Where previous 'patent plans' have been 'the medium of delusion and improvident speculation', those of the CCC were 'tried on a practical scale ... while it has received the unqualified approbation of the intelligent and the scientific, its principles are sufficiently plain, and its superiority so obvious, as only to require a short explanation to enable almost any person to discern and appreciate them'.[31] In this sort of case, where does some sort of effective patent agency start and stop? It is certainly noteworthy that both the academic proponents were very much in the public eye well beyond the confines of their official positions – Hodges was a major founder and activist in the Royal College of Chemistry in London from 1839, Brande had risen from humble apprentice apothecary to FRS, chief officer to the coinage department of the Mint, joint editor of the *Quarterly Journal of Science* and member of the Senate of London University. These were neither quiet nor slothful folk.

As we suggested in the introduction to this collection, agency became greater assured, refined and identified in cases of patent litigation, especially in industries such as cotton, lace and engineering where the veracity and provenance of many very competitive patented incremental advancements were challenged in the courts. Thus the two foremost agents before 1851, William Newton (above) and A. Carpmael were closely involved in the important case of 1841 concerning the status of Samuel Draper's 1835 patent for the application of perforated substances to lace machinery which was a product of both an extensive experimental partnership with John Hind and the Scottish linen manufacturer Andrew Wilkie in Nottingham as well as the extensive agency advice of Carpmael.[32] The 1841–2 case was a legal challenge by Hooton Deverill resulting for his own 1841 patent, which he claimed as the first successful application of the Jacquard apparatus to bobbin net. What is notable is the expert stance taken by both agents, Carpmael in particular quoting a number of related patents from the mid-1830s, which he argued were together distinct from the Draper breakthrough. Quoting several previous cases he argued that using Jacquard in the Deverill manner would be an infringement. In turn, Newton used similar expertise and case studies, particularly drawing from the use of Dawson's wheels and the chime barrel, etc., and focusing on the legal distinction between intention and actual mechanism to show that novelty must lie only in the exact 'means of applying that old contrivance', and that this was insufficiently explicated in the Draper patent. For him, then it followed that 'according to my views of the patent laws, and the practice of the courts, that all other modes, forms, and combinations of mechanism for connecting the principles of a Jacquard with a bobbin lace machine, are open to the inventive world to modify and adapt as they please'.[33] Newton's judgement prevailed.

A final mode by which agency became formalized and better assured was through mutual association. Thus the Inventors Aid Association of Beauford Buildings, the Strand was established with a large capital of some £50,000 and a managing committee including such frequent patentees as the civil engineer Frederick Braithwaite, the chemist Richard Coad (a series 1835–48) and the chemical manufacturer Charles Watt (1818–51) and his son John Watt of the Bolingbroke Works, Surrey and editor of the *Chemist*.[34] In a real sense the 1851 Exhibition itself promoted mutual association and a new agency. Thus William Murray and Co., civil and mechanical engineers of the Adelphi offered their engineering services to exhibitors and patentees, erecting and maintaining constructions, negotiating sales on inventions, constructing models 'before being made public or prior to patenting'.[35] Again, patentees and patent agents Phillip Le Capelain and Joseph Steele, from their patent agency on Chancery Lane, were well placed to assist patentees and inventors 'as to sale, and their obtaining the assistance of capitalists'.[36]

In 1847 the engineer William Spence was warning that patent specifications must be proof against both 'persons of ability, science and learning' and 'men intimately acquainted with the manufacture, but totally unskilled in science, or learning'.[37] From thence, with the more technical requirement demanded by the reformed patent system in Britain after 1851, the two attributes were to be increasingly combined in patent agencies. The problem for judges was that scientific evidence came usually from 'depositions of opinions from persons who have received *ex parte* instructions' and was thus liable to serious defect.[38] Even in the case of the comparatively simple criterion of previous knowledge of the patent in determining its acceptance, expert questions arose as to whether this was to be by previous specifications, by books or by folklore. In the case of Wood versus Zimner this prompted the exclamation of Lord Chief Justice Gibbs that 'some inventions almost baffle discovery'. Immediately after the patent reform of 1851–2 it was claimed that the new legislation alleviated the financial burden on the artisan of securing provisional protection, but in the absence of informed decisions there was still little facility for enforcing patent rights. A relatively minor failure in specifying the chemical process at work led to the House of Lords allowing an infringement on Heath's important patent for manufacture of steel.[39] Information and rights went hand in hand. Arguing that the legal mind 'is altogether at fault in following an inference in mechanics or chemistry, or detecting and exposing a sophistry therein', the agent William Newton lobbied for a special patent court to replace the confused complexity surrounding the Courts of Queen's Bench, the Exchequer and Common Pleas, to be paid for through the sales of patent literature 'in the chief manufacturing towns'.[40] This was not so very fanciful – the annual cost of printing specifications had reached £30,000 by the early 1850s.

CUNNING ARTIFICERS: URBAN SITES AND AGENCIES IN BIRMINGHAM PRIOR TO 1851

It has been all too often claimed that London was the greatest inducting city known to Europe, swallowing skilled immigrants by spawning civic places, shortening the avenues of their social acceptance and multiplying the marks of their commercial success, creating thereby a great emporium of fresh initiatives. But the English provinces proved to be even greater assets to industrializing Britain. William Hutton recalled entering Birmingham for the first time as a young worker way back in 1741, where townsfolk possessed 'a vivacity I have never beheld; I had been among dreamers but now I saw men awake. Their very step along the street showed alacrity: every man seemed to know and prosecute his own affairs: the town was large, and full of inhabitants and those inhabitants full of industry'.[41]

At the time that the young Hutton entered, bewildered, into Birmingham, the town already offered a range of evening schools and associations that were providing discussions or basic instruction in natural and experimental philosophy and their applications in arts and crafts, as prime movers, and in a range of manufactures.[42] But the provision of useful knowledge was not to be left to the designated teachers. From the early years of the great industrial century, local manufacturers and workshop owners were producing works designed to bring useful knowledge to the operative mechanics upon whom they depended for accurate and reliable work. Thus Robert Brunton of Horsley Iron Works just outside Birmingham, who regarded himself as 'one of their number' had the intention of providing a text book for operatives during a period of 'the rapid advance of knowledge among Mechanics, and the many excellent opportunities they now have for its attainment', for the time was at hand 'when Mechanics shall not only be acknowledged cunning artificers, but men of science: when the word Mechanic shall convey the idea of wisdom and understanding, – and the profession, highly fraught with good to man, shall be honoured and respected.'[43]

There can be little doubt of the manner in which this artisanal culture forged the distinctive character of the urban patent agency as the town grew; by the beginning of the century physical and experimental science, mechanics and practical engineering were allied to trade concerns in major forums for discussion and experiment. From an early stage Birmingham associations included those designed specifically for technical innovation, this particularly associated with the progressive movements of the 1790s formed around such major national issues as the abolition of the African slave trade or the Repeal of the Test and Corporation Acts.[44] As one local commentator wrote in 1791, 'the dissenting system in all its parts is highly favorable to democracy. It is a body animated by a democratic soul'.[45] The soul was nurtured in such forums as the Birmingham Society for Free Debate on Temple Row or the Birmingham Liberal Society at the Shakespeare Tavern.[46] The secretary and spirit of the latter association was James Bisset (1762–1832), artist and art worker and publisher. This new, reformist urbanity spawned evening schools, libraries and lecture courses, including those of John Warltire in 1789, whose 12 evening lectures at the Assembly Rooms included 'Philosophical, Mathematical and Mechanical Recreations' at 1/- the course.[47] Philosophy for the artisan happily entered the pub; Warltire's more specialized course on Philosophical and Chemical Subjects two months later was hosted at the Coffee Pot Tavern, Cherry Street, and demand was such that they were repeated at the same more modest venue a few weeks later.[48] Later in the same year James Burton repeated earlier visits to Birmingham with his course in Natural and Experimental Philosophy (physics and chemistry) delivered from the Shakespeare Tavern, which was also a venue of the republican Constitutional Society of Birmingham from 1789.[49]

Here was a precise locus or symbol of the urban complex of rational religion, radicalism and philosophy, but within the precincts of the artisan. Joseph Priestley's (1733–1804) published works, ranging from his *Defence of Unitarianism* and his *General History of the Christian Church* to his *Experiments and Observations on Different Kinds of Air* were being advertised in the local press and by handbills just at the same time as it was planned that he address a public meeting to commemorate the fall of the Bastille at a dinner of the Constitutional Society of Birmingham at the Shakespeare Tavern in July 1791. A crowd that had assembled to attack his guests became a riot which destroyed his house at Fairhill and his laboratory and library. It seems that many of the 'church and king' urbanites of Birmingham already felt left behind by the progressive sites, which had been formed in local taverns and pubs as well as coffee houses and assembly rooms, that linked a new world of useful and reliable knowledge with artisan skills, intersecting with radical social alternatives and fast-moving money makers. Such congeries and sites deserve far more acknowledgement in the writing of the urban and industrial history of industrializing Britain.[50]

Not only were a huge number of cheap publications on the arts and trades being sold in town, local artisans such as W. Richardson were writing them and distributing them through local booksellers and news-agencies. Richardson's *Chemical Principles of the Metallurgical Arts*, also sold from his house on Newton Street, covered gilding and silvering and the preparing of Prussian Blue dye, and was designed specifically for 'manufacturers'. Cheap translations of Euro-wide compilations, dictionaries, trade books and encyclopaedias carried useful industrial and chemical knowledge directly in to the artisanal heart of the town. At the local agent and bookseller Thomas Pearson's could be found 1/- and 2/- translations from the German of special editions of Crell's *Chemical Journal*, in which might be found very recent patented breakthroughs and demonstrations by Karl Wilhelm Scheele and Martin Heinrich Klaproth in chemistry, Thomas Beddoes in metallurgy or James Watt's experiments on madder,[51] as well as advance notices of coming local events such as the lectures on Experimental Philosophy (chemistry) of John Banks, who could demand a minimum of 50 persons in his audiences prior to his arrival, and whose successes prompted repeated deliveries in large venues such as the New Public Rooms at the bottom of Cannon Street as well as at local pubs.[52] Among all this the artisan inventors were traveling out from the town to any part of the country to give assistance in setting up new workshops, others were threatened with imprisonment for assisting Jacobin revolutionaries by supplying them with weapons – thus the 20,000 daggers supposedly supplied to the Jacobin cause in London by a Birmingham producer![53]

The more gentlemanly clubs of the later eighteenth century, epitomized by the famous and oft-quoted Lunar Society (1775–98), had by the 1820s given way to a culture of urban technical association increasingly dominated by patenting.[54] So the Birmingham Philosophical Society founded in 1800 by a group including James Watt, focused on lectures in 'mechanism, chemistry, mineralogy and metallurgy', which by 1818 had 'contributed in a considerable degree to the improvement of gilding, plating, bronzing, vitrification and metallic combination', while the contemporary Physiolectical Society had been founded in 1803 'for the purpose of improving its members in natural philosophy by lecture, experiment and discussion'.[55] Prior to the Great Exhibition in London in 1851 the Birmingham Institution and the Birmingham Polytechnic Institution boasted memberships of over 600 persons.[56] Active members of the Birmingham Philosophical Institution, which had been founded in 1803, included such leading patentees and innovative industrialists as George Parsons, J. F. Ledsam, A. Follet Osler, Arthur Ryland, Joseph Wickedden, James Timmins Chance, John Percy MD and George Frederick Muntze, several of whom delivered classes and lectures before the mainly artisan membership. Charles Dickens for one visualzsed the Birmingham Polytechnic of the 1840s as working for artisans on 'the principle of comprehensive education'.[57] The associational culture that forged together patent agency and useful and reliable knowledge was to become the hallmark of Birmingham as an inventors emporium.

Within all this the innovating, upwardly mobile artisan dominated. The capture and ownership of technological knowledge was becoming essential to small business formation and success; the industrial revolution in Birmingham was forged more out of this institutionalized formation of *human* capital than out of the earlier Marxist conception of original accumulation of fixed capital. Even as early as the 1780s Birmingham's new wealth creation seemed to be emerging from resources of personality rather than inherited mercantile or landed capital. When Hutton calculated the wealth of the richest 209 men of the town around 1783, ranging from 96 persons with over £5,000 to 3 persons with over £100,000, he reported that 71 had significant wealth to begin with, 35 had possessed small fortunes, but 103 had arisen by their own initiative.[58] Where in the great factories, warehouses and banks of the Liverpool and Manchester merchants and manufacturers huge fortunes changed hands and determined the rate of commercial progress, in cities such as Birmingham or Sheffield, small capitals were enough to continue efficient domination of a host of trades right through the century, and a secure income was best insured through innovation, an accumulation of technological skills and workshop assets as human capital, and upward social mobility. From the late eighteenth century local plating manufacturers were now expecting that their apprentices would pay a 'genteel Premium' for that privilege and bring with them basic skills of literacy and accounting.[59] In Birmingham, and through inventiveness alone, men such as

Henry Clay or William Whitemore moved from journeymen status to ownership of their own engineering firms, Edward Thomason passed from the trade of button-maker to the position of large manufacturer and many others moved upward from journeyman status to become engineers, brass and iron founders and merchants.[60] Such movements of men changed the political soul of the town – Henry Clay's 1772 patent for *papier mache* made his fortune as a manufacturer and in 1790 he became High Sheriff of Warwickshire, by which time he was employing 300 hands at a huge personal profit.

Such patents as that of Henry Clay were a good way to capture technology and to mark an act of innovation and business acumen. The annual average of Birmingham patenting during the 1770s to 1800s was relatively low, but then doubled in the 1811–30 period, doubled again during the 1830s, and had by the 1840s reached 13 times the levels of the late eighteenth century.[61] In those later eighteenth century years such local patentees as the iron masters Richard Jesson, Richard Dearman, Jonathon Taylor, William Bell and John Wright, or the brass-founders Thomas Whitehurst, John Ashton and John Marston, had registered a series of innovations in casting metals, rolling iron from pig, and stamping plated metals that together represented a significant chain of technical improvement in the locality. By the 1790s Birmingham easily outranked Manchester, Sheffield or Newcastle in the number of patent lodgments per capita. Few of the Birmingham patentees registered themselves as engineers, the exceptions being the great James Watt (1784, steam engines) and Matthew Boulton (1791, press), and William Whitmore (1792, mashing machinery). At this time the majority of Birmingham patentees were tool makers, brass founders, iron founders and manufacturers, or were small masters in buckle and button making or japanning, and this pattern was not much disturbed into the 1830s. Increasingly, groups of patentees were drawn from surrounding areas of the town – West Bromwich, Islington, Edgbaston, Ashted, Smethwick and Winston.[62] Metal-based invention had itself become an industry.

In Birmingham, urban development resulted largely from the evolution of a system of machinofacture that was to spread throughout industrializing Europe during the rest of the century. It becomes clear that group of industries centring on the working of metal by machinery, dominated the industrial world of the late 1830s and beyond, and thus the huge diversity of final products which emerged was dependent upon a relatively small number of universal operations – turning, dieing, boring, drilling, milling, planing and polishing. A relatively small number of machines rather than men could perform these functions once a common group of technical problems associated with power transmission, control, feed mechanisms and friction reduction had been resolved or reduced. It was the machine tool manufacturers who, in essence, did 'normal technology', that is solved the day-to-day puzzles involved in improving the machinofacture operations of cutting, planing, boring and shaping of metal parts. This was at the very heart of the indigenous technological system. The incremental improvements in these processes, gadgets and machines were at the hub of technical enquiry in Birmingham workshops and the basis of the national patent system in the years from around 1830, both of which accelerated in the later part of the century.

There is every reason to emphasize the importance to global technological change of the years approximately 1830–50.[63] Of total British patentees for these two decades, some 37 per cent were from skilled trades, 25 per cent were self-styled engineers, 22 per cent were self-styled gentlemen and esquires, with another 10 per cent as mostly small- and medium-scale manufacturers. In the six major industrial counties of the north and midlands, where patenting was very intensive, 40 per cent of patentees were tradesmen and artisans, some 28 per cent were engineers, 18 per cent manufacturers and 10 per cent were classified as gents. So in this period the social distribution of innovators varied significantly between regions, and we might suggest that in industrial areas such variation related mainly to the transitions involved between individuals as they moved from tradesman to manufacturer status, as in Birmingham, where 26 per cent of patentees were manufacturers.[64] In such places as Manchester, engineers emerged from the trades, and shared many of the same apprenticeship experiences, associations and street cultures as did the artisans.

In the unreformed patent system prior to 1852, Birmingham was second only to London in total patenting activity, falling behind Manchester to third place between 1852 and 1881. However, in per capita terms after 1852, Birmingham yet ranked ahead of both London and Manchester. We might judge that Birmingham was a leading centre of innovation throughout the period in which a more formalized engineering emerged as a predominant source of technical change. In Birmingham, where artisan invention was of especial importance during the 1830s and 1840s, so too was there a disproportionate emphasis on small metal product improvements – 43 per cent of patents in those two decades related to advances in design, materials or use of equipment of such items as decanters and other glassware, firearms, lamps and gas-burners, woodworking and furniture making, inkstands and ornamental items. It was the generally skilled Birmingham engineers who were more likely to be taking out patents in actual machine processes – from improvements in steam engine manufacture and steam locomotion (John Jones, Henry Davies, Charles Heard Wild, the Soho Company, Emanuel Wharton, Isaiah Davies, Thomas Edwards, Thomas Craddock, George Heaton, William Baker, Charles William Siemens, Samuel Fisher) to pipe and tube manufacture, thrashing machinery, fire proofing and printing, to bolt building, metal shaping and cutting, shearing and punching, gilding and plating, manufacture and working of metallic alloys and improvements in planes and metal surfaces. Several such patentees were using a general engineering expertise across a field of activities, a good example being Henry Adcock of Summer Hill Terrace, Birmingham, variously a toy manufacturer, engineer, and traveling lecturer on physics and mechanics, who brought out a varied series of patents between 1824 and 1851.[65] Those engineers who were more concerned with products such as pipe manufacture, cooking apparatus, needle manufacture or clothing were now themselves moving into the manufacturer category, a good example being the civil engineer Richard Prosser who brought out a series of varied product innovations and had established his Birmingham Patent Iron Tube Co. at Smethwick near Birmingham by 1851.

A major feature of Birmingham was the very large number of its art products and trades, which over the next years were to produce much of the British style of arts and crafts and *art nouveau*.[66] From the earlier years of the century, artisan creativity and manufacturing ingenuity had coexisted in a wonderful enterprise of patented inventions, making the town one of the leading centres in Europe for new art technologies. The early years of the century saw fortunes made in the patenting of hitherto traditionally crafted goods. Thus the fall of gilt and metal button makers after 1825 may be related to the patent of B. Sanders Jr. for a flexible shank cotton or silk button, manufactured at huge profit. This was offered another boost in 1837 with William Elliott's patent for fancy silk buttons – at one time production under that patent alone employed 60 looms in London to provide Birmingham with the necessary cloth for it. In an area such as ornamental work, patented advances were having striking impacts. Through Thomas Horne's ornamental stamping and cornice manufacturing patent of 1844 many existing manufactures and craftsmen were forced to acknowledge his rights and to pay huge royalties – during the period of his patent the inventor himself made some 16,000 pairs of Cornice ends – but in particular, the Birmingham electricians engaged in electrolysis, using metallic deposits to provide a great range of hitherto expensively crafted goods. Henry and G. R. Elkington were from 1838 depositing gold and silver on ornaments made of other metals.[67]

At mid-century Birmingham was home to some 500 separate skilled trade categories, providing a living for thousands of middling families, whose lives depended upon the imaginative application of their skills in metal, leather, wood and textiles. But while such a large community was composed very much of the artisans of the labour aristocracy it gave employment to a host of shopkeepers on one hand, surgeons and the lower professionals on the other. Because of this the scientific and technical culture of the city was spread across a wide social level, pluralist though sexist in its composition, but an epitome of the new modernity of the industrial revolution. Although this was bound to be a city of strife and conflict, the competing interests of the working classes and aggressive capitalist employers was not so marked as in factory-based cities such as Leeds or Newcastle, and was not so dramatically polarized during the 1840s as to prohibit cultural association and competition across almost the entire range of the urban society. So in his famous comparative study, Asa Briggs demonstrated that the large reforming Birmingham Political Union was not monopolized by radical commercial interests as in other cities, but rather represented a 'political consciousness in radical causes' stretching across simple class lines.[68] Despite the absorption of many such small shops in amalgamations during the 1850s and 1860s, a leading patentee-manufacturer of the town could naturally comment in 1866 on how the town's social and political freedoms were extreme because 'the large number of small manufacturers are practically independent of the numerous factors and merchants they supply . . . in no town in England is comfort more common, or wealth more equally diffused'.[69] It was within this context that a vibrant culture of innovation continued to evolve as a multitude of urban agencies.

There seems to be good qualitative evidence that the rise of innovation in Birmingham was strongly associated with increased facilities for knowledge circulation and testing, and for basic technological training, which went well beyond our familiar distinctions between the tacit knowledge of apprenticeship and the trades on one hand, and a higher scientific training on the other. Between such extremes lay an urban culture of information circulation that was constantly tested and reformulated by a competitive culture of innovation pursued by those intent on rising 'above the Lathe and File' within one of the most intensive patenting cities in the world. Prior to 1851 this was the environ of patent agency. And this was itself a component of a wide process of machinofacture.

Birmingham was clearly an earnest and energetic place, which by the 1860s would have disturbed a young William Hutton much more than in the early eighteenth century. Artisans were now bustling everywhere, but they did not undertake their innovations as a plot against the world, new patents were not seen as 'colonial' or expansive by their originators, but were in fact very much viewed within a perspective of immediate urban survival. Furthermore, the high technology that emerged was clearly not any direct result of learned English university experimentation or of government interference or funding within Britain. Elite Britain had no impress on urban Birmingham. We would claim the contrary. The culture of machinofacture was absolutely inherent within the social processes of British industrialization and involved subtle informal linkages with many productive sites in Europe (see below). Through such networks knowledge and intellect were brought to bear on technique in a myriad of ways. Of course, elite bureaucracy and colonial technocrats, experts in diplomacy, foreign languages and commercial stealth, would soon enough take ownership of the expansion and application of such technologies during the following years, those of what is now often called the Second Industrial Revolution.

URBAN SITE AND AGENCY: ALEXANDER PARKES, BIRMINGHAM AND THE WORLD

So, where does agency begin and where does it end? Informed colleagues or competitors who provide expertise, information or experience, those who are paid to publicize or guide, are most clearly agents. But in the years prior to a greater formalization of the patent systems, all supports within micro-sites of inventive activity are surely at least candidates for inclusion? This appears as a reasonable generalization but only detailed case studies can serve to define terms and boundaries. Peering within the climes of Birmingham at one site of invention may exemplify the historical complexities.

Alexander Parkes was born in Suffolk Street, Birmingham, the son of a brass lock manufacturer, so was from the beginning of his life embedded quite precisely in the urban artisanal machinofacture described above. Samuel Harrison, hailed by Sir Josiah Mason as the inventor of the split-ring (or key-ring) and widely credited with the invention of the steel pen, was his great-uncle. Parkes' younger brother Henry (1824–1909), a trained chemist, assisted him in many of his experiments during a collaboration lasting more than 50 years. During the 1840s Henry was trained as an experimental chemist under August W. Hofmann (1818–92, FRS) the brilliant German organic chemist, who had earlier delivered quite dramatic lectures on a tour of England and become Professor of Chemistry at the Royal College of Chemistry in London, a novel and expensive British centre combining training and experimental laboratory work and geared to original research.[70] Hofmann at that time was patenting applied advances in chemistry – such as his method for preparing aniline dye from benzene in 1845 – and there can be little doubt that in the partnership between Alexander and Henry Parkes, the latter would have brought greater experimental rigour to the patenting projects from the very beginning.

His *Dictionary of National Biography* entry labels Alexander Parkes as chemist and inventor and divides his many patents (at least 80 in all) into the long series related to the deposition of metals by electricity, the method of using zinc for the desiliverization of lead in 1850 and the inventions after that leading to the discovery and application of celluloid to industrial uses. His own description of his early life shows him as a busy tinkerer, working from home on kites, fireworks, kaleidoscopes and designs for ornaments and fabrics. He also assisted his father in his workshop, showing talent for the understanding and repair of complex locks and gadgets. Not unexpectedly he was apprenticed locally as an art metal worker to a firm of brass founders, Messenger and Company, where he learnt the arts of casting from models in plaster, wax, sulphur and metals, becoming expert during his apprenticeship in drawing, painting, woodcarving and modelling.

After serving his articles Parkes became the head of the casting department of Elkington Mason and Company, who had just at that time begun the development of electroplating. This was a typical Birmingham enterprise, its core being the technological partnership of the cousins George Richard Elkington (1801–65) and Henry Elkington (1810–52), whose series of patented inventions earned the company some real comparative advantage in a highly competitive environment. These two effectively founded the industries of electroplating and electrogilding in Britain on technically viable grounds, at first using a traditional voltaic pile of the late eighteenth-century type. So, the move to Elkingtons immediately transferred Parkes into Birmingham's high-tech, especially as directed towards design and art products.

From the turn of the century major natural philosophers turned applied scientists such as William Hyde Wollaston (1766–1828), a Fellow of the Royal Society from 1793, had taken to metallurgical applications of electricity. Indeed, as soon as Wollaston switched from medicine to chemistry during 1801–4 he alighted on the electrical deposition of metals, using the new process for producing pure platinum and welding it into vessels usable for experimentation, out of which he had made a fortune of £7,000 by 1815.[71] During the 1830s a group of practical electricians in Birmingham independently revived this early work, especially revolving around the use of John Frederic Daniell's (1790–1845, FRS) newly developed constant battery of 1836, invented during his tenure as Professor of Chemistry at King's College, London, and the patent of 1842 of John Stephen Woolrich of Birmingham, which developed the use of the dynamo. This latter is of direct concern to us as it fixed the character of the high-tech site in which Parkes was to operate from then on.

The Russian, Moritz Hermann von Jacobi is properly identified as the initial discoverer of electroplating as a chemical process in 1837, but with the Swiss obtaining the first patent for manufacture. It was this patent that was in turn licensed to John Wright of Birmingham in 1840, and so he can be named the first really practical electroplater in England. His early activity suffered as he obtained his charge from the old-style voltaic piles. However, in 1842 Woolrich obtained his patent for electroplating using a magneto-electrical generator while he was employed as Professor of Chemistry to the Royal School of Medicine at Birmingham. Its design was clearly based on the theory of electromagnetic induction which had been developed in 1831 by Michael Faraday (1791–1867), the result of an experimental programme in the laboratory of the Royal Institution in London that had begun as early as 1812.[72] In the 1830s Woolrich had patented a series of discoveries from Birmingham in industrial chemistry, including the production of carbonate of baryta (barium hydroxide) and an improved process for manufacturing carbonate of lead (white lead), but in 1840 he started in the town a small works for making magneto-electric machines or dynamos, and showed how the current from these could be employed for the electro-deposition of silver.[73] In 1908 Kershaw could claim that this was 'in fact, the commencement of the large and important electro-plating industry, which now flourishes in the midland city'.[74] In 1844, Thomas Prime & Son, another Birmingham firm of electroplaters, made the patented machine to Woolrich's design, although some working details differed considerably from his patent of 1842. The generator was powered by steam, and it appears that this was the one used by the Elkingtons to electroplate on a commercially viable basis; they immediately adopted it to fabricate a huge range of decorated articles.

Within the year the Elkingtons were publishing on their advances, reporting particularly the prime importance to them of the work of Jacobi at St Petersburg from around 1838, Grahams's *Elements of Chemistry*, and the practical experiments of Thomas Spencer in Liverpool on electrolytic depositing.[75] Such advances had been rejected by Birmingham die-sinkers, but Spencer continued and announced his larger results at the Liverpool Polytechnical Society on 12 September 1844. It was this paper that brought the earlier work of Jacobi to the attention of British technicians and described a series of experiments from 1837 using zinc and copper plates for coating with copper, following experiments of Faraday and others.[76] Although both the 1836 and 1840 patents of the Elkingtons were periodically infringed by French technicians, leading to a period of litigation between 1841 and 1843, the Elkington precedence was generally recognized and indeed proclaimed in France with the award of the *Academie des Sciences* prix of 6,000 francs. By 1844 a suggestion at the Royal Institution in London led to the conjoining of patent rights, and so two Parisian firms were 'extensively carrying out the [Elkington] process'. According to the firm itself, the advanced Birmingham technology was easily superior to others as there was no limit to the design or the metal upon which plating occurs nor any need for iron dies for silver leaf molding; furthermore pure depositing meant the product was indistinguishable from silver and exact copies could be multiplied on the large scale and great intricacy obtained without the need of high skills or expert casting and chasing.[77]

So, it seems clear that the new tools were first taken up in the town by Parkes' new employers, who by 1838 were quite successfully depositing gold and silver on ornaments made of a widening range of metals, and that this was a result of an astute but complex combination of skills, tacit understandings and formal knowledge. The Elkington patent of July 1838 coated copper and brass with zinc by means of an electric current generated by a piece of zinc attached to the articles by a wire, which was then immersed in a metallic solution with them. This was the first patent in which a separate current of electricity was employed for plating. It was in this production process that Parkes was directly employed as an experimentalist alongside Dr John Wright, and together they patented in 1842 their discovery of the use of cyanides in a solution of metals to produce thick deposits, especially of silver.[78] It was this and the subsequent local improvements that stimulated the fast development of the German silver industry in Birmingham, which together with the nickel and gold manufacturers was by the early 1860s employing over 7,000 workers in the town.[79]

Wright seemed to be a major influence here in linking the local practical manoeuvring in Birmingham with the theoretical developments that were Europe-wide. Gill claims that Wright and Parkes together were 'constantly engaged in electro-deposition experiments' and Wright had earlier read a chemical essay by the great Swedish chemist Karl Wilhelm Scheele (1742–86, see above) which had pointed to the suitability of the cyanides of gold and silver for electroplating.[80] At an earlier point Wright had submitted his results to George and Henry Elkington and it was embodied in their patent of March 1840 on the coating of metals, and it was this patent that became the firm basis for the following development of applied electroplating.[81] The spectacularly precocious German metallurgist and engineer William Siemens (1823–83) visited the Elkingtons' workshops in 1843 on his trip to introduce to Britain an electroplating process invented by himself and his brother Werner Siemens (1816–92). The Elkingtons immediately adopted the process and Siemens then suggested some further improvements in the firm's technique, and from around then the original plan of licensing the Elkington patents for direct royalties altered to that of manufacturing and sale, and from this point in 1844 Josiah Mason (1795–1881), patentee-manufacturer, designed and built a new factory for the firm on Newhall Street and – for plating technology only – another on Brearley Street. At the same time Siemens himself made Birmingham his home, becoming naturalized in 1859, and setting up a great chain of experiments at mechanical works near Birmingham before going into full-time practice as an engineer from 1851.

Within this complex agency network, in which scientific, artisan and business acumen mixed freely, Parkes own first single-authored patents (number 8,905 of 1841 and 9,807 of 1843) were for a method of electroplating flowers and fragile objects by dipping them in a solution of phosphorous in carbon bisulphide, and subsequently in a silver nitrate solution. This sequence covered the objects with a coating of reduced silver upon which 'any desired quantity' of copper, silver or gold could be deposited electrolytically. The family tradition was that when Prince Albert visited the Elkington works in 1844 he accepted the gift of a silver spider's web which had been plated by Parkes' own process. But perhaps the most notable feature of this first patenting was that it contained a large number of discrete inventions and sequences and products, claiming also the waterproofing of fabrics with rubber dissolved in carbon bisulphide. From this time a good proportion of Parke's inventions took the form of compound patent registrations in an effort to cover all possible applications of core ideas or processes, and in this he was clearly informed by the local information and competitive environs.

This first phase of inventive activity during the 1840s included some fundamental advances. In 1846 he patented under the title 'Vulcanisation with Sulphur Chloride and Oxides of Nitrogen' the 'cold cure' process for vulcanizing rubber, identified by Thomas Hancock as 'one of the most valuable and extraordinary discoveries of the age'. This consisted of immersing rubber in a solution of sulphur dichloride in carbon disulphide and throughout the twentieth century was used for surgeons' gloves, balloons ands bottle teats.[82] Although this clearly represented a major technical advance, the carbon disulphide and sulphur chloride required for the process were then costly, and so his next work aimed to reduce such costs. In 1843 carbon disulphide sold at just over £2 per lb, reduced by Parkes to two shillings or to less than 5 per cent, and there were seminal Birmingham-based reductions in the price of sulphur chloride by 1844–5.[83]

Although this series of patents might seem at first glance to be distinct from those later directed at plastic materials, the total inventive programme has some significant common ingredients – the emphasis on coating with and of materials, the compound character of patenting, the clear importance and internalization of relatively recent advances in formal science especially chemistry, the essential attributes of skilled manipulation and artistic flair, and the eye to cost, especially the costs of materials – as we shall see below, this latter feature of the Parkesian inventive programme may well have determined the failure of his own early attempts at manufacturing of celluloid products of his own invention.

The bulk of the dozen or so patents by Parkes from 1841 to 1852 covered the fields of electrodepositing in works of art, applications of India-rubber, and the general depositing of metals; on that basis his contemporary R. B. Prosser labelled Parkes one of the greatest of those Birmingham inventors who were patenting advanced methods of depositing metals and alloys.[84] In 1844 Parkes registered the first of 66 metallurgical patents.[85] It described the white alloys of copper, nickel, zinc and silver, but also claimed the novel use of a bath of fused salts for metallic electrodeposition, a method anticipated by Faraday in 1833. Two years later he pioneered the addition of small quantities of phosphorus to metals and alloys, and developed phosphor-bronze in a patent of 1848, taken out jointly with his brother Henry Parkes.[86] This invention of phosphor bronze and other alloys, created by adding about 2 per cent of phosphorous to alloys of copper, zinc, tin, nickel and tungsten and thereby increasing fluidity when fused, increased solidity when cold and improved power of resisting oxidation, was probably the most important of this early series of experiments.[87]

But most of this was of lesser distinction than his discovery of the method for desilverizing lead. His 1850 patent which developed the 'Parkes Process' for economically desilvering, with additional patented refinements in 1851 and 1852, dominated the industry throughout the world. With its later improvements it was worked with great effect in Germany and the United States by adding a small fraction of zinc to the melted lead, which could almost entirely remove all silver.[88] Possibly something over half the lead used in the world in the early twentieth century was desilvered by the improved Parkes' process.[89]

However, as in so many such cases, there is no evidence that Parkes exploited this breakthrough commercially, and between 1849 and 1856 he remained employed with Elkington and Mason in building a copper smelting works at Pembray in South Wales. In the construction of this he used bricks manufactured from local shale and erected a stack of 280 feet in height. At this time he had already established a friendship with Henry Bessemer, and just after the latter's introduction of the basic process which produced inexpensive steel in 1856, Parkes persuaded him to Birmingham on a promise that he could press a disc of Bessemer mild steel in his own recently invented tube-making machine, which he did with aplomb. Parkes was obviously ranging widely. Just months previously, during the end-games of the Crimean war, he invented a powerful new explosive which received a public trial in August 1855. Comparing the results with those for the government's shells the *Times* reporter on the spot agreed with the inventor's claim that his powder had three times the explosive power of the common powder and was more resistant to damp.[90]

The third phase of Parkes' inventive life centres on his development of plastic materials from the mid-1850s, but especially the key later years of 1862–5, when he established the importance of the camphor process in the production of what was later to be called celluloid (Essentially celluloid is the same cellulose nitrate as guncotton but less nitrated, so not explosive). This required the nitrating of cellulose fibres, more simply the soaking of cotton or wood or other cellulose sources, in nitric acid with the addition of one of a number of feasible solvents. The chemical background to this work was primarily French and Swiss, initiated in 1832 by the production of water-resistant film through the effect of concentrated nitric acid on cotton fibres in experiments by Henri Braconnot (1781–1855), professor at the Lyceum at Nancy. Later in the 1830s T. J. Pelouze of Paris suggested that this reaction between cotton and nitric acid could be utilized in the manufacture of explosives.[91] In 1846, by treating paper with a mix of nitric and sulphuric acids C. F. Schönbein, an established authority at the University of Basle obtained a transparent and malleable substance that he reported to Faraday at the Royal Institution in London in March 1846. This was cellulose nitrate, commonly called guncotton, to become a foundation of the late nineteenth century explosives industries. As a result of this advance, Pelouze returned to his work, experimenting with nitric acid and a variety of cellulose, obtaining a substance he called pyroxylin, without any commercial outcome. Schönbein was very active in the international patenting of what seems to have been an accidental discovery, giving exclusive rights for the manufacture of the explosive in Britain to the unfortunate John Hall and Sons of Faversham, whose factory blew up while experimenting with the new material in July of 1847. Similar disastrous factory explosions occurred in France, Germany and Russia. Somewhat randomly, a little later John Taylor, Schönbein's British patent agent, mentioned cellulose nitrate to Alexander Parkes, and presumably directed him to the Schönbein British patent filed on 8 October 1846.[92]

Parkes seems to have speedily seen this as a potential solution to a problem just then facing all electroplaters as well as the practical electricians of Birmingham more generally. The need was for more reliable insulators than the very expensive horn, shellac or gutta-percha then in use. With his working background, and given the character of his patenting programme, Parkes would also have seen the opportunity of developing plastic substances for ornamental and artistic productions. But the clear problem confronting Parkes was that cellulose nitrate was dangerously inflammable if not explosive. Between 1855 and 1868 Parkes made literally 'thousands of experiments' with plastic masses of nitrocellulose, developing alternative plasticizers and solvents, and on his own evidence given in 1878 experimented with camphor from the beginning, but there is no evidence of the production of any rolled mass containing camphor and nitrocellulose until 1865.[93] In 1856, he patented in England and France 'Parkesine' – the first thermoplastic – a celluloid based upon nitrocellulose treated with a variety of solvents. The semi-synthetic cellulose nitrate material – that had been named after the Birmingham inventor by a French chemist – was an early form of celluloid, and could be molded or pressed, turned, carved, and rolled into sheets, and was waterproof. The artisan trade applications that he identified as appropriate to the new material included spinners pressing or embossing rolls, knife-handles, combs, shoe-soles, walking-sticks, buttons, bookbinding, waterproof sheets, coating for telegraph wires and so on. The pyroxyline could be made from any vegetable fibre, from cotton and flax waste to rags. The solvent was naphtha solidified with chloride of sulphur.[94] Although specimens across this range seem to have been available from 1856, they apparently made little impact until he cleverly launched a range of products in this 'new material and manufacture' at the 1862 London International Exhibition and was awarded a bronze medal for a very varied range of products that anticipated many of the modern aesthetic and utility uses of plastics. His prize medal certificate explained that Parkes as yet had no 'systematic manufacture for the material' but that the final product could be made

> hard as ivory, transparent or opaque, of any degree of flexibility, of the most brilliant colours, can be used in the solid, plastic or fluid state, may be worked in dies and presses, as metals, may be cast, or used as a coating to a great variety of substances; can be spread or worked in a similar manner to India rubber . . . the most perfect imitation of tortoise-shell, woods, and an endless variety of effects can be produced'.[95]

It is this prize and its associated list of products that is most often cited as Parkes' real claim as the discoverer of a usable cellulose nitrate. As has often been acknowledged by later writers, if Parkes had been less determined on continuing his metallurgical experiments he might have himself become a chief beneficiary of the industrialization of celluloid and its related products and processes.[96]

The industrial chemist J. N. Goldsmith caught the spirit of this inventive trajectory when he argued that Parkes was especially at that time and place well qualified for the invention of some form of plastic composition, for his 'discoveries had made him familiar with the machinery used in rolling, dissolving and spreading rubber, he was expert in moulding, tube making and modelling, as an artist he could take advantage of the unlimited variety of form and colour obtainable for the first time in the history of the arts by his invention of a plastic substance based on gelatinized nitrocellulose.' [97]

In these years he further developed parkesine, his patent dated 11 May 1865 was for 'Improvements in the manufacture of parkesine or compounds of pyroxyline, and also solutions of pyroxyline, known as collodion'. The following patent of 8 December 1865 was for the invention of 'improvements in preparing compounds of xylodine or gun-cotton, and in the apparatus employed'.[98] Four days later he presented to the Royal Society of Arts in London objects made from plasticized cellulose nitrate which now contained the new key ingredient of camphor. At the RSA meeting he made things clearer in his talk which highlighted

> the employment of camphor, which exercises an advantageous influence on the dissolved pyrolyline, and renders it possible to make sheets etc with greater facility and more uniform texture, as it controls the contractile properties of the dissolved pyroxyline; camphor is used in varying proportions according to requirements, from 2% to 20%.

In his lecture he claimed that by using very cheap waste cotton he was producing parkesine for 1/- per lb.[99] His imagination here was superb and confirmed over the next decades when he suggested that the possible uses of the new Parkesine, a list wider than that of his International Exhibition claims of 1862, embraced

> knife handles, combs, brush-backs, shoe soles, floor-cloth, whips, walking sticks, umbrella and parasol handles, buttons, brooches, buckles, bookbinding, chemical taps and pipes, photographic baths, battery cells, philosophical instruments, waterproof fabrics, sheets and other articles for surgical purposes and for works of art in general'.[100]

The artist in Parkes could not be gainsaid. Only months later, in 1866 he became managing director of the Parkesine Company at Hackney Wick, London, for bulk low-cost production, involved some commercial association with Henry Bessemer and with G. Maule of Simpson Maule and Nicholson, a large manufacturer of aniline dyes.

The story so far, then, brings into effective proximity a number of leading European scientists – the earlier work of J. F. Daniell, J. S. Woolrich, August Wilhelm von Hofmann, Moritz Jacobi, Michael Faraday or K. W. Scheele that together helped establish Parkes' experimental programme in Birmingham, and the later influences of C. F. Schönbein and T. J. Pelouze in the field of cellulose nitrate. Intertwined with this formal, reported and registered knowledge were the skills and dexterities and patented ownership of technique of the men around him, such as John Wright, Henry and G. R .Elkington and Josiah Mason, embedded deeply in the machinofacture of Birmingham and brimful with success – Mason alone acquired a huge fortune, founded Mason College, established many almshouses and orphanages, and was knighted in 1872. Nor was he any sort of a free-rider within this inventive site – his chain of patents from 1877 to 1885 were all on chemical metallurgy.

How do we differentiate knowledge from technique and urban savvy when trying to understand a man like Parkes? His energetic but highly informed research programme with John Wright, the longer association of Parkes with his own brother Henry, surely measured the work of the 'mindful hand' *in situ*, amid patent agency widely defined but closely proximate?[101] Again surely we can not now presume to define William Siemens in Birmingham circa 1843 as 'merely' a mechanician? We are not describing a benign 'bringing' of scientific knowledge to a passive space or loose 'association of interests'. Although both the Royal Institution and the Royal Society for the Advancement of Arts were indeed associated with this urban site as loci of reliable information and places of demonstration, they did not issue any orders or prescriptions, fund any activity or determine any outcomes. We are nearer to describing a particular, urban site of technological endeavour and patent agency. But none of this means that we have somehow buried Parkes. Apart from his eminently inventive abilities, it was Parkes who, however commercially inept, pursued a determined research programme, speedily mounted an effective publicity machine through the use of national associations and prizes and used his chain of patents in selling products and forming companies. Within a particular urban site he could command his own agency as well as receive it from others His personal fortune remained modest but the social returns to his private interests were very extensive indeed.

For knowledge to come to technique requires something more than temporal and spatial proximity. The forging of technological utilities awaits also something of social and cognitive proximities. Thus Schönbein – our archetypical scientist of this story – writing to Berzelius in 1846, noting that several German academic chemists were working on guncotton, himself clearly seeing its potential commercial value, fearing the resultant disputes over priority, then confessed that 'in certain respects it is almost a misfortune to have made an important practical discovery; it completely destroys one's peace of mind. Faraday and Grove told me the same thing: they continually stood in fear of coming across something which would bring them in contact with the practical world, as I have done'.[102]

There is a lot wanting here. There can be no doubt that although Parkes was himself untrained in the higher chemistry, his position within his particular urban culture exposed him to not only general expert knowledge but to specific experimental expertise at the then European level of excellence. The emergence of camphor technology with his work was at the intersection of euro-wide scientific knowledge with the tacit, artisanal expertise of Birmingham industries. The technological advancement was not a process of the state or of great patronage. It was not part of that elitist culture that so preoccupied Martin Weiner when he approached the subject of 'industrial decline'![103] But it was one that involved networks of intellect that many of the world's state bureaucrats later in the century would have either killed or died for. Scheele, Hofmann and Siemens, in a manner, congregated around a very specific site of patent agency, one within a cultural neighbourhood dominated by a highly competitive, urban machinofacture enterprise. The human capital of the industrial revolution was not accumulated only on an individual basis but within competitive sites in which no-one, certainly no great leader, was imposing any distinctions between knowledge and technique.

Such a narrative analytic account of Parkes does serve to illustrate one more, larger theme that deserves to be better acknowledged and explored among professional historians. The life of Parkes yields nuance to the economists' clever old query: 'If the knowledge you have is so new, useful, reliable, and potentially lucrative, why ever cooperate in its formation, why demonstrate its reliability, or share it in use?' Why should there be any unprotected agency? In more modern parlance, why ever write the book and release the CD or e-book on *How to Succeed in Business without Really Trying*? Well, the answer is just not going to *be* straightforward, is it?

Most of the activists in our Birmingham story were well-enough covered – many had patents and others were well-protected by publication. Several had been rewarded for their ingenuity either by university and institute positions and promotions or by reasonable personal returns on their own actual production of products or through processes that were fairly securely owned. At the same time, knowledge (even as mere information) expands and alters with discussion and usage, and in this way contrasts starkly with the using up in production of physical capital or land. There were many people who made substantial fortunes out of the experimental work of Parkes and others like him, but Parkes gained from those others, from Wright and the Elkingtons, from John Taylor or his own brother Henry. The patent trajectory became more focused through time and clearly more sensitive to the patent agency of the city of Birmingham at large. It is true enough that Parkes' own business ventures were mediocre affairs, but his work led directly to the formation of new firms in new industries quite as much as did any injections of physical capital from those taking lesser risks and possessing lesser ingenuities. As Goldsmith caught it in his manuscript of 1934, he was 'a born experimenter, his workshop was his own house', and after the period of working for Josiah Mason he 'lived by the sale of his patents . . . His time was so occupied with experimenting that he never attempted to be the man-of-affairs'.

This man could live quite well by giving information away. Even partial intellectual property rights combined with a personal publicity machine ensured enough of an income to generate two great compensations for income – a deserved reputation and the admiration of Birmingham folk, together with the enjoyment of working all his life as an artist, as one who 'never overlooked the possibility of producing a decorated or colored material' – Parkesine products included an intricately carved head of Christ, crowned with thorns, in imitation amber. He may at least once have been threatened with penury, but was never reduced to it, and according to his son Alexander Parkes J, his rule was to 'dispose of an invention without as a rule any provision for payment of royalties. He went on from one invention to another, always confident in the versatility of his ideas'.[104] But he was not anyone's fool, he sold his very first patented invention of 1843, and another of 1846, for 'obtaining and applying solutions of india-rubber' to that famous water-proofer Charles Macintosh (1760–1843) in the year that the latter died. So this was no backwoods or backyard adventurer, an isolated hero turning coat-hangers into barbed-wire. Not at all. Parkes was as fully representative of all that was Birmingham, of all that was becoming the fabled Workshop of the World, as was any James Watt or Henry Bessemer or William Siemens. He made less immediate markers and much less of a fortune, but his ultimate impact on the character of the coming second industrial revolution was enormous and lasting.

CONCLUDING POINTS. AGENTS, INSTITUTIONS AND KNOWLEDGE

We postulate, then, that the sites and agents of the useful knowledge culture were also the sites of technological innovation, especially of those incremental improvements referred to as 'ordinary inventiveness' by McCloskey.[105] As the engineer John Farey put it in 1835, the patented incremental improvements of the time were 'the origin of a number of considerable trades in Birmingham, Sheffield and in London'. A few years earlier he had emphasized 'the very expressive nature of the technical language that is used among all our artisans; also the established habit that the English have, more than any other people, of associating themselves into bodies and societies to act in concert to effect a common object'.[106] Here, then, was a fairly clear statement of the linkages between workshop culture, urban associative agencies surrounding the diffusion and discussion of reliable knowledge and the process of technological change.

We can conclude with some more specific points. When accounting the history of registered invention, we must consider more than patentees – those who, especially in the unreformed earlier years of the patent systems, were general activists, organizing the patent systems into optimality by dispersing information, monitoring and improving patents, acting as partners and agent-consultants and so on. Much of this work was outside of the patent system regulations, but ancillary and important to patenting itself. Patentees were organizational animals who – directly or through intermediaries – used advertising, exhibitions, lectures and associations to maximize their impact within and beyond particular urban locations.

We might accept that after the reform years of the 1830s–1850s it is more feasible to capture agency wholly within the workings of patent systems, with the addition of non-patent courts and other legal elements. The law courts become a prime site of comparative investigation – thus the difference between Britain and the United States, where the former was far more prone to allow final status and legitimacy of particular patents to be formed in the challenges to patentees by the competitors and expert witnesses of the non-patent courts.

The period prior to reform also suggests that there might be organizational advantages in institutional imperfection! The very imperfections of the pre-1850 British patent system called up the need for forms of agency, training, advertisement and information dispersal that together did congregate as more or less informal knowledge systems, ones that were on the whole inexpensive, inclusive and adaptable to circumstance. The Birmingham material illustrates this well. It might be that as institutional reform tended to formalize and regulate the forms of agency within patent systems, so too it may have separated the patent system from its earlier information base.[107]

Birmingham and other examples point to the possibility of comparisons of urban sites of patenting across national systems as well as within them. If agency lies beyond the patentees and patent agents of formal institutions, then an ideal site for examining the conjuncture of agency is the wider urban context. Urban location of clusters of patents and of innovation in private enterprises includes elements such as industrial employment, training, knowledge associations and channels of information diffusion and how these influenced or even determined activities of patentees and patent agents.

How far were these extra-system features – both before and after reform – part of the organizational resource utilized by patentees and agents to optimize their position within the inventive and commercial culture? North postulates that agents play optimizing games as organizations *within* their institutions. We might also develop an argument that incorporates extra-institutional elements if we recognize that associations and information systems outside the patent systems assisted patentees (i.e. acted as agents) operating within them.

How far might it be argued that patents and patent agency (as here defined) between them assisted in the identification of useful and reliable knowledge during years in which industrialization was primarily based upon a system of machinofacture? This would point to the limitations of any generalizations stemming from this sort of material or approach. In combination our latter two queries seem to suggest possibilities for a firmer comparative approach to both locations of technical innovation and the role of intellectual property systems.

Notes

1. Douglass North, *Understanding the Process of Economic Change* (Princeton, NJ, 2005), 59, 61.

2. William Newton is of especial interest as editor of the *London Journal of Arts*, which reviewed all patents annually from series 2, Volume 1, 1828. See *A Memoir of the Late Mr William Newton*, reprinted from Newton's *Journal of Arts* for August 1861 (London, 1861).

3. This society was closed down under the act against seditious meetings, prohibiting the delivery of a chemical lecture by Michael Faraday.

4. For this see also William Felkin, *History of the Machine-Wrought Hosiery and Lace Manufacture* (Nottingham, 1867) and more generally his *The Exhibition in 1851 of the Products and Industry of all Nations. Its Probable Influence on Labour and Commerce* (London, 1851).

5. *Newton's London Journal of Arts and Science*, 1859, X: 129–34, 257–63.

6. R. K. Dent, *Old and New Birmingham* (Birmingham, 1880), 218–19.

7. The mechanics' institutes have often been seen as merely expressions of middle-class cultural dominance. That they may also have acted as providers of education and information resources to artisan and engineering innovators, has in the main been ignored. See however Ian Inkster, *Scientific Culture and Urbanisation in Industrialising Britain* (London, 1997).

8. *Atheneum*, 5 April 1845, 340.

9. *Times*, 1 January 1851, 2.

10. *Times*, 1 February, 1851, 1; 25 February 1851, 3.

11. For example, *Times* 1 January 1826, T. W. Burr, science lecturer and frequent patentee (1820–39, rolling and manufacturing sheet lead) or its Secretary, George Stacey (patents in the 1850s for reaping and mowing machines).

12. *Times*, 1 January 1851.

13. *Atheneum*, 1 March 1845, 256, 281.

14. *Atheneum*, 5 April 1845, 553.

15. Nottingham Collection of Addresses and Posters, Volume 1, 1791–1810, British Library bound volume 1888. c. 18, Folio 91.

16. *Atheneum*, 7 January 1843, 3.

17. *Times*, 1 January 1851, 2.

18. *Times*, 4 November 1843, 6.

19. *Times*, 2 July 1787, 1.

20. See especially the range from the *Atheneum* to the *Polytechnic Review and Magazine of Science, Literature and Arts*. See also for early material or references Hugh Woodrow, *Tales of Victoria Street. The Story of the Association of Consulting Engineers* (London, 2003).

21. *Times*, 1 January 1851, 3. For Calvert in particular see patents, 11: 126, 12: 427, 13: 658.

22. John Bourne, *A Treatise on the Steam Engine and its Applications* (London, 1851); *Times*, 13 March 1851, 10.

23. 1849–50, 140. Savage is not found patenting pre-1852, with his first patent in 1855, no. 1,877, when he is registered as of Eastcheap, machinist, with improvements in the means for treating tea, sugar, coffee, etc. for separation and mixing. This patent was sealed on 26 November.

24. *Sheffield Iris*, September–October 1808, *Liverpool Mercury*, 12 October 1808, *passim*.

25. *Derby Mercury*, 30 November 1809.

26. Charles Sylvester, *An Elementary Treatise on Chemistry, Comprising the Most Important Facts of the Science, with Tables of Decomposition on a New Plan, to which is Added, an Appendix giving an Account of the Latest Discoveries* (Liverpool, 1809), 50–1, 73–4.

27. *Derby Directory*, 1829, various pages and references.

28. *Derby Mercury*, 13 April 1825; Ms Cash Book Derby Literary and Philosophical Society 1815–19, Derby Public Library, Ms 7,625.

29. John Farey, Westminster to MacVey Napier, February 1814, BM Add Ms, 34,611, Napier Letters, vol. I, 1805–16, 43–4.

30. *Times* 17 March 1851, 3.

31. *Morning Chronicle* 24 April, 213, 7 May, 1, 1817. William and Martin Bevan of Morriston, near Swansea, were the patentees.

32. John Hind had been involved in funding earlier Nottingham patenting, but in this case his funding amounted to thousands of pounds for the patents of 1834 (6,683) and 1835 (6,907), and by the later 1850s he had seemingly patented his way into poverty. Heathcoat also purchased rights in the patent when it was working on pattern-making in a Whitemoor workshop and employed Draper at Tiverton, but he eventually gained nothing by it in any direct financial sense. After funding and experimenting with the second Draper patent, Wilkie too died soon after in humble circumstances. Draper's patents basically demonstrated the applicability of Jacquard pierced cards to bobbin net machines. At one point the first scarf made by Draper on this Jacquard-ed machine was held as a specimen in the collection of what was then the South Kensington Museum.

33. John Felkin, *Hosiery and Lace Manufactures* (Nottingham, 1867), op. cit., 360–75.

34. *Times* 30 January 1851, 3.

35. *Times* 10 January 1851, 2,

36. *Times* 1851 21 January, 9

37. William Spence, *A Treatise on Principles Relating to the Specifications of a Patent for Invention* (London: V & R Stevens and G. S. Norton, 1847), 43.

38. William Spence, *Patentable Invention and Scientific Evidence* (London: Stevens and Norton, 1851), x.

39. The process used carburet of manganese, which reduced the cost of manufacturing cast steel by up to 50 per cent. In Sheffield, Heath had found that using its chemical elements was sufficient for they fused in the crucible. His failure to make this distinction in the original allowed the successful challenge by Unwin. This case gave reformers an argument for adopting French procedures where the patentee was allowed to substitute an improved for a defective specification.

40. *Newton's London Journal of Arts and Science*, 1859, X: 129–34, 257–63.

41. W. Hutton, *An History of Birmingham to the Year 1780* (Birmingham, 1781), 63

42. John Money, 'The Schoolmasters of Biotrmingham and the West midlands 1750–1790', *Historie Sociale-Social History*, 1976, IX: 1–23; John Money, 'Taverns, Coffee Houses and Clubs: local Polutics and Popular Articulacy in the Birmingham Area', *Historical Journal*, 1971, XIV146–62.

43. Henry Brunton, *A Compendium of Mechanics or Text Book for Engineers, with a Treatise Particularly Adapted for the Use of Operative Mechnics* (6th edn) (Glasgow, 1837), xii.

44. For the dissenting issues, science and technology in this decade see Ian Inkster 'Under the Eye of the Public: Arthur Aikin (1773–1854), the Dissenting Mind and the Character of English Industrialization' in *Religious Dissent and the Aikin-Barbauld circle 1740–1860*, eds, Felicity James and Ian Inkster (Cambridge, 2012), 126–55.

45. Anonymous, *Thoughts on the Late Riots at Birmingham* (London, 1791), 24.

46. *Aris' Birmingham Gazette* (henceforth Aris), 30 April: 3, 1 October: 3, 1792.

47. *Aris* 28 December 1789, 1.

48. Ibid., 8 February, 22 February, 1790: 3.

49. Ibid., 21 September 1789, 3, 14 February, 1791, 3.

50. Ian Inkster, 'Association, provincialisme et sociologie du progrès technique: le cas de la Grande-Bretagne, entre 1780 et 1914' in *Encourager l'innovation en France et en Europe*, eds, Serge Benoit, Gérard Emptoz, Denis Woronoff (Paris, 2006), 327–49.

51. *Crell's Chemical Journal* should not be confused with *Crelle's Journal*, only published from 1826 which was founded by August Leopold Crelle and was the first periodical devoted exclusively to high level research in pure mathematics.

52. *Aris* 16 January, 1792, 2.

53. Ibid., 22 October 179, 3.

54. Robert E. Schofield, *The Lunar Society of Birmingham. A Social History of Provincial Science and Industry in Eighteenth Century England* (Oxford, 1963).

55. J. Drake, *The Picture of Birmingham* (Birmingham, 1825), 36; C. Pye, *Modern Birmingham* (Birmingham, 1818), 37–8; R. K. Dent, *The Making of Birmingham* (Birmingham, 1894), 323–5.

56. List of the Literary and Scientific Institutions from which Returns were Procured at the Census of 1851, *Population Census of Great Britain*, Sessions 1852–4, (London, House of Commons, 1851), 237f; E. P. Blakiston, 'Observations on the Diffusion of Scientific Knowledge in Large Towns', *The Analyst. A Quarterly Journal of Science, Literature and Fine Arts*, 1838, 8: 83–103.

57. *Report of the Birmingham Philosophical Institution for 1836* (Birmingham: J Belcher, 1844), henceforth, BPI.

58. Dent op. cit.,261.

59. *Aris*, 14 March, 1791, 3.

60. Prosser op. cit., 81.

61. Conrad Gill, *History of Birmingham* (Oxford, 1952), 292.

62. Samuel Timmins, 'The Industrial History of Birmingham', in *The Resources, Products and Industrial History of Birmingham, A Series of Reports*, ed., Timmins (London, 1866), 207–24.

63. Bennet Woodcroft, *Titles of Patents of Invention Chronologically Arranged*, 1617–1852 (London, 1854). Unless otherwise stated all patent data in this paper up to 1851–2 is taken from the work of patent officer Bennet Woodcroft, compiled mostly in the 1850s. Material from 1855 to 1914 is derived from the original British patent applications, each one of which has been sighted and summarized in an EXCEL spreadsheet system. All social data mentioned here is taken from complete analysis of the years 1852, 1855, 1860, 1865, 1870, 1875, 1880, 1881–2. All other data unless mentioned is derived from data in *The Commissioner of Patents Journal*, annually from 1852 to 1883.

64. Ian Inkster, 'Engineers as Patentees and the Cultures of Invention 1830–1914 and Beyond – The Evidence from the Patent Data', *Quaderns d'Historia de l'Enginyeria*, 2004, VI: 25–50.

65. *The Patent Journal and Inventors' Magazine*, 5 October 1850.

66. Timmins op. cit., 1866, 536–51.

67. Ibid., 294–5.

68. Asa Briggs, *Victorian Cities* (London, 1963), 43.

69. Timmins, 1866, 207–24.

70. J. Bentley, 'The Chemical department of the Royal School of Mines: Its originsand development under A.W. Hofmann', *Ambix* 1970, 17: 153–81.

71. Ian Inkster and S. Bryson, *Industrial Man. The Life and Works of Charles Sylvester* (Las Vegas, 1999), 82–5.

72. K. Beauchamp, *Exhibiting Electricity* (London: Institute of Electrical Engineers, 1997), 90–3.

73. *New Monthly Magazine*, 1836, 533; *Iron*, 1836, 304; *Civil Engineers and Architects Journal* (London, 1837–38), 390. See also James F. W. Johnston, 'On the Composition of the Right Rhombic Baryto-Calcite, the Bicalcareo-Carboniet of Baryta of Dr Thomson', *Philosophical Magazine*, January–June 1837, X: 373–6.

74. J. Kershaw, *Electro-Metallurgy* (San Francisco, 1908).

75. Elkington and Co. [George Richard Elkington], *On the Application of Electro-Metallurgy to the Arts* (London, 1844); see also Thomas Spencer, 'Experiments upon Forming Copper Plates for Printing, Medals and other Metallic Designs, by Galvanism', *The Mechanics' Magazine*, October 1839–May 1840, XXXII: 54–61 which gave the detailed results of experiments over a two year period at the Liverpool Polytechnic Society, eventually announced as a result of publication of Jacobi's experiments. Lardner had blocked Spencer's planned demonstration to the British Association for the Advancement of Science in 1837.

76. A.Watt, *Electro-Deposition. A Practical Treatise, and Chapters on Electro-Metallurgy* (London, 1886), 54–62.

77. Elkington, op. cit., 1844, 23.

78. Timmins op. cit., 405–6, 674.

79. Ibid., 489–52.

80. For context and technical details see Graham Williams, 'The cyanides of gold. The history of their key role in elecroplating', *Gold Bulletin*, 1978,11: 56–9.

81. George Gore, *Chemistry* (London, 1856); Gore, *Copy of the Correspondence between the Committee of the Birmingham and Edgbaston Proprietary School and George Gore FRS, Lecturer on Chemistry* (Birmingham, 1871); Gore, *Electrolytic Separation of Metals* (London: Electrician Offices, 1877 and 1890).

82. *Landmarks of the Plastics Industry* (London: Imperial Chemical Industries Ltd., 1962), 9. This publication was intended to mark the centenary of Alexander Parkes' 'invention of the world's first man-made plastic': 9)

83. J N Goldsmith, *Alexander Parkes, Parkesine, Xylonite and Celluloid* (London, 1934), 30 (British Library 8233 d 6)

84. Prosser, op. cit., 1881, 118, 213–26.

85. P10, 366, 1844.

86. M. Kaufman, *The First Century of Plastics* (London, 1963).

87. P12, 142, 1848.

88. J. A. Phillips and H. Bauerman, *Elements of Metallurgy* (London, 1887), 641–6;

89. Goldsmith, op. cit., 1934, 31; Kaufmann, op. cit., 1963, 17.

90. *Times*, 27 August 1855, 8.

91. See for context P. S. Bulson, *Explosive Loading of Engineering Structures* (London, 1997), especially chapter 1.

92. P11407, 1846.

93. Goldsmith 28; P1, 313, 1865; Alexander Parkes, *Parkes' Evidence for the Defendant in Spill v The Celluloid Manufacturing Co.* (New York, 1878), 164.

94. Timmins, op. cit., 1866, 668.

95. Prize Medal, *International Exhibition 1862 (London)*, Class IV, Official Catalogue No. 1112 (Birmingham, 1862).

96. *Landmarks*, op. cit., 1962, 7.

97. Goldsmith op. cit., 1934, 33.

98. P3163, 1865.

99. Alexander Parkes, 'Origin and Uses of Parkesine', *Journal of the Society of Arts*, 1865, 14: 81–4.

100. Landmarks, op. cit., 1962, 9.

101. For the mindful hand see Lissa Roberts, Simon Schaffer and Peter Dear eds, *The Mindful Hand: Inquiry and Invention from the Late Renaissance to Early Industrialisation* (Amsterdam, 2007).

102. G. E. Kahlbaum, ed., *Letters of JJ Berzelius and C.F Schonbein*, trans. F. V. Darbishire (London, 1900), 88–9.

103. Martin J. Weiner, *English Culture and the Decline of the Industrial Spirit* (Cambridge, 1981).

104. Goldsmith op. cit., 35–6.

105. D. McCloskey, 'The Industrial Revolution 1780–1860: A Survey', in *The Economic History of Britain since 1700*, ed., R. Floud and D. McCloskey (Cambridge, 1981), volume 1 1700–1860, 103–27, seepage 117.

106. William Newton, *Letters and Suggestions Upon the Amendment of the Laws Relative to Patents for Invention* (London, 1835), quote 78–9; *Report of Select Committee on the Law Relative to Patents for Invention* (London, 1835), 132.

107. Ian Inkster, 'Introduction. An Imperfection of Institutions', *History of Technology*, 2002, 24: xvii–xxi.

Patent Agents in Britain at the Turn of the Twentieth Century. Themes and Perspectives

ANNA GUAGNINI

Università di Bologna

Hardly could a metaphor be more appropriate for describing the patent agents than the one forged by Ian Inkster: 'the legal beavers and engineers of Southampton Buildings and Chancery Lane'.[1]

He was referring to the London-based patent-agents, but the metaphor applies equally well to the professional community as a whole, in Britain and abroad: to their colleagues at work in St. Vincent Street in Glasgow, in the area of the Conservatoire des Arts et Métiers in Paris and of the Brandenburg Gate in Berlin. Wherever they operated, their work was made apparent by the constructions they produced; they, the agents, remained largely invisible – not least to historical analysis.[2] And yet, even this elusive community has began recently to attract the attention of the historians – economic and law historians and historians of technology.[3] The attempt to unravel the process by which innovation is transmitted and consolidated has been extended beyond the traditional 'front-line' protagonists to include other, less prominent but vital actors who played a role in the management of innovation: among them legal experts, consulting engineers and patent agents.

Most of the observations, especially with regard to Britain, have focused on the mid-nineteenth century and on the early stages in the development of patent agency as a new profession. The role of the agents, by the very nature of their occupation, was to transfer information, and they carried it out at the interface between different social, economic and occupational milieus. The role of patent literature as an effective instrument of technical information, and more specifically of agents as information brokers, has already been discussed by Inkster in the present volume.[4] The second aspect to which attention has been directed is the role that patent agents played in the development of patent practice and norms. Already in the mid-nineteenth century patent agents were involved, along with lawyers, in the collection and notation of patent cases and in the publication of manuals and handbooks based on their professional experience. And yet they were not only assimilating the outcome of court decisions and making available a substantial body of knowledge on patent literature and practice. They were actively engaged in the gradual transformation of such body of knowledge and of practical norms, drawing on their practical experience as translators of technical inventions into texts.[5] The participation of patent agents in the debate on the reform of the patent law which culminated in the passing of the Patent Amendment Act of 1852, and in the patent controversy of the mid-nineteenth century has also been duly noticed and discussed.[6]

Less attention has been devoted, in both respects, to what happened in the second half of the century and especially after the Patent Act of 1883. And yet patent agents continued to be proactive players in the evolving game of patent law and practice in the late nineteenth and well into the twentieth centuries; they did so no longer in the prevalent form of loosely associated individuals as in the pre-1850 period, but as organized pressure groups. After all, the 'promotion of improvements in the patent laws and regulations' was one of the aims of the first professional association, the Institute of Chartered Patent Agents (of which more below). Their involvement in the further developments of the reform of the patent law, their position and the nature of their vested interests and how those positions coalesced or conflicted with those of other agencies and actors, are also awaiting to be analysed in-depth.

The observations that follow touch upon questions that are preliminary to that sort of analysis. As players in the complex game of the patent business, at the interface between its techno/scientific, legal and commercial sides, their task was to interpret and mediate the interests and the objectives of the other players involved in the game, institutional and individual. At the same time, in the last quarter of the nineteenth century they were a highly composite group of practitioners, especially in consideration of the way in which their activity was carried out. Not surprisingly, their professional interests, occupational outlook and economic concerns were also diverse. The assumption from which these observations stem is that the analysis of the internal dynamics of this small but diverse group can tell us much not only about the profession itself and how the characteristics of the practitioners evolved but also about the changes that took place within the network of the other players involved in the patent business.

PATENT AGENTS AS A PROFESSIONAL GROUP

Already before the mid-century the qualification and standards of practice of the patent agents, and the very nature of the profession, had been the object of discussion among the practitioners and other interested parties, especially inventors and solicitors.[7] As I pointed out above, in the third quarter of the century they were still relatively few, but they operated in a rapidly expanding market. By reducing the cost of obtaining protection for inventions and simplifying the procedure, the Act of 1852 brought about dramatic increase in the number of applications; the Act of 1883 caused a further surge in the rush to the Patent Office. The result was an increase in the demand for expert technical and legal assistance, but also a growing competition among the practitioners who offered it. At that point the definition (and delimitation) of the occupational group, which had already been the underlying theme of the debate on the professional identity of the patent agents, came to the fore. Other closely related professions, the lawyers, the engineers and the accountants, had already gone through that process: the Incorporated Law Society was created in 1825, the Institution of Civil Engineers and the Institution of Mechanical Engineers were created respectively in 1818 and 1847. However the existence of well-established models did not make the process any easier; a main problem was the considerable diversity in the way in which patent agency was carried out.

The presence of contrasting positions emerged clearly in the process that led to the creation of a register of the patent agents. In 1862, when a Royal Commission was appointed to inquire into the working of the law relating to letters patents for inventions, one of the commissioners, William Hindmarch, Queen's Counsel and an expert on patent law and practice, recommended to establish a register and a procedure for ascertaining the qualification and the professional behaviour of the people who practiced as patent agents. The main reason he adduced in support of his proposal was the prevention of cases of malpractice: as he argued, the opening up of new opportunities for the people who made it their job to offer assistance to inventors was being exploited also by individuals whose competence was questionable and whose intentions in some cases were less than honest. In his denunciation Hindmarch gave voice to the main practitioners in the field, and those who were most determined to use the experience and reputation they had already achieved as a tool against the competitors.[8] His recommendation did not receive the support of the other members of the Commission, but nevertheless it was presented as a minority report by the proponent alone.[9] The definition of the qualification required in order to carry out patent business and of a professional code of behaviour as antidotes to incompetence and misconduct still remained an open problem; it was discussed again in the evidence given before the Select Committee on Letters Patent of 1872, but as on the previous occasion no measure was adopted. Clearly the attempt to control the way in which patent agency was conducted arose suspicion both from within the occupational group and from outside, not the least from the powerful lobby of the solicitors. As for the Board of Trade and the Patent Office, they kept aloof from a direct involvement in the regulation of this or indeed any professional community.

While the request of regulations remained unanswered, a group of patent agents resolved to move forward on a voluntary basis. The initiative came from a small group of well-established practitioners, most of them London-based. In 1882 the Institute of Patent Agents was created in the capital: prominent among its aims was the definition of code of practice, the acceptance of which was a condition for the admission of members.[10] Explicit reference was made to the association of the solicitors and the engineers and their regulations.[11] Right from the start the institution adopted strict criteria with regard to the qualification of the members: they were expected to have practiced for five years on their own account, or to have been engaged as assistants to fellows of the Institute for seven years. The Institute organized also examinations, the passing of which constituted the third route for the admission of new fellows.[12] Following the example of other professional institutions, a class of Associate members was also set up, mainly for patent agents who were not yet senior partners of well-established firms nor practicing their account, as well as a class of foreign members.

While this remained a private initiative, the pressure for the creation of a roll of the practitioners, controlled by a public body such as the Patent Office or directly by the Board of Trade, did not relent.[13] Not surprisingly, the members of the Institute were among the most vigorous advocates of such measure. A boost to the proposal came from a most prestigious voice, namely the physicist and inventor/entrepreneur James Thomson (the future Lord Kelvin). In 1887, in his evidence to the Committee set up by the Board of Trade to discuss the Patent Act, Thomson argued in favour of some form of control over the professional qualification of patent agents. Eventually, in 1889, the Board of Trade complied with the request by creating a Register and issuing rules for the admission of candidates.[14] As a result of this measure, no person was entitled to describe himself (no women were involved)[15] as a patent agent unless he was registered; however people who did not join the Register were at liberty to offer their services, so long as they avoided using for themselves the title of patent agents. The scope of the measure was therefore limited, namely to allow prospective patentees to make an informed choice as to the practitioners they were consulting, without preventing them from asking – if they wanted to – the advice of people who were not enlisted in the Register. Moreover the qualification required for admission was minimal: it was enough to demonstrate 'to the satisfaction of the Board of Trade' that the candidate had been *bonâ fide* practising as a patent agent before the passing of the act; in fact, it was sufficient to prove that the candidates had filed one complete specification. Inclusiveness, it was argued, was meant to guarantee a form of control, for the Registered agents who were found guilty of malpractice could be struck out.[16] The result was a roll of 257 people who, in accordance with entrance requirements, carried out patent related business in a variety of different forms: as pointed out above, by 1889 there were already several individuals and well-established firms whose occupation consisted exclusively in patent agency (dealing also with designs and trademarks); however many practitioners continued to combine it with other occupations – most notably engineering consultancy.

Obviously the interests of the public could hardly be overlooked by the parties involved; nobody objected to the necessity to prevent and to sanction misconduct. However the decision to create a Register had other and more controversial implications: what was at stake was the definition of who was entitled to practice in a publicly recognised and therefore legitimized way. The fact that, along with the Register, the Board of Trade established also examinations as a procedure for the admission of agents, to be adopted subsequently to the first round of enrolments, suggested that they were moving in that direction. And yet neither that body nor the Patent Office took upon itself the responsibility of conducting the examinations: that task, as well as the keeping of the Register, were delegated to a private association, the Institution of Patent Agents; the same association was also entrusted with the task of levying the registration fees and organizing the examinations.[17]

These decisions brought to light the tension between the different components of the occupational group that had been brewing for more than two decades. The assumption was that, on the strength of the responsibility bestowed on them by the Board of Trade, the Institute would inevitably try to extend to the entire occupational group their own professional standards and rules. It was clear to contemporary observers that the members of the Institute were the élite of the profession; far from resenting it, it was a self-image that they cherished. The 46 founding fellows were partners of firms that had been in existence for considerable time and their activity consisted exclusively of patent agency.[18] Their dominant position rested not only on their experience and reputation but also, and above all, on their extensive practice. In 1894, when the total number of Registered patent agents was 245, the membership of the Institute consisted of 70 Fellows;[19] and yet, according to an estimate given by the President of the CIPA, as many as 45 per cent of the total number of complete specifications filed at the Patent Office in London were processed by members of the CIPA.[20] The promotion of high professional standards was part and parcel of their business strategy: reputation and trustworthiness we regarded as main assets, and by adopting a strict code of behaviour they were determined to preserve them as their distinctive hallmarks. The granting of the Royal Charter in 1891, as a result of which the association became the Chartered Institute of Patent Agents, was undoubtedly a prestigious public recognition of the distinction they had sought to achieve as a professional group; nevertheless in the eyes of the other practitioners they were and remained a private association.[21]

The tension erupted in open conflict in 1893 when a rival association was created, the Society of Patent Agents (SPA). Its aim, explicitly stated, was to challenge the way in which the management of the Register had been arranged by the Board of Trade, and in particular the role of CIPA.

The objections raised by the SPA were clear: in their view the Institute consisted of a small group of the practitioners, and therefore it was not entitled to represent and still less to control them as a whole. The members of the new association, who were also Registered agents, not only denounced the privileged position achieved by the Institute by virtue of having received from the Board of Trade the administration of the Register;[22] they also resented its self-appointed status as a 'super-professional' body. The Society, which also published a journal,[23] remained a comparatively small association, reaching as its highest 40 members. However they sought to present themselves as spokesmen of the majority of the practitioners, the 'outsiders' who had not joined the 'élite club', and they were determined to make their voice heard – with the support of few but influential allies. In fact, an in-depth study of the people who supported the SPA in its attack to the CIPA members, their political, economic and industrial interests, would be most revealing.[24]

In 1893, as an attempt to solve the situation, two Bills on patent agency were submitted to the House of Lords, one by the Institute and one by the Society.[25] The discussion of the Bills was referred to a Select Committee especially appointed in 1894 by the Board of Trade. That was the occasion on which the positions of the two parties, not only their different interests and agendas but more generally the heterogeneity of positions within the occupational group, came to the fore – some of them clearly expressed by the actors involved, others less explicitly.

THE PRACTITIONERS

The background of patent agents was by and large common: among those who entered the business before 1870 there were some solicitors, and assistance with regard to trademarks was also offered by printers, but the majority of them, both the élite and the 'outsiders', had some form of technical training, in civil or more frequently in mechanical engineering. After 1870 a growing number of patent agents received their training as pupils or assistants of patent agents, sometimes integrating it with work carried out in chemical or mechanical works. Solicitors too carried out some agency work, and they were determined to safeguard their access to that market, even when it became clear that it was being taken over by a new category of experts. For their part, both CIPA and SPA carefully avoided antagonizing their association; a compromise was reached as a result of which practicing solicitors who engaged in patent business were exempted from registration.[26] It is also the case that some patent agents, especially among the CIPA fellows, had a legal background: for example, John H. Johnson, one of the founding fellows of that institution, was a solicitor, and his son, James Yate, followed in his steps before joining him as partner in 1888.[27] Nevertheless they were a minority; clearly the divide was not between agents with a legal and with a technical background.

The main cleavage consisted rather in the way in which the work was carried out, between practitioners whose occupation consisted exclusively with patent applications and related business (all the fellows of CIPA belonged to that category) and those who carried out patent agency more or less occasionally and as a complement to other kinds of activity. The regulations adopted by the Board of Trade allowed representatives of the latter group to qualify as patent agents; and in fact many of the registered agents belonged to that category. The cleavage between exclusive and non-exclusive practice intersects with another major partition, this one of a geographical character. As Inkster points out, the capital was undoubtedly the main hub of patent agency business: in 1882 31 of the 46 founding Fellows of CIPA were heads or partners of London-based firms;[28] the proportion did not change significantly at the end of the century: in 1897, when their number had risen to 90, 58 of them operated in the capital.[29] As for the Registered patent agents, in 1894 more than half (128 of the total 246 practitioners) were based in London.[30] The intersection consists in the fact that many of the practitioners for whom patent agency was an exclusive profession operated in London, whereas the 'non-exclusive' tended to operate in the urban provincial areas. One of the issues that was repeatedly raised by the opponents to CIPA was precisely that whereas that association represented effectively the interests of the 'exclusive', London-base agents, it did not take into account those of the practitioners who worked in the provincial towns. For the latter, it was argued, an occasional involvement in patent agency was not a matter of choice but rather of necessity: the demand for that kind of activity was not enough to justify specialization.[31]

In reality, in spite of their self-appointed role as the paladins of the provincial and non-exclusive agents, the geographical/occupational cleavage affected also the membership of SPA; so much so that eventually it became one of the causes of internal friction even within that association.[32] Moreover, among those who did not join the CIPA 'élite' circle there were not only representatives of the 'non-exclusive' and provincial practitioners but also some prominent individuals like William Gadd and Joseph Wilson, both consulting engineers and patent agents in Manchester, and firms like Herbert, Haddan & Co. and Fairfax & Wetter, both London-based. So other professional interests were also at the root of the tension, intersecting but not coinciding with the two partitions mentioned above.

Certainly the networks within which patent agents operated differed according to their geographical location; and different was also the portfolio of their clients. It is clear that the London-based agents intercepted a good deal of the foreign patentees intent on finding their way to the doorsteps of the London Patent Office. In 1870 they represented 27 per cent of the total number of patents issued;[33] and the main beneficiaries of that lucrative business were mainly the old, established firms like Haseltine, Lake & Co., Abel & Imray and Ernest De Pass' Office for British and Foreign Patents. But what were the other differences in the portfolios of the patent agents? It would be interesting to examine, from the patent agents' perspective, what the characteristics of the inventors market were and how collaborations between patentees and agents were established; and what proportion of 'élite patents' were filed by élite patent agents.[34] The question, more specifically, is to what extent ambitious, well-informed and expert patentees and, especially from the late nineteenth century, corporate patentees, opted for particular patent agents; what factors affected their choices, and to what extent reputation, so eagerly cultivated especially by CIPA fellows, was an effective asset, paying back the expected dividends. Anecdotal evidence suggests the existence of fairly consolidated patterns of collaboration between high-profile inventors (British and foreigners) and high-profile patent agents.[35] More importantly though, it would be interesting to examine if and to what extent the interests of the patent agents coincided with those of their main clients. The question, in particular, is whether the interests of the 'élite patentees' and, especially towards the end of the century when industry became more concerned with intellectual property, those of corporate patentees corresponded to the professional standards upheld by the leading practitioners represented by CIPA. Conversely, the question that remains to be addressed is whether the positions of the 'outsiders', of the non-exclusive agents or those at work in provincial areas, somehow corresponded to the interests of the particular sectors of the patentees market they catered for.

As for the second question, namely how the internal tension evolved over time, any suggestion is even more tentative. Undoubtedly the SPA achieved some of its objectives; in particular they staved off the attempt of the CIPA to preclude the access to the Patent Office to non-registered practitioners. The other main result they obtained was to reopen the Register to new admissions with the same rules of 1888, namely to the individuals who could claim to be engaged in patent practice. For its own part, the CIPA tried to take off the edge of its critics' pressure by reducing the admission fees for all its categories of membership, so as to encourage more Registered agents to join the association; witness of their tactful mood is the particular attention they paid to the provincial agents, whose fees were set at a lower level than their London colleagues.[36]

If that was a success for the SPA, it was a self-defeating one: gradually more Registered agents joined the ranks of the CIPA and by 1904 the 'rebel' association ceased to exist, thus leaving the CIPA as the only professional association.[37] In that year already 60 per cent of the 262 Registered patent agents were members of the CIPA.[38] Was it the sign of a gradual acceptance by an occupational group of the professional standards advocated by the CIPA? And what happened with regard to the non-registered people who offered their service to inventors under various labels such as 'patent experts', 'patent offices', 'inventors' agents' and other allusive denominations? The advertisements published in technical journals and magazines indicate that this form of activity continued well into the twentieth century, in London as well as in the provinces. In the late nineteenth century scientific and technical magazines published also a flurry of advertisement of special facilities for inventors. Although they did not openly suggest an involvement in patent agency, they offered laboratory space and equipment, as well as technical expertise, in the service of prospective patentees. In London the General Engineering Company, set up by G. W. von Tunzelmann in London, offered facilities for experimenting mechanical, electrical and chemical patents and constructing models;[39] and the firm Braun & Co., Inventors' Model Makers and Scientific Experimental Engineers, announced that they undertook to develop inventions but also, very intriguingly, 'to form companies to work mechanical patents in all parts of the world'.[40] In 1893 15 per cent of the total patents granted in Britain was filed without the assistance of registered agents, either by the inventors themselves or with the undeclared assistance of some kind of 'experts';[41] if that estimate is correct, the share of the market that was left for them was limited, but not altogether insignificant. But who were the clients? Is it correct to assume that they were targeting/exploiting the lower layer of the patentees, the amateurish and occasional type?

FORMATION AND HOMOLOGATION

Another perspective from which the evolution of the occupational group can be considered – albeit limitedly to the Registered agents – is the mechanism by which new enrolments were made. As I pointed out above, according to the rules of 1889 admission to the Register for those agents who were not already in practice was conditional to the passing of an examination; the same rules indicated also the two routes by which candidates were admitted to the examination: they had to prove that they had been pupils or assistants of a Registered patent agent for seven years, or that they had passed preliminary examinations at recognized institutions of higher education.[42] Originally they were the matriculation examination at any university in Britain, the Oxford and Cambridge middle class senior local examination or the examinations of the Civil Service Commissioners for admission to the civil service; subsequently other institutions, offering scientific and technical degrees, were added to the list.[43]

In spite of the strong dissatisfaction of some of the 'outsiders' with the role of the CIPA in the organization and administration of the examination, once the system became operational it remained solidly in the hold of that association. On the other hand, the objections raised, especially by the members of the SPA, to the level at which the examinations were originally pitched were heeded:[44] as a result adjustments were made which reduced the difficulty of the tests, especially those on scientific and technical subjects. A change was also introduced with regard to one of the routes of access to the examination: according to the CIPA it was due to 'external pressure' that in 1901 the period of apprenticeship was the reduced to five years.[45] However even after those modifications the examinations were, according to the reports published in the *Transactions of the CIPA*, comprehensive and thorough, occupying no less than six hours per day for five days; in the mid-1890s the subjects included 'Law and practice relating to patents, Preparation of Specifications, Case law, Foreign Patent Law and Practice, Manufactures, Applied Mechanics, Electricity, Chemistry and Heat' (mechanical drawing was included in 1898).[46] The candidates who passed the examinations were entitled to apply for enrolment in the Register; they were eligible for admission to the CIPA, if they wanted to enter that association.

Having established a procedure for the assessment of the qualification of the candidates, a main problem remained though, namely their formation before the examination, and especially the combination of technical and the legal aspects of the patent business. At the end of the century the debate on the form of training and education that could best serve that scope, and on the institutions that could offer it, was intense within the occupational community. In this sector, as with regard to scientific and technical education more generally, Germany became a model to which some of the patent agents looked with admiration when, in 1900, regulations were issued with regard to the qualification of the patent agents to be admitted to the newly established Register kept by the German Patent Office. In order to be admitted, candidates had to prove not only that they had practical experience having worked for at least one year in an industrial concern and two years experience in matters relating to patenting but also that they held a degree of a technical high school, a university or a mining college.[47] In Britain, by contrast, the problem remained an open-ended one: no prescriptions were issued about the course of instruction and the task of ascertaining the qualification of the candidates remained deferred to the examiners.

This does not mean that the importance of the formal education of the new generations was underestimated; in fact, especially for the élite agents, education could be more than a way of obtaining relevant instruction. The case of the Carpmael family is particularly interesting for the attention paid not only to formal education as a source of potentially relevant professional instruction but also for the social benefit that could ensue from a carefully selected educational curriculum.[48] All the six sons of the founder, William Carpmael, were channelled through Clapham Grammar School where they were expected to benefit not only from the particular attention paid to scientific education[49] but also from the association with a distinctly middle-class milieu: among their contemporaries at Clapham there were Arthur Rücker, (from a family of prosperous colonial merchants, later to become professor of physics at Yorkshire College, Leeds), and two of Charles Darwin's sons, George and Frank. On leaving Clapham, the first three sons began to prepare for their professional career: two joined their father, the other was introduced to a firm of solicitors (of which he soon became a partner). However for the last three sons Carpmael chose Cambridge, where all of them sat for the Tripos, the prestigious examination that was the nursery of several among the most famous and successful barristers of the time. One of the young Carpmaels was 'lost' to science, but the others became respectively a partner in the family firm and a successful solicitor specializing in patent law. It is hard to imagine that the scientific education they received at Clapham and Cambridge was of much use in dealing with the technical side of the patent business, but certainly as a result of their dwelling in the lofty halls of those institutions they were not altogether unfamiliar to the kind of people they were later to encounter in the law courts.

Admittedly the very high-profile pattern adopted by the Carpmaels was unusual, even among the CIPA élite group. However a superficial survey of the biographical memoirs of patent agents who were admitted to the Register before the end of the century suggests that access to the examination via the route of higher education was becoming more common: in the period from 1889 to 1900 105 candidates were examined; 63 of them had been pupils for seven years, 42 had passed recognized preliminary examinations, most of them having attended college level scientific or technological courses.[50] Even the candidates who were admitted via the apprenticeship route showed a growing level of education. That said the most important aspect of the future agents' instruction, namely the acquisition of the skills and expertise required for dealing with the patent business, and especially with regard to its legal side, was and remained essentially based on practice. There is no doubt that the offices of the patent agents were the real 'high schools' that prepared for the profession. It is telltale of the strength of that tradition that in their advertisements patent agents indicated their employment with some of the most prestigious firms previously to their setting up in business on their own account, as a testimony of their qualification.

This debate, and the development of an hybrid form of instruction and training at the interface between technology and law, is in itself a subject that deserves to be examined in-depth. It also prompts questions on the different approaches adopted in other countries, most notably in Germany and the United States. Although a degree of higher education was required in order to gain admission to the Register of patent agents of the Imperial Patent Office of Berlin, both in Germany and Britain the main emphasis was on scientific and especially technical experience and competence. On the other hand, in the United States, as in Britain, no requirements were specified with regard to the educational background and training of the future practitioners; it has been argued that a distinctive feature of the American patent business, especially in the second half of the nineteenth-century, was the tension between lawyers and nonlawyers, and the prevalence of the legal over the technical expertise.[51] The implications of these similarities and discrepancies in the attempt to define the background of patent agents and the balance between technical and legal formation remains to be explored in a comparative perspective. However the issue I want to highlight here is more narrowly focused: it is the impact that the introduction of the examination had on the profile of the Registered agents. It is not unreasonable to assume that this procedure, not only the examination as such but also the formation by apprenticeship before and after the examination, favoured a growing homologation in the characteristics of the new, post-1883 generation of patent agents. If that was the case, did such homologation extend not only to the characteristics of their profile but also more generally to their approach to the profession? And did that have an impact on the evolving pattern of patent procedures and specifications, favouring the emergence of distinctive and possibly more homogeneous standards?

BROKERAGE IN THE MARKET FOR INVENTION

A main question remains, and that is how do British patent agents compare to their US colleagues as brokers in the market for invention. The role of patent agents as intermediaries in the US market for technology in the late nineteenth and early twentieth centuries has been examined by Naomi Lamoreaux and Kenneth Sokoloff.[52] Drawing on both quantitative and qualitative data, their analysis highlights the contribution of American patent agents to the commercialization of invention in the United States. In reality, the very dimension of the market for patents, its characteristics and the way in which it operated is just one of the aspects that needs to be ascertained, both with regard to assignments and licences. Contemporary observers commented on the reluctance of British firms and companies to buy patents.[53] The fact that the validity and the value of patents depended, more than in other countries, on their capacity to stand litigation, and the awareness that their strength rested to a large extent on the determination of the patentee (or the patent holder) to invest money in their defence, made potential licensees and assignors more cautious.[54] However, in the absence of quantitative surveys comparable to those available for the United States, it is also difficult to ascertain the role played by patent agents. In his study of the pre-1852 period, Dutton argued that one of the ways in which patent agents assisted inventors was by acting as intermediaries, introducing them to manufacturers and capitalists.[55] He draws his evidence from the work of people who typically, in that period, combined patent agency with consulting as civil or mechanical engineers. The problem, when we move to the late nineteenth century, is to what extent brokerage became an organic and recognized part of the patent agents' business. The observations that follow are therefore more on their propensity to act as brokers than on their actual involvement in that kind of activity.

It is certainly true that the services they provided extended beyond the preparation and filing of applications. Agents were asked to provide documents certifying the validity of patents when they were in the process of being sold, or when public companies were set up whose aim was their commercial exploitation; such documents were normally attached to the prospectuses issued to prospective shareholders, along with similar documents by scientific experts and lawyers. The same kind of documents were probably required also for licensing agreements. They also provided advice when patentees considered litigation and, in collaboration with lawyers, when the validity of their patents was challenged in court. In fact assistance in preparing for law court proceedings must have been a considerable source of income.

As to acting as brokers, however, the positions of patent agents were by no means homogeneous. Some of them did not regard it improper to participate in the creation of syndicates, whether to provide the funds that were required to test an invention or to bring it to commercial fruition. In some cases they also became partners or shareholders in such ventures. In the mid-1860s John H. Johnson, who assisted the Belgian inventor Jean Joseph Étienne Lenoir in obtaining a British patent for his gas engine, took a direct interest in that invention.[56] Johnson, a founding member of the Institute of Patent Agents and its first president, helped Lenoir in launching the production of his engines on British soil 'by taking shares and otherwise'. A company was set up and according to Johnson 300 or 400 engines left the works, although in the end the company did not prove successful.[57]

It was a behaviour that some of his colleagues disapproved. It was not only the correctness of a direct involvement in a client's venture that was questioned; the offer of financial support, or of contacts with people interested in the purchasers of inventions, before or after filing a patent, was regarded by some patent agents as the bait with which unscrupulous practitioners tried to lure naïve patentees. To avoid advertising the sale or license of patents was one of the recommendations given by the CIPA to its fellows.[58] This view found supporters also among the 'outside' Registered agents. Reginald Haddan was partner in the London-based firm Herbert Haddan & Co. whose founder (his father) had stood aside from both CIPA and SPA. He was the author of a textbook, first published in 1894, in which the commercial aspects of patenting and of the management of patents were discussed in more detail than in other similar manuals, and in which he made scathing comments about combining patent agency and patent selling:

> There are no recognised 'patent brokers,' or persons who truly make a business of buying and selling patents [. . .] There is a class of practitioners who make a great pretence of negotiating patents. Such business is entirely foreign to the proper avocation of a patent agent, and it is to be feared that it is resorted to in many instances simply to attract business from inventor. The principal patent agents do not hold themselves out as sale agents, though in their connection they will often number manufacturers interested in patents to whom they are not averse from introducing inventors with genuine novelties.[59]

The same view was held by Marks & Clerk who, in the booklet mentioned above, informed American attorneys (and their clients) that:

> the business of selling or negotiating the sale of a patent is not part of the business we undertake. Our practice is to obtain patents, not to exploit them. The attorney or agent who offers to sell a patent will sooner or later disappoint himself or annoy or loose clients.

That said, they were willing to pass on information to 'merchants and factors' who dealt especially with that sort of activity.[60]

Not all patent agents took such a resolute stand against brokerage. The existence of discordant opinions surfaces clearly in the discussion triggered by a paper offered by Frederick Walker, patent agent in London, at a meeting of the SPA. 'The question has been raised from time to time whether a patent agent, as a professional man, should make a practice of exploiting or dealing with patents commercially'.[61] He argued that one thing was for an agent to assist a patentee in finding a partner and financial support, quite another to do it as part of his business, and to be paid for it. In the discussion that followed his view was shared by Reginald W. Barker, also practising in London. Others, on the other hand, argued that they did not see moral or professional objections to providing assistance to clients, especially those who did not have the benefit of industrial and financial connections. Thomas Wilkins, patent agent in London, had no qualms in admitting that he arranged agreements between manufacturers and patentees, and also in the formation of syndicates; where he drew the line was at profit sharing because that would have biased the judgement of the agent.[62] As for Joseph Lockwood, who practiced in Glasgow, he regarded assistance in the sale of patents as particularly valuable for his clients who, in that part of the country, would have found it otherwise difficult to find an outlet for their inventions: 'an ingenious but unpecunious inventor in Scotland is obliged to look to his patent agent for help and suggestion in launching his invention before likely parties'.[63]

As a matter of fact, in the late nineteenth and early twentieth century the offer of assistance in the commercialization of invention (before and after patenting) remained one of the facilities offered by some agents, and occasionally indicated in explicit terms in their advertisements. In the 1890s John G. Wilson & Co. of Manchester, registered patent agents, consulting engineers and scientific experts, offered 'special facilities for the purchase and sale of inventions'.[64] There is no reason to believe that Wilson & Co., later to become the well-established firm Wilson Gunn firm, acted less than correctly; however the behaviour of other agents corroborated the worst views of the critics. In the late nineteenth and early twentieth century Edmund O. Eaton, head of the London-based Inventors' Patent Office, informed potential clients that he had a finance department for 'Sales of Patents, Designs, Unpatented inventions, Patents placed on Royalties'; however he turned out to be a 'share-pusher' and an adventurer 'specialized in buying up small worthless companies and selling their shares through the mails'.[65] Other agents presented themselves specifically as patent brokers, although probably they acted also as agents; this was the case of offices like the Patent Exploitation Ltd of Liverpool.[66]

The disparity of attitudes must have remained a lingering problem among the agents if, more than 15 years later, the newly appointed president of the CIPA, R. B. Ransford (a partner of Carpmael), in his reflections on the state of the profession, indicated as one of the professional principles he regarded as fundamental that 'a patent agent should refrain from having any commercial interest in a patent or in any concern or business connected with a patent'.[67] Clearly even the patent agents who disapproved of mingling with their clients' commercial activity and of embarking upon brokerage as part of their professional activity might well have assisted their clients in non-official ways, for example by establishing out-of-office contacts between independent inventors and manufacturers. However the point I would like to suggest here is rather that the different attitudes among the practitioners seem to bring back the problem outlined before, namely that also their involvement in intermediation might somehow relate to specific characteristics and professional interests of different segments of the professional community, and to what they regarded as the prevalent interests of their clients. It is reasonable to assume that the market for inventions was sector-specific, and also that the attitudes towards both patentees and licensors varied according to the state of development of a particular technology. The attitudes of patent agents whose portfolio was closely associated to particular sectors might have reflected or responded to the interests of their particular clientele. The involvement of patent agents in the sale or licensing of patents and in the procurement of agreements between inventors and financial or industrial partners, appears to be more common in the provinces; but the evidence is anecdotal, and it might well be the result of the fact that provincial agents were keen to promote that aspect of their activity. Was the argument offered by agents like Gadd, namely the lack of interest in the market for invention and the distance from the city and its financial hubs, an adequate and sufficient explanation? In any case, if patent agents were not as actively engaged in brokerage as their colleagues in the United States, what remains to be explained in more detail is how the market (or the markets) worked, and who the intermediaries were. But an answer can only emerge from a more systematic research on the licensing and sale of patent rights in Britain, and on how the negotiations were carried out.

CONCLUDING REMARKS

As I indicated at the start, the aim of the chapter is to suggest themes for future research on the development of a professional community whose history has so far remained relatively little explored. The themes that have been outlined are the occupational and geographical characteristics of the practitioners, how such characteristics affected the emergence of a new professional group and the debate on the standards and formation of the patent agents and their position with regard to the market for invention. The result is a broad-brush survey, and by no means comprehensive; the role they played in the transfer of technologies across national boundaries (as pointed out in the essay by Pretel and Saiz in this volume), is another promising direction for further research. So is the role they played in the international arena, in the attempt to overcome the difficulties arising from different patent regimes and regulations.

Because it has been cast as a survey, the questions that emerge from this essay remain open-ended. The changes in the profile of the patent agents at the turn of the century and in the early twentieth, and the process by which their professional interests and agenda were negotiated and defined, deserve to be examined on the basis of a more systematic empirical research. So does the way and the extent to which they their interests were brought to bear, along those of the other 'players', on the evolution of the 'rules of the game' – the patent system as an institution, to stick to North's image evoked in Ian Inkster's introduction. My final comment is methodological: it arises from the very nature of the work of patent agents as intermediaries operating at the inter-face between a variety of professional and occupational groups, and of patent agency as an hybrid occupational activity drawing on technical as well as legal expertise. The themes outlined above can undoubtedly be explored from dif-ferent perspectives, but their analysis would benefit considerably from a close collaboration between historians – historians of the techno-sciences, legal, eco-nomic and social historians.

Notes

1. Ian Inkster, 'Discoveries, Inventions and Industrial Revolutions: on the varying Contributions of Technologies and Institutions from an International Historical Perspective', *History of Technology*, 1996, 18: 39–58, at 50.

2. There are exceptions, of course. Patent agents were among the occupational groups included in Alexander M. Carr-Saunders and Paul A. Wilson's study *The professions* (Oxford, 1933), 58–64. Harold I. Dutton discussed the early history of patent agency in *The Patent System and Inventive Activity during the Industrial Revolution 1750–1852* (Manchester, 1984), esp. Chapter 5, 86–100. So did Dirk van Zyl Smit in 'Professional Patent Agents and the Development of the English Patent System', *International Journal of Sociology and Law*, 1985, 13: 79–105.

3. Naomi Lamoreaux and Kenneth Sokoloff, 'Intermediaries in the U.S. Market for Technology, 1870–1920', in *Finance, Intermediaries, and Economic Development*, eds, Stanley Engerman, Philip Hoffman and Kenneth L. Sokoloff, (Cambridge, 2003), 209–46. Gabriel Gálvez-Behar, 'Des Médiateurs au Coeur du Système d'Innovation: Les Agents de Brevets en France (1870–1914)', in *Les Archives de l'Invention: Ecrits, Objets et Images de l'Activité Inventive*, eds, Marie-Sophie Corcy, Christiane Douyère-Demeulenaere and Liliane Hilaire-Pérez (Toulouse, 2006), 437–47; and by the same author *La République des Inventeurs. Propriété et Organization de l'Innovation en France (1791–1922)* (Rennes, 2008), 50–1 and 116–18. Kara W. Swanson, 'The Emergence of the Professional Patent Practitioner', *Technology and Culture*, 2009, 50: 519–48. Frequent references to the work of German patent agents are also in Margrit Seckelmann, *Industrialisierung, Internationalisierung und Patentrecht im Deutschen Reich, 1871–1914* (Frankfurt am Main, 2006).

4. See also Ian Inkster, 'Engineers as Patentees and the Cultures of Invention 1830–1914 and beyond. The Evidence from the Patent Data', *Quaderns d'Història de l'Enginyeria*, 2004, 6: 1–27; and 'Machinoculture and Technical Change: The Patent Evidence', in *The Golden Age: Essays in British Economic and Social History, 1850–1870*, eds, Ian Inkster, Colin Griffin, Jeff Hill, and Judith Rowbotham (London, 2000), 121–45. The contribution of patent agents to technical change was also intense in other countries; see for example Gálvez-Behar, 'Des Médiateurs au Coeur du Système d'Innovation', *op. cit.* (3); and Lamoreaux and Sokoloff, *op. cit.* (3).

5. van Zyl Smit, *op. cit.* (2).

6. Ibid.; Dutton, *op. cit.* (2). On the participation of patent agents, and especially of A. V. Newton, in the patent controversy see also Victor Batzel, 'Legal Monopoly in Liberal England: the Patent Controversy in the Mid-nineteenth Century', *Business History*, 1980, 22: 189–202; and Christine MacLeod, 'Concepts of Invention and the Patent Controversy', in *Technological Change*, ed., Robert Fox (Amsterdam, 1996), 137–53.

7. Dutton, *op. cit.* (2), at 94–6.

8. Cases of incompetence and malpractice were already exposed in the *Report and Minutes of Evidence taken before the Select Committee of the House of Lords, Appointed to Consider of the Bill Intituled 'An Act further to Amend the Law Touching Letters Patent for Inventions'* (London, 1851); for example by Paul R. Hodge, 'practical engineer, inventor, patentee, patent agent', 84–5 (Q 482–6); and William Spence, a patent agent, 141 (Q 884–6). However there are no precise indications of how common such cases were, and what their nature was.

9. *Royal Commission to Inquire into the Working of the Law relating to Letter Patent for Inventions*, British Parliamentary Papers, 1864, XXIX; William Hindmarch, Minority Report, 335–7.

10. 'Memorandum of Articles of Association', *Transactions of the Institute of Patent Agents*, 1882–3, 1: 1–32. J. H. Johnson, 'Inaugural address', *Transactions of the Institute of Patent Agents*, 1882–3, 1: 35–43. The Institute became in 1891 the Chartered Institute of Patent Agents, and the journal the *Transactions of the Chartered Institute of Patent Agents* (see below). I shall refer to them as CIPA and *Transactions of the CIPA*.

11. In 1843 the Solicitors' Act established a Roll of Attorneys and Solicitors; subsequent acts dealt with malpractice (1874), and admission examinations (1877). Richard L. Abel, *The legal profession in England and Wales* (Oxford, 1988).

12. According to the original statute, candidates to the Fellowship were required to pass an examination in patent law and practice, mechanical drawing and other technical subjects, and that the examination was to be conducted by members of the Council of the Institute or by external experts appointed by them. In reality, the first formal examination was held in 1889, after the creation of the Register.

13. *Report of the Committee appointed by the Board of Trade to inquire into the Duties, Organisation, and Arrangements of the Patent Office under the Patents, Designs, and Trade Marks Act* (London, 1887, c. 4,968), Minutes of Evidence, William Thomson, at 16 (Q 398).

14. *Patents, Designs, and Trade Marks Act, 1888* (51 & 52 Vict. c. 50), s. 1. In the Unites States a register of patent attorneys, including 'nonlawyer' agents, was established in 1897; Swanson, *op. cit.* (3) at 543. In Germany a similar initiative was adopted in 1900; Seckelmann, *op. cit.* (3) at 310–3. In France the creation of a roll was delayed by the reluctance of the Office National de la Propriété Industrielle to create division within the practitioners; Gálvez-Behar, *La République des Inventeurs, op. cit.* (3) at 219–20.

15. In reality there was at least one exception, namely Eliza Orme. By the time she graduated in law at the University of London, Orme was already conducting what her entry in the ODNB describes as a prosperous business, '"devilling" for lawyers as a conveyance and a patent agent'. Leslie Howsam, 'Liza Orme', *Oxford Dictionary of National Biography* (Oxford, 2004).

16. *Special Report from the Select Committee on the Patent Agents Bill. Together with the Proceedings of the Committee*. Minutes of Evidence, Appendix and Index, (London, 1894), F. Hopwood, secretary of the Board of Trade, at 8, (Q 83–94). In fact, only two agents were expelled, ibid., 14, (Q 199–200).

17. The fees required for admission to the Register were £5 on entrance and £3 for the annual subscription. The equivalent fees set by the Institution of Mechanical Engineers were £2 and £3 respectively.

18. 'List of Members', *Transactions of the Institute of Patent Agents*, 1882–3, 1: vi–viii.

19. *Special Report, op. cit.* (16) at iv.

20. W. Lloyd Wise, 'The present position of the profession', *Transactions of the CIPA*, 1893–4, 12: 97–112, at 111. According to the same source, 40 per cent of the patents were filed by Registered agents who were not members of the Institute, and only 15 per cent by the applicants themselves.

21. 'Charter of Incorporation', *Transactions of the CIPA*, 1891–2, 10: 3–25.

22. *Special Report, op. cit.* (16) in particular J. S. Fairfax, 92–101; and W. Gadd, 107–16.

23. *Transactions of the Society of Patent Agents*, first published in 1894; in 1900 it became the *Journal of the Society of Patent Agents*. For consistency I shall refer to it as *Journal of the SPA*.

24. 'Patent agents' (Editorial), *The Electrician*, 1894, 39: 12–3. Among them there were Albert Rollit, barrister and Conservative MP, later to become president of the Law Society, William F. D. Smith, from 1891 head of the newspaper-distributing business of W. H. Smith & Son, and Reginald Hanson, former Lord Mayor of London, Conservative MP and senior partner of the wholesale grocery business, Samuel Hanson & Son.

25. A third Bill was prepared by a third party of patent agents who did not agree entirely with either of the two parties, but it was not submitted. *Special Report, op. cit.* (16), F. Hopwood, 12 (Q 160–1).

26. As William Lloyd Wise, in his capacity as the president of the CIPA, pointed out on occasion of the discussion of the Bill, 'that very powerful body, the Incorporated Law Society, would have opposed them tooth and nail if they had not made concessions'. W. Lloyd Wise, 'The President's Statement', *Transactions of the CIPA*, 1894–5, 13: 68–86, on 84–5. For similar remarks by a member of the SPA see William Gadd's evidence, *Special Report, op. cit.* (16) 110 (Q 1873–4).

27. John H. Johnson, 'Memoirs', *Transactions of the CIPA*, 1899–1900, 18: 265–6; James Y. Johnson, 'Memoirs', *Transactions of the CIPA*, 1935–6, 54: 224. George B. Ellis, one of the two candidates who passed in the first examination set up by the Board of Trade, was also a solicitor who practiced both as a patent agent and a solicitor; 'Memoirs', *Transactions of the CIPA*, 1938–9, 57: 198–9.

28. 'List of Members', *Transactions of the CIPA*, 1882–3, 1: vi–viii.

29. 'List of Members', *Transactions of the CIPA*, 1896–7, 15: x–xv. The geographical concentration was even higher for the 28 Associate Fellows, 26 of whom were London residents.

30. *Special Report, op. cit.* (16) Lloyd Wise, 49 (Q 737).

31. *Special Report, op. cit.* (16) especially Fairfax, 93 (Q 1527–31).

32. 'Patent Agents' Watch Committee' (Editorial), *Journal of the SPA*, 1901, 2: 176–80.

33. Inkster, 'Machinoculture and Technical Change', *op. cit.* (4) at 133–4.

34. Inkster describes them as patents that were lodged by particular categories of individuals or partnerships, or extended to seven and then 14 years beyond the initial granting, or lodged in foreign patent systems; Inkster, 'Machinoculture and Technical Change', *op. cit.* (4) at 136–7. He suggests that in the period 1850–70 'probably between 10% and 20% of all patenting may be regarded as an élite activity'. Here I do not suggest to consider only the presumed financial value of a patent, but also the 'quality' of the applicants, their expectations and ambitions and also their social status and their position within influential economic, techno/scientific and political networks.

35. The electrical inventor and entrepreneur Sebastian Ziani de Ferranti, for example, choose consistently the Carpmaels as his patent agents; Abel & Imray had among their regular clients Westinghouse and Meister Lucius & Brüning.

36. Originally the fees were £6 on admission and £4 for the annual subscription for the Fellows, and £3 and £2 respectively for the Associates. The reduction brought them down to £3 for admission and £3 for the annual subscription for 'town Fellows' and to £2 and £2 for 'country Fellows'. H. Howard Graham, 'On the Progress and Work of the Chartered Institute of Patent Agents', *Transactions of the CIPA*, 1900–1, 19: 113–52, at 115.

37. The Patents and Designs Act of 1907 confirmed the responsibility of the CIPA for the keeping of the Register and the organization of the examinations.

38. George G. M. Hardingham, 'The President's Opening Address', *Transactions of the CIPA*, 1904–5, 23: 43–56, at 54.

39. The General Engineering Company, Advertisement in *Nature*, 1899, 61: ii.

40. Braun & Co., *Journal of the SPA*, 1903, 3: 668.

41. Lloyd Wise, 'The Present Position of the Profession' *op. cit.* (20), at 111.

42. Thomas Terrell, *The Law and Practice Relating to Letters Patent for Inventions* (3rd edn) (London, 1895), Register of Patent Agents Rules, 460–7.

43. People entitled to practice as solicitors before the Supreme Court of Judicature in England and Ireland, or as law agents before the Court of Session in Scotland, were also admitted to the examination.

44. For comments on the excessive difficulty of the examinations see *Special Report, op. cit.* (16) Fairfax, 97 (Q 1637–40). For the revised regulations see Thomas Terrell, *The Law and Practice relating to Letters Patent for Inventions* (4th edn) (London, 1906), Register of Patent Agents Rules, 538–67.

45. Hardingham, 'The President's Opening Address', *op. cit.* (38) at 23.

46. The examiners were members of the CIPA as well as prominent barristers and scientific and technical experts (John Hopkinson, Silvanus Thompson, Ambrose Fleming). H. Howard Graham, 'On the Progress and Work of the Chartered Institute of Patent Agents', *op. cit.* (36) at 123–4.

47. Hardingham, 'The President's Opening Address', *Transactions of CIPA*, 1903–4, 22: 16–27, at 21–3. On the Act on Patent Agents of 1900 (Gesetz betreffend die Patentanwälte) see Seckelmann (2006), *op. cit.* (3), at 310–13.

48. Anna Guagnini, 'Patent Agents, Legal Advisers and Guglielmo Marconi's breakthrough in wireless telegraphy', *History of Technology*, 2002, 24: 171–201. The Cambridge pathway was also followed by the successive generations of Carpmaels, among them William Percy and Robert B.

Ransford, a grandson and a grand-nephew of the founder, who joined the firm in 1887 and in 1893 respectively.

49. The headmaster was Charles Pritchard, a Cambridge mathematician who left Clapham in 1862 to return to Cambridge as Savilian Professor of Astronomy. He was replaced as headmaster of the school by another Cambridge mathematician, Alfred Wrigley. Many of the students from Clapham entered Cambridge and Oxford.

50. Howard Graham, 'On the Progress and Work of the Chartered Institute of Patent Agents', *op. cit.* (46) at 123.

51. Swanson, *op. cit.* (3), at 537–44.

52. Lamoreaux and Sokoloff, *op. cit.* (3).

53. See for example Rankin Kennedy, 'Progress and improvements in patents', *The Electrical Review*, 1901, 48: 786–7. Kennedy was a well-established electrical manufacturer and a patentee.

54. This is one of the points raised, especially with regard to chemistry, by Johann P. Murmann, *Knowledge and Competitive Advantage. The Coevolution of Firms, Technology, and National Institutions* (Cambridge, 2003).

55. Dutton, *op. cit.* (2) at 92–3.

56. Patent N. 335, 8 February 1860, 'Improvement in obtaining motive power' 1860; and Patent N. 107, 14 January 1861 'Machinery and apparatus for obtaining motive Power', both communicated from abroad by Jean Joseph Étienne Lenoir.

57. J. H. Johnson, 'Discussion on Mr J. Imray's paper' ('On novelty of invention'), *Transactions of the CIPA*, 1884–5, 3: 136–8. Lenoir's engines were produced in Britain by the Reading Iron Works Ltd; it is not clear whether that was the company to which Johnson referred. See Dugald Clerk, *The Gas and Oil Engine* (7th edn) (New York, 1896), at 15.

58. *Special Report*, Lloyd Wise, *op. cit.* (16) at 50 (Q. 759).

59. R. Haddan, *The Inventor's Adviser and Manufacturer's Handbook to Patents, Designs & Trade-marks: Being an Instructional Guide to the Commercial Development* (4th edn), 3 vols (London, 1898), at 64–5. Haddan eventually became a fellow of the CIPA in 1898 and its President in 1924–5.

60. Marks and Clerk, *British and Foreign Patent Laws and Practice for American and Canadian Patent Attorneys only* (London, 1904) at 48. The booklet was issued in order to provide American patentees with instructions about the particular procedure and rules for patenting in Britain. It is significant that they felt it necessary to inform their potential clients about their own attitudes (but arguably consistent with those of other British agents) towards brokerage.

61. Frederick Walker, 'Patent Agents and Patent Brokers', *Journal of the SPA*, 1902, 3: 39–42, Discussion, 51–5.

62. Ibid., 55.

63. Lockwood pointed out that this was also due to the fact that 'Scotch manufacturers are very unwilling to adopt *another* person's invention either upon royalty or by purchase. English houses are more liberal-minded'. Ibid., 41–2.

64. Advertisement in *Slater's Manchester & Salford Directory*, [Part 2: Trades, Institutions, Streets, etc.] (Manchester, 1895), at 186. A similar case was Percy R. J. Willis, a non-registered agent who, operating under the alluring name of 'Patentees' and Finance Company', and 'Universal Patent Disposal Company' frittered away the remittances of 553 patentees (mainly American), ending up with a bankruptcy amounting to £2,277. George B. Ellis, 'Protection of Invention', *Journal of the SPA*, 1900, 1: 174–5.

65. George Robb, *White-Collar Crime in Modern England: Financial Fraud and Business Morality 1845–1929* (Cambridge, 1992), at 89. Information on his activity as a patent broker is drawn from his correspondence with the Marconi Wireless Telegraph Co.; letterhead, E. Eaton to Marconi, 24 September 1903; Oxford, Bodleian Library, MS Marconi Archive His 212–13.

66. *Kelly's Directory of Liverpool & Birkenhead*, [Part 2: Birkenhead and Trade & Court Directories] (London, 1894), at 154.

67. R. B. Ransford, 'The Profession of Patent Agency', *Transactions of the CIPA*, 1919–20, 38: 15–35, at 25.

1573: The Oldest Patent Granted in Mexico and Latin America

MANUEL MÁRQUEZ

L. L. & M. M. Consultores S. C.

The Patents or Letters Patent were the documents by which His Majesty the King of England granted preferential or exclusive rights to any of his subjects within his territory. These 'open letters' were written on large sheets, signed and sealed by the authority and were then exhibited so that the people could see them and use them as reference to enforce the will of the authority and to guarantee, among some other rights, a monopoly or any other exclusive right granted by the State. Because of their well-known function for granting exclusive rights and privileges to their subjects or the people under their rule, the 'open letters' became the ideal way to protect an invention if it was created by any of them. In that way, the State would announce the exclusive right of use and grant the inventor a certain period of time to be the only one to use and reap the economic benefits arising from the application of a new technique. In the course of history, there was plenty of evidence that inventors were granted such exclusive rights.

The oldest evidence (fourth century BC) was registered in the Greek colony of Sybaris, where those who had invented a new dish or drink were granted the privilege of being the only ones that could prepare them for one year. It is known that in 1449 King Henry VI granted an exclusive privilege to Juan de Utynam to produce stained glass in England and to put it on the market in London. Another historical precedent, and likewise recognized, is the Venetian Patent Statute from the mid-sixteenth century, concerning the privilege requested by Galileo to the Grand Duke of Venice, so that the mill he had built would not be 'of common use by everyone', since building it had cost him considerably and he wanted to recover such expenditure. This happened in the year 1594. It is quite interesting to see how the modern historian Nicolás García Tapia accounts in his book *Patentes de Invención Españolas del Siglo de Oro* (Spanish Patents in the Golden Century, Ministry of Tourism, Trade and Industry, 2008) the manner in which Queen Isabel the Catholic granted a privilege to Pedro de Azlor on February 24 of 1478, so that he could obtain the benefits of his invention for a term of 20 years. This was the first patent in Spain known so far.

Another major European antecedent is the French patent statute in the year 1791. In North America, particularly in the United States, the registration and granting of patents started in 1790. It is important to say that, in the year 1785, King Charles III created the General Archive of the Indies, whose purpose was to concentrate all the documents associated with the Spanish colonies, which had been previously kept in the Archives of Simancas, Cadiz and Seville. This is very important because of new evidence found in the General Archive of the Indies in Seville (Spain) associated with a document which, even though there is no record of it throughout history, is an acknowledgment and privilege – stated in the original document as 'granting a favour' – bestowed to the inventors Don Fernando de Portugal and Leonardo Fragoso by His Excellency, the Viceroy of New Spain, Don Martín Enríquez concerning an invention for a benefit from mercury and silver. This cannot be taken as a Royal Charter, since this concession was granted by the Viceroy. This document, was dated 1573, that is 21 years before the privilege granted to Galileo in Venice and 220 years before the commencement of the grant of patents in America by the U.S. Patent Office. This 'Favor' of 1573 granted by the Viceroy of New Spain, Martín Enríquez de Almansa was rescued from the General Archive of the Indies. While there is still no evidence of similar documents or 'Favors' being granted to inventors by a Viceroy in the Spanish Colonies or bestowed before that time in any other colony in America, and since there is no antecedent in the General Archive of the Indies, we can reasonably conclude that this exclusive right is not only the oldest one in Mexico, but in all America.

It is important to note the existence of other exclusive rights granted to inventors before that patent of 1573, but those were granted by Royal Charter (in Spain) and not by any Viceroy (of 'the Indies'). Nonetheless, it is important to emphasize that the Mexican Patent Office and the formal sequential record only started after 1890, although patents were already granted on the grounds of the first legislation for this type of industrial protection, which was the decree of Spanish Courts of 1820. However, the first Mexican Law was dated May 1832. An interesting aspect in this document recently found in the General Archive of the Indies, as can be observed from its transcription, is that it fully complies – just like many other Spanish documents of that period – with the current requirements of an invention: a) a novelty (technology that has no antecedent); b) an inventive step (which adds something new to current knowledge and allows the solving of a technical problem); and c) for industrial application (which can be commercially profitable).

This can be observed in the selected transcription of said 'favor' below and in the original manuscript reproduced fully at the end of this commentary:

> . . . in view of the loss of mercury and silver that is incorporated in metals, they have sought a way and procedure due to which they can now set these apart and have discovered a new secret to separate the mercury and silver that is incorporated in metals in order to obtain dry silver without it being exhausted by mercury, or spending very little of it, for the obtaining of at least two hundred and fifty silver marks separated per quintal of mercury . . .

It continues elsewhere in the same document:

> . . . and to obtain from the quintals of mercury and silver that are separated a
> profit in silver and more quintals of mercury for the benefit of New Spain, as this
> has previously represented a loss of more than eighty thousand silver marks which
> required two thousand quintals of mercury, but this will now be remedied through
> said invention and separators; hence, considering how burdensome it was the time
> and work they have put on this, I have been asked to acknowledge them above any
> other person that could use their knowledge without recognizing their right and
> who would use it without paying any amount . . .

It is clear then that the inventors asked the Viceroy to acknowledge them – just
like the request of European inventors concerning third parties – on the one
hand in their character as inventors, and on the other hand to prevent 'others'
from taking advantage of the concerned novelty and breakthrough, except in
the case that they paid some royalty for use of such invention to the inventors
in recognition of their innovation.

However, in this document there is one significant issue that was not mentioned in other previous documents by means of which exclusive rights for
inventions were granted in Europe, which concerns proof that the invention
works, as stated in this document:

> . . . I instructed the inventors to demonstrate the Performance of this new inven-
> tion, which they did before me, thus proving that what they said was true, then in
> the name of His Majesty and in my own, I acknowledge that the inventors of this
> new invention are Fernando de Portugal and Leonardo Fragoso, and that it has
> not been used before now. Neither third parties nor us shall make use of it without
> obtaining their license and express consent to use it across the territory of New
> Spain during the first fifteen years from this date onwards . . .

From the above paragraph we can observe how other elements of modern patents are also incorporated: first, the 'temporality', that in this case represents a
privilege for 15 years; second, the 'territoriality', which in this document is limited to New Spain, which means these are not eternal or universal documents;
and third, 'novelty', which in our current legislation provides that if from a
patent description a third party cannot repeat the same invention, the patent is
invalid, but in this case the same invention was reproduced and, therefore, the
exclusive privilege is considered valid.

How much would someone pay for using this new invention?

> . . . and the people who are granted with permission to use it should pay for each
> water mill a maximum of one hundred and twenty silver marks, plus ten additional
> marks from profit; and for each mill operated by mules or horses, or those beasts of
> burden, sixty silver marks; the rest of the people who might have a mill operated by
> hand or feet should pay eleven silver marks for each mill; and all other Individuals
> who would use such industrial application, but would not have any of the above
> mentioned mills, should pay two silver marks; and all those who might have any of
> such mills, of more or less marks, should pay according to the amount of marks,
> provided it does not exceed such amount, and with said statements, less water
> should be used from any person or state, whatever quality and condition they may
> have, so they can use this invention but never without a license from the inventors

under penalty of paying in silver marks according to the use they might have given to it and to the mills used with such invention, hence the Justice Authorities are instructed to immediately observe and enforce payment in silver marks as detailed here . . .

How much was paid by the inventors for the protection they were granted?

> . . . due to which the above mentioned Fernando de Portugal and Leonardo Fragoso in use of their free will and consent shall give the nuns of the order of Mary in this town, whose church is commended to the Holy Trinity, a tenth part of the royalties coming from this invention, and an additional amount to buy sixty . . . [nb, a word that has no translation] for those nuns, according to the instructions they may give. Either done by the Authorities of the mines or the government of New Spain, wherever this invention is applied, a book shall be used to record the royalties to be collected every week, which should be safely kept so the nuns or any other person appointed on their behalf may come to receive any payable amounts, to comply with the instructions of His Excellency [the Viceroy] . . .

It was clear, then, that as ordered by the Viceroy, 10 per cent of the weekly collection should be handed over to the nuns of the Holy Trinity, besides the purchase for them of 60 items [comprising a word that has no translation] from the very beginning. Compared to the current patent protection system, inventors must pay an annual fee for the protection they are granted by the State and throughout the whole term of the protection period. It is also important to note that in modern practice of patent protection it is acknowledged that the exclusive rights provided to inventors by the State is in exchange for making their invention public to the rest of the inventors and researchers in that technical field, so they know about the existence of said invention as 'state of the art' and can develop more new inventions from that one without falling into conflict with what has been already registered as an invention.

This invention was made public in the following way:

> In the City of Mexico, on the seventh day of September of 1573, I certify that Leonardo Fragoso and Joan Vanegas, as free town criers of this city, by means of their undeniable voices out loud, have announced three times this mandate of Mexico in the presence of different people, one next to the Royal Hearing in this city, and at the entrance of the street leading to the main square, and from the public square of the Marquiz (as it is so called) to the town of Tacuba, accompanied by people while playing trumpets. Witnessed by Carlos de Montoya, Martín de Siguza, Diego de Villegas, Alonso Hernández de Carmona, Domingo Castellanos, and Diego de Morales, neighbors of this city and being present.

Surely there could be nothing better for inventors than hearing that they were receiving protection for their invention from an 'undeniable' voice out loud and accompanied by the sound of trumpets and a boost in local fame! This is not known to be any sort of a common patent practice at that time in Europe. It should be noted that this protection to such invention was granted only 52 years after the conquest of Mexico by the Spaniards in the year 1521. Nevertheless, the places mentioned in this document where this mandate was made public are easily identifiable nowadays. The Church of the Holy Trinity is near the Balderas Metro Station, The Royal Hearing is currently the National Palace, the street leading to the Main Square is now identified with the name of Seminario Street (next to the Museum of the Historic Center) and the Square of the Marquiz of Apartado just across from the current National College in Donceles Street, which continues ahead leading in the direction of Tacuba.

And finally, the acknowledgments and signatures of the witnesses and the scribe:

> Being said, taken, amended and agreed to, this was compared against the original charter. It was signed, executed, endorsed by the scribe, Joan de Cueva, with testimonials and exclaimed public announcements, so the request of Fernando de Portugal and Leonardo Fragoso is accepted and considered to be faithful, and through the very illustrious Don Fernando de Arriba y General as secretary, designated by order of His Majesty in this City of Mexico, where he claimed his authority and judicial competence for the City of Mexico, on the first day of the month of October of 1573, the witnesses passed in order to take and amend this according to its original.

> The witnesses, Alonzo Vernárdez y Diez, Regent and Master; and Melchor de Herrera, from Mexico Fernando Derriba General [signature]. I, Antonio Alonso, hereby certify the number of this city of Mexico by Mandate of his Majesty for further drafting and amendment jointly with Alonso Torre, which I certify with my Seal [Transcriber's note: There is a sign in the manner of an official seal] in witness of the Truth [an illegible signature], presented before me.

Sources and special thanks to:

This official document from the sixteenth century was written in the Castilian Language of that time, and thanks to the transcription work of Mr Guillermo Medina Lamadrid (guillermemedina@yahoo.com.mx) it can be read in a comprehensible way.

The original document is kept in the General Archive of the Indies in Seville (Spain), and thanks to the support and advice of Archivist, Mr Manuel Álvarez Casado, we were able to access a graphic version of the original document that is available at:

HYPERLINK http://es.wikipedia.org/wiki/Archivo_General_de_Indias

The translation of this article from Spanish to English was by Patricia Siller Olvera, Professional Translator (psiller_traducciones@yahoo.com).

http://es.wikipedia.org/wiki/Archivo_General_de_Indias, consulted on 8 November 2010.